ISBN 978-1-333-62619-8
PIBN 10527989

For support please visit www.forgottenbooks.com

1 MONTH OF
FREE
READING

at

www.ForgottenBooks.com

By purchasing this book you are
eligible for one month membership to
ForgottenBooks.com, giving you
unlimited access to our entire
collection of over 700,000 titles via
our web site and mobile apps.

To claim your free month visit:

www.forgottenbooks.com/free527989

English
Français
Deutsche
Italiano
Español
Português

www.forgottenbooks.com

Mythology Photography **Fiction**
Fishing Christianity **Art** Cooking
Essays Buddhism Freemasonry
Medicine **Biology** Music **Ancient**
Egypt Evolution Carpentry Physics
Dance Geology **Mathematics** Fitness
Shakespeare **Folklore** Yoga Marketing
Confidence Immortality Biographies
Poetry **Psychology** Witchcraft
Electronics Chemistry History **Law**
Accounting **Philosophy** Anthropology
Alchemy Drama Quantum Mechanics
Atheism Sexual Health **Ancient History**
Entrepreneurship Languages Sport
Paleontology Needlework Islam
Metaphysics Investment Archaeology
Parenting Statistics Criminology
Motivational

All the Worthingtons in America are believed to have descended from Nicholas, who came to New England in 1649, and from Capt. John, who is first known of in Maryland in 1675, and who died April 9, 1701, leaving several sons. Both, probably, descended from the Worthingtons of Lancashire, and such is the tradition of both families.

In this genealogy will be found only those who are descended from Nicholas, and, as it is most probable that he belonged to the Shevington branch of the family of Worthington, of Worthington, County Lancashire, England, I have given the "Herald's Visitations" of that branch down to 1650, at which time Nicholas was in New England.

The origin of our name as given in the "Heraldic Journal, 1868," is Wearth-in-ton, from three Saxon words, meaning Farm-in-town. The old Hall at Worthington, where the family resided for seven hundred years, was recently pulled down.

The Coat of Arms here given are those of the Worthingtons of Lancashire and Cheshire. While I have been exceedingly anxious to secure accuracy and completeness, many errors and omissions must necessarily occur in a work of this kind. If all corrections and omissions, together with any additional records which may be in the possession of some hitherto uninterested member, or one who may not have received my "Genealogical Inquiry," will be forwarded to the compiler, addressed to 775 Case avenue, Cleveland, Ohio, within the year, it will be printed as an addition to the present records. It is hoped that an earnest effort will be made to complete those family lines which are here unfinished.

WORTHINGTON.

In Burke's 'Landed Gentry of Great Britain,' we find the following account of the early family of Worthington:

In the Hundred of Leyland, Parish of Standish, and Palatinate of Lancaster, is situated the Manor of Worthington, which at an early period gave name to a family seated in the direct line, as well as in its various branches, for centuries in the same locality, maintaining a distinguished position amongst the chief Lancashire proprietors, and allying with its most eminent houses. The main stock established at Worthington is recorded in the "Herald's Visitations," and can be traced through the public archives as far back as the time of Henry III. In the 20th of that monarch's reign [1236] the name of William de Worthington occurs in the Testa de Nevill, and in the 15th, Edward II. [1322], by the same authority, fol. 397, William de Worthington held half a knight's fee in Worthington. In the 5th of the next reign William de Worthington is mentioned; and in the 20th, Hugh de Worthington and John de Heton as holding half a knight's fee in Worthington, in the Hundred of Leyland.

The Hundred of Leyland was formerly called Leylandshire. It was in Saxon times a royal possession of great extent, as appears from the Domesday survey. King Edward, the Confessor, held the Hundred of Leyland. It was divided into twelve divisions, which twelve freemen held as twelve Manors or Lordships. The Manor or Lordship of Worthington was one of the twelve manors of Leyland Hundred. In the History of Lancashire, under the head of the Manor of Manchester, is the following:

A. D. 1322.—This Court of Manchester is held every three weeks, at which the Lord of Childwall, the Lord of Wittington, the Lord of Harewood, the Lord of Undeswood and Pilkington, the Lord of Worthington, etc., are judges of the Court of Ancient Customs, etc.

Of the derivative branches of this most ancient family, the oldest is that of Henry de Worthington of Blainscough; the second, Chris.opher Worthington, Esq., of Crosshawè; third, William Worthington of Shevington, in Standish Parish, County Lancaster, described in the "Herald's Visitations" as a younger brother of the family of Worthington of Worthington. In this third branch the rather. uncommon name of Nicholas appears for the first time.

This William Worthington of Shevington was wit ess to deeds of the Manor of Adlington, in the parish of Standish, ninth year of the reign of Edward IV., 1470. He married a daughter of Bradshaw of Litherland, County Lancaster, who was a descendant of Sir John Bradshaw, a Saxon living at the time of the conquest. Their son, Nicholas of Shevington, married Jane, daughter of Richard Langtree, Esq., of Langtree, and had issue:.

Alexander,
Margaret,
Catherine,
Lowry,
Grace.

Alexander, of Shevington, married Amarv or Marion, co-heir of Thomas Duxbury of County Lancaster, and was suc ceeded by his son, Nicholas Worthington, Esq., of Shevington, 1567, who, by deed dated April 21, 7th James I. (1610), conveyed the Manor of Shevington to Robert Kesketh, Esq., of Rufforth, County Lancaster. He marrrid Agnes, daughter of Richard Worthington, Esq., of Worthington, and was father of a daughter and heiress, Margaret Worthington of

Shevington, who married 14th Elizabeth (1592), Edward Chisnell of Chisnell.

RICHARD WORTHINGTON, Esq., of Worthington (father of Agnes, who married Nicholas of Shevington), of whom Edward, Earl of Derby, in 15th Henry VIII. (1524), held the Manor of Copull, by the service of a red rose, and of whom Roger Ashton, Esq., 33rd Henry VIII. (1542), held lands in Copull, married a daughter of Holcroft of Holcroft, County Lancaster, and was succeeded by his son, Thomas Worthington, Esq., of Worthington, whose wife was Anne, daughter of Richard Ashton, Esq., of Croston, County Lancaster. By this lady, who was buried at Standish, 6th February, 1600, Thomas Worthington, who was buried at the same place, nineteenth November, 1595, had issue:

 I. Edward.
 II. Thomas, buried at Standish, sixth February, 1593.

Thomas Worthington was succeeded by his son,

EDWARD WORTHINGTON, Esq., of Worthington, who married Margaret, daughter of John Orrell of Torton, County Lancaster, and by her had issue:

 I. Thomas.
 II. Richard.

Edward Worthington was succeeded by his son,

THOMAS WORTHINGTON, Esq., of Worthington, who married Isabel, daughter of Gilbert Langtree of Langtree, County Lancaster, and by her had issue:

 .I. William.
 II. John, buried at Standish, eighth December, 1667, father of Edward.

Thomas Worthington (who was buried at Standish, twenty eighth December, 1626), was succeeded by his son, :

WILLIAM WORTHINGTON, Esq., of Worthington, who mar-

ried Margaret, daughter of —— Halsall, Esq., of Alker,
County Lancaster (buried at Standish, seventh January,
1667), and had issue:

    I. Thomas Worthington, Esq, of Worthington buried at
          Standish, 14th Dec., 1670.
  II. Edward, living 10th Dec., 1670.
III. William, living 10th Dec., 1670.

"There is in the possession of the descendants of Rev. William
Worthington, a grandson of Nicholas, an ancient silver
tankard or pitcher, which has descended in the family for
many generations. Its massive mould and antique shape
would indicate an age coeval with the settlement of our
country. Deeply, though rudely, engraved on the front, are
the ancient arms of Worthington, described in heraldic terms
as follows, viz. :

Argent—Three dung forks, sable.

Crest—A goat stantant, argent; holding in the mouth an
    oak branch, vert.

Motto—Virtute dignus avorum."

    (Worthy by the virtue of their ancestors.)

These arms are still borne by the Worthingtons of Lancashire and Cheshire.

"No attempt has been successful in connecting our New England ancestor with the parent stem in England by document-
ary proof, but circumstantial evidence of such connection is
not wanting. According to family tradition, transmitted to
Rev. William Worthington of Saybrook, Conn. (grandson of Nicholas), was by him transmitted, through his
daughter, Elizabeth (Worthington) Chauncey, to her son,
Worthington Gallup · Chauncey of Durham, Conn., an
accurate preserver of historical facts and traditions, and by
him, prior to his death in 1858, communicated to the present
writer.

"Nicholas Worthington was a considerable landholder near Liverpool, in County Lancaster. He fought in the Cromwellian wars, in which conflicts his estates were confiscated."

He was the first, and probably the only Worthington who came early into New England, settling first at Saybrook, Conn., 1649 or '50, then at Hartford, Conn. (by proceedings of the county court of Hampshire county, March 28, 1870, he was called "of Hartford"), and finally at Hatfield, Conn., where the county records show the name of "Nich. Worthington" as having taken the oath of allegiance, February 8, 1678.

FiRsT GENERATION.

NICHOLAS WORTHINGTON of Hatfield, Conn., married first, about 1668, Sara White, daughter of Thomas Bunch, Sr., of Hartford, Conn., and widow of John White, Jr., of Hatfield. Mrs. Sara Worthington died June 20, 1676, and Nicholas Worthington married, second, Susanna ——, who, after his death, married Captain Jonathan Ball of Springfield. Mass., Feb., 1684, and by whom she had several children, Captain Ball died May 21, 1741.

Nicholas Worthington died, Sept. 6, 1683.

Mrs. Susanna Worthington Ball died March 9, 1727.

THOMAS BUNCH, Sr., father of Sara (Bunch) White, who was the first wife of Nicholas, is first known of in 1636. The next year he served well in the Pequot war. Married Susannah, daughter of Thomas Bull, under whom he had served during the war. They had children.

I. Thomas.
II. John.
III. Sara, who m., first, John White; second, Nicholas Worthington.

IV. Mary, b. September 17, 1645, m. Thomas Meakins of Hatfield, and afterwards John Downing.

V. Elizabeth, who m. Jacob White, of Hartford, Conn., brother of John, who was the first husband of Sara.

THOMAS BULL of Hartford, Conn., father of Susannah, and grandfather of Sarah (wife of Nicholas) was born in England in 1606. Came to New England in the ship "Hopewell," under Captain Babb, embarking at London, Sept., 1635. He was first of Boston or Cambridge, but in the following May accompanied Hooker, serving in the Pequot war in 1637. At the taking of the fort, May 24, 1637, Lieutenant Bull had a narrow escape, thanks to a piece of hard cheese in his pocket, which arrested the flight of an arrow. In 1675 he was in command at Saybrook, Conn., when Andros unsuccessfully attempted to gain the fort for the Duke of York. Captain Bull died in 1684, his wife, Susannah, having died in 1680, aged 71. There is a tradition that he was the brother of Henry of Roxbury, who came from South Wales in 1636, and was one of the original purchasers of Aquineck, Rhode Island, Governor of Rhode Island colony in 1685 and 1689, and died in 1693.

CHILDREN BY FIRST WIFE:

†1. WILLIAM,   born 1670.

2. ELIZABETH,   born ——, m. —— Morton.

3. MARY,   born January 24, 1673-4. Died in early life.

CHILDREN BY SECOND WIFE:

†4. JONATHAN.

†5. JOHN,   born Aug. 17, 1679, in Springfield, Mass.

SECOND GENERATION.

I.

WILLIAM WORTHINGTON of Hartford, Conn., removed about 1717 to Colchester, Conn., which town was incorporated in 1699. Married, 1693 or '4, Mehitable Graves Morton,

---

† Record continued under same number in next generation.

widow of Richard Morton, Jr., of Hatfield, Conn., and Daughter of Isaac Graves of Hatfield. She was born October 1, 1671, married Mr. Morton in 1690, who died in 1691. William Worthington served in the Falls fight under Captain William Turner, and died at Colchester, May 22, 1753.

Mrs. Worthington died at Colchester, March 22, 1742.

Thomas Graves, father of Isaac and grandfather of Mehitable, who married William Worthington, was of Hartford, Conn. Not an original proprietor, was, on account of old age, excused from training. In 1645, he removed to Hadley, Mass. His children, whom he probably brought from England, were:

    I. Isaac.
    II. John.
    III. Samuel.
    IV. A daughter, name unknown.
    V. Nathaniel.

All except Nathaniel accompanied him to Hadley. He died Nov., 1662. His widow, Sarah, died 1666.

Isaac, eldest son of Thomas Graves, was born in England; made freemen 1669; married Mary, dau. of Richard and Ann Church, and was killed by the Indians in 1677. Had ch.,

    I. Mary, b. July 5, 1647.
    II. Isaac, b. August 22, 1650.
    III. Rebecca, b. July 3, 1652, d. July 6, 1653.
    IV. Samuel, b. October 1, 1655.
    V. Sarah.

They moved to Hatfield, Conn., and their children born there,

    VI. Elizabeth, b. 1662.
    VII. John, b. 1664.
    VIII. Hannah, b. 1666.
    IX. Jonathan, b.
    X. Mehitable, b. October 1, 1671, who m., 1st, Richard Morton, Jr., and, 2nd, William Worthington.

Richard Church of Hartford, Conn., father of Mary and grandfather of Mehitable, who married William Worthington, was an original proprietor in Hartford, Conn., in 1637. His former residence is not known. He was a freeman in Conn. in 1688, and was one of the sixty persons who moved to Mass. for the purpose of founding Hadley, in 1659, and died there in 1667. His widow, Ann, died in Hatfield, Mass., March 10, 1684, aged 83 years. In his will he mentions four children, probably all born in England, as there are none recorded in Hartford.

   I. Edward of Hartford, Norwalk, New Haven and Hadley.
  II. John, died in Hartford.
III. Mary, who married Isaac Graves.
 IV. Samuel, lived in Hadley.

Richard Morton, Sr., of Hartford, Conn., father of Richard, Jr., who was the first husband of Mehitable Graves, was freeman in Hartford in 1669. Of his children, two were born there.

  1. Richard, Jr.
 II. Thomas.

He removed to Hatfield and had children born there.

 III. John, b. 1670, died early.
 IV. Joseph, b. 1672.
  V. John, b. 1674, died young.
 VI. Abraham, b. 1676.
VII. Elizabeth, b. 1680.
VIII. Ebenezer, b. 1682.
 IX. Jonathan, b. 1684.

He was made freeman in Hatfield, Mass., in 1690, and died in 1710. His widow, Ruth, died in 1714. All of his sons, excepting Thomas, lived at Hatfield.

CHILDREN OF WILLIAM AND MEHITABLE WORTHINGTON.

†6. WILLIAM   born Dec. 5, 1695, in Hartford, Conn.
†7. DANIEL   born May 18, 1698, in Hartford, Conn.
8. MARY,   born Sept. 23, 1701, in Hartford, Conn.; married, 1st, Oct. 13, 1720, Daniel Jones of Colchester, Conn. (born Feb. 2, 1693), son of Josiah Jones of Watertown, Mass., and Abigail Barnes of Marlbor-

ough. Josiah Jones was son of
Josiah and Lydia (Treadway)
Jones, and grandson of Lewis
Jones, one of the first settlers of
Watertown. Daniel Jones died
June 18, 1740. He was the
brother of Abigail Jones, who
was the second wife of Colonel
Ephraim Williams, father of the
founder of Williams college. Colonel Ephraim Williams married,
1st, Elizabeth Jackson, by whom
he had two sons—Colonel
Ephraim, Jr., and Dr. Thomas.
Colonel Ephraim Williams, Jr.,
born Feb. 23, 1713, in Newton,
Mass., was killed on Sept. 8,
1755, during the last French
war. Williams college derived
its name from him and he endowed it. In Albany, N. Y.,
July 22, before starting upon
what proved to be his last campaign, he made his last will.
After several bequests to rela
tives and friends, he orders
"that the remainder of his lands
should be sold, at the discretion
of his executors, within five
years after an established peace;
and that the interest of moneys
arising from the sale, and also
the interest of his notes and
bonds, should be applied to

the support of a free school in a township west of Fort Massachusetts, forever; provided the said township, when incorporated, shall be called Williamstown." Colonel Ephraim Williams, Sr., died Aug., 1734, in Deerfield, Mass Mrs. Abigail Williams died Dec 4, 1784.

Mrs. Mary Jones married, 2nd, June 15, 1741, Captain Benjamin Lathrop of Norwich, Conn. She was his second wife. He married, 1st, Mary, (born Aug 27, 1694, died March 26, 1740), daughter of Thomas Adgate of Norwich, Conn., whom he married Nov. 13, 1718.

Mrs. Mary Lathrop died Aug. 4, 1770, in Norwich, Conn.

Children by her first husband.

1. Mary Jones, b. May 26, 1724, d. June 13, 1729.
2. Amasa Jones, b. Oct. 2, 1726; was twice m., 1st, July 12, 1749, to Elizabeth. Chamberlain, dau. of William of Colchester, Conn., who d. Sept. 23, 1753; 2nd, Aug. 27, 1754, to Hope (b Nov. 22, 1736, in Middletown, Conn,), dau. of Epa-

phrus Lord of Colchester,. Conn

Amasa Jones d. Feb. 24,. 1785, in Hartford, Conn.

Mrs. Hope Jones d. Dec. 11, 1798, in Hartford, Conn.

Children by first wife:

1. Rhoda Jones, b. Oct. 5, 1750, m., July 3, 1766, Major Bulkeley.
2. Daniel Jones, b. May 27, 1752, d. Oct. 27, 1753.

Children by second wife ·

3. Daniel Jones, b. Aug. 28, 1755; was of Hartford; m., 1st, March 11, 1781, Olive Tinker of E. Haddam, Conn. She d. Feb. 7, 1788.. M., 2nd, Oct. 7, 1798, Rho-- da, dau. of Dr. Charles Mather of Hartford. Daniel Jones d. Feb. 1, 1802. Mrs Rhoda Jones d. Nov. 26,. 1847.

   Olivia, dau. of Daniel and Olive Jones, m. Sept. 24,. 1811, Rev. Dr. Jeremiah Day of New Haven, Conn., and president of Yale college.
4. Amasa Jones, b. July 27,. 1757; m. Cynthia Jones, dau. of Isaac Jones of Adams, Mass. Amasa Jones died in 1808. Had 8 chil dren.
5. Samuel Phillips Jones, b.. Sept. 23, 1759.

6. Hope Jones, bap. Nov. 1, 1761, m. Horace Seymore of Lansingburg and New York, N. Y.

7. Epaphrus Jones, bap. Feb. 19, 1764.

8. Richard L. Jones, bap June 14, 1767; m. Hannah Hooper.

9. Abigail Warren Jones, bap. April 23, 1769; m. Charles Selden of Troy, N. Y.

10. George Jones, m. a Miss Bogardus of Catskill, N Y.

11. William Jones, m. Eunice Buckland, dau. of Aaron of East Hartford, Conn.

12. Mary Jones, died unm.

13. Hannah Jones, m. Josiah Sherman of Albany, N. Y.

3. Mary Jones, 2nd, b. June 13 1729, d. unm.

4. Abigail Jones, b. May 1, 1732.

5. Ann Jones, bap. Oct. 5. 1735; m., April 20, 1758 Nun Clark of Lyme, Conn.

6. Elizabeth Jones, bap. Sept. 24, 1738; m., Oct. 25, 1757, Nathaniel Clark of Colchester, Conn.

9. MEHITABLE,   born July 18, 1706, in Hartford, Conn., supposed to have died unmarried, as no mention of her is made in her father's will.

†10. ELIJAH,   born June 16, 1710, in Hartford, Conn.

IV.

JONATHAN WORTHINGTON of West Springfield, Mass. was twice married. 1st. Feb. 19, 1708, to Elizabeth, dau. of John Scott and Sarah Bliss of West Springfield; 2nd, March 21, 1744, to Experience Fowler.

Jonathan Worthington died ———.

Mrs. Elizabeth Worthington died Sept. 18, 1743.

JOHN SCOTT, father of Elizabeth, married, July 20, 1659, Sarah, dau. of Thomas Bliss and Margaret ———, and had children

   I. Sarah, b. Oct. 19, 1663, married, Feb. 9, 1680, Benjamin Leonard.

  II. John, b. Jan. 4, 1666 (the last figure is uncertain).

 III. Hannah, b. Oct. 16, 1668, married, Oct. 30, 1695, John Fowler.

  IV. Margaret, b. Feb. 25, 1670, Springfield, Mass.; married, but name of husband is not known.

   V. Ebenezer, b. Aug. 3, 1673.

  VI. William, b. Aug. 8, 1678, who was one of the first settlers of Palmer, Mass.

 VII. Mary, b. Dec. 29, 1678; m., July, 1701, Ebenezer Nash.

John Scott removed, about 1680, to Suffield, where, 8, Elizabeth was born, and where he died Jan. 2, 1690. Of his sons, William only had children. His widow, Sarah, married the same year Samuel Terry, and died Sept. 27, 1715.

THOMAS BLISS of Hartford, Conn., father of Sarah and grandfather of Elizabeth Scott, wife of Jonathan Worthington, was an early but not an original settler. Nothing is known of his coming from England. His first residence was in that part of Boston called The Mount, afterwards Braintree, now Quincy, in 1639 or '40. He is first mentioned in Conn. at the same time with his son, Thomas, Jr., who may be the freeman of May 18, 1642, in Mass., and there left by his father, whose death is early heard of but date not known. His widow, Margaret, after two or three years, removed to Springfield with all her children, excepting Thomas and Ann, and died Aug. 28, 1684. Of their nine children, probably five were born in England.

  I. Mary, m., Nov. 20, 1646, Joseph Parsons.
  II. Thomas.
 III. Nathaniel, d. Nov 8, 1702.
 IV. Laurence, d. 1676.
  V. Samuel, d. March 27, 1720.
 VI. Sarah, m., Julv 20, 1659, John Scott.
 VII. Elizabeth, m., Feb 15, 1670, Miles Morgan, being his
   second wife.
VIII. Hannah, d. unm., Jan. 25, 1662.
 IX. John.

CHILDREN BY FIRST WIFE:

11. ELIZABETH, born Feb. 17, 1710; m., Jan. 3,
          1730, Samuel Gaylord of Had-
          ley, and died in 1759.

12. MARGARET, born Feb. 2, 1712; m., Dec. 1. 1733,
          Jonathan Purchase of Walling-
          ford, Conn.

†13. JONATHAN, born June 17, 1715.

14. NICHOLAS, born July 26, 1717, died Feb. 23, 1720.

†15. WILLIAM, born Jan. 16, 1720.

16. AMY,   born Nov. 3, 1825, died Feb. 20, 1743.

CHILDREN BY SECOND WIFE.

17. OLIVE,   born April 17, 1750.
18. BEULAH, born April 7, 1752, died in infancy.
19· BEULAH, 2nd, April 2, 1754.

V.

LIEUTENANT JOHN WORTHINGTON of Springfield, Massachusetts, married, May 22, 1713, Mary (b. May 24, 1677), dau. of John Pratt and Mary Andrews of Saybrook, Connecticut. John Pratt married, August 10, 1676, Mary Andrews and had six children.

  I. Mary Pratt, born May 24, 1677.
  II. Martha Pratt, born January 16, 1679.
 III. Daniel Pratt, born January 13, 1680.

    IV. Jonathan Pratt, born December, 1682.
    V. Hannah Pratt, born June 14, 1688.
    VI. John Pratt, born March 19, 1691.

Lieutenant John Worthington received from the English government a large tract of land, a part of which was included in the city of Springfield, Massachusetts. The first street laid out in that city ran through the grant and was called Worthington street. The land descended, by right of the English law of entail, to the eldest son, John, who, leaving no sons, it passed to his daughters.

    Mr. John Worthington died Dec. 30, 1744.

    Mrs. Mary Worthington died Oct. 29, 1759.

CHILDREN.

20.	JOHN,	born Oct. 26, 1714, died Mar. 1, 1717.
†21.	JOHN, 2nd	born Nov. 24, 1719, in Springfield.
22.	TIMOTHY,	born July 1, 1722, died Nov. 25, 1724.
†23.	SAMUEL,	born July 11, 1725, in Springfield, Mass.
24.	MARY,	born March 8, 1728, m., May 20, 1762, Ebenezer Hotton.
25.	SARAH,	born Jan. 27, 1732, m., Dec. 10, 1755, Rev. John Hooker of the Congregational church of Northampton, Mass. Rev. John Hooker, died Feb. 6, 1777, aged 48 years. Mrs. Sarah Hooker died April 5, 1817 Judge Hooker of Springfield, was a son, whose son, Josiah Hooker, also lived in Springfield.

THIRD GENERATION.

VI.

Rev. William Worthington, first of Stonington, Conn., afterwards pastor of the Congregational church of that part of Saybrook, Conn., now called Westbrook. He graduated at Yale college, in the class of 1716, was ordained at Saybrook, June 29, 1726, married twice. 1st. Oct. 13, 1720, to Elizabeth (b. May 6, 1697, d. Jan. 1, 1725, in Stonington, Conn.), dau. of Capt., afterwards Major Samuel Mason, and his second wife, Elizabeth Peck, of Rehoboth, Conn.

2nd. Sept. 20, 1726, to Temperance (b. Feb. 1, 1701), dau. of William Gallup and Sarah———— of Stonington.

Rev. William Worthington died Nov. 16, 1756, in Saybrook.

Mrs. Temperance Worthington died March, 1778, in Durham, Conn.

One Hundred Years Ago—An Early New England Wedding.

Of the broad spirit and good cheer among the best settlers of Stonington, Conn., we may give a story from the lips that proudly cherished the family tradition, of a golden day in the town's history. A marriage occurred in the family of Mr. William Gallup, who lived in the best of style, for his day, on his ample estate on the left bank of the Mystic river—his mansion being on the present White Hall farm, the fine mansion probably receiving the old English name, White Hall. His daughter Temperance was married to the Rev. William Worthington, one of the first ministers in the northern portion of the township. As a measure of affluence had sprung from the virgin soil of the valley, and colonial life was blooming into a degree of luxury and taste befitting the inherited qualities of the Puritan planters, the wedding was made to comport with the dignity of the large plantation and the blood of the families to be united. Mr. Gallup extended an invitation to the settlers of the town to be present at the nuptials. Arrangements, broad and generous, were accordingly made. Field and fold, stall and cellar, purse and pantry, were widely opened.

The day chosen was September 20, 1726, a golden autumn day in a prosperous year. The invitation was honored. By road and bridle-path came saddlers and pillions with gayest riders in old English costume, as high civic and military rank belonged to the family whose great mansion doors now stood ajar. With the settlers and their families, came also the friendly remnant of the Pequot Indians, then occupying reserved lands in the northern portion of the town. Mr. Gallup found himself more popular than he supposed. The Pequots were his friends and admirers, and had an inherent relish for large and abundant feasts. The guests of rank filled the mansion, and the glad ceremony was duly performed to the joy of all parties. But Mr. Gallup was compelled to explain to his aboriginal friends, and asked them to visit him the next day, when they should receive his attention and find full proof of his hospitality. As they wound their way back to their wigwams, in open Indian file after their native manner, the line extended from the Gallup mansion well on to the head of the river, near a mile. On the following day the Pequots returned, plumed and mantled in their best, and closed the festive scenes by haring all that had been promised them. None went away hungry or thirsty.

Mr. Gallup's father was the brave Captain John Gallup, who led the friendly Mohegans in King Phillip's war and fell at their head during the great swamp fight in South Kingston, Rhode Island, Dec. 19, 1675.

The family of his daughter, Temperance Worthington, became conspicuous in Conneeticut history. One of her grandsons became governor of the state.—*From the Providence (R. I.) Journal.*

In Westbrook, Conn., is a tombstone bearing the following:

In memory of ye Rev. William Worthington, first minister of ye West Parish of Saybrook, who died Nov. 16, 1756, in ye 61 year of his age and 31 year of his ministry. Who lived beloved and died lamented by all who were happy in his acquaintance.

Major John Mason, grandfather of Elizabeth, born in England about 1600; lieutenant in the English army; served in the Netherlands under Sir Thomas Fairfax; emigrated to America about 1630, and settled in Dorchester, Mass., representing that town in the general court. In Oct., 1635, he removed to Windsor, Conn., in company with Rev. John Warham, Henry Wolcott and others of the first settlers of that town, where he was elected an assistant magistrate of the colony in 1642.

In May, 1637, he commanded the successful expedition against the Pequots, near New London, for which he was called " Conqueror of the Pequots." He married, about 1640, Anne————, and in 1647, removed to Saybrook. In 1660 he became one of the first settlers of Norwich, Conn., where he was deputy governor and major general of the forces of the colony.

He died Jan. 30, 1672, at Norwich, where his widow died soon afterwards. They had 3 children.

   I. Priscilla.

  II. Samuel, b. July 6, 1644, in Windsor, Conn.

 III. John, b. Aug., 1646, m. Abigail Fitch.

Samuel Mason married twice, his first wife's name is unknown. They settled at Stonington, Conn., where he was Major of Militia, and assistant of the colony, and where his wife died. They had three children.

   I. John, b. Aug. 19, 1676, in Stonington, d. March 10, 1705. Unm.

  II. Anne, who m. her first cousin, Captain John Mason, Jr., son of Captain John Mason and Abigail Fitch.

 III. Sarah, who m. her first cousin, Joseph Fitch.

Samuel Mason m. 2nd, July 4, 1694, Elizabeth Peck of Rehoboth. Died, March 30, 1705, at Stonington, and was buried at Lebanon, Conn. His widow married Gershom Palmer of Stonington, Conn.

Children of Samuel and Elizabeth (Peck) Mason.

  IV. Samuel, b. Aug. 26, 1695, in Stonington, d. Nov. 28, 1701.

  V. Elizabeth, b. May 6, 1697, in Stonington, and m. Rev. William Worthington.

CHILDREN OF REV. WM. WORTHINGTON AND HIS FIRST WIFE :

26, MARY,   born Aug. 18, 1721, in Stonington, Conn.; m., Feb. 14, 1745, Hon. Aaron Eliott of Killingworth, Conn. (b. March 15, 1718, in

Killingworth), 2nd son of Rev.
Jared Eliott, D. D., of that town,
grandson of Rev. Joseph Eliott,
minister of Killingworth,
and great grandson of John
Eliott, the minister of Roxbury,
and "Apostle to the Indians."
Hon. Aaron Eliott was a Physician and Colonel of Militia at
Killingworth, was frequently
elected to the General Assembly.
Died at Killingworth, Dec. 30
1785.

Mrs. Mary Eliott died June
18, 1785.

CHILDREN.

1. Hannah Eliott, b. Aug. 31,
    1746, in Killingworth; m.,
    Nov. 23, 1773, at Amenia
    N. Y., Gen. Reuben Hopkins
    (b. June 1, 1748), a lawyer.
    They settled at Charlotte,
    removing to Goshen, N. Y.,
    where he was a Brig.-Gen.
    of Militia, and commanded
    a brigade in the U. S. service
    at Plattsburgh, in the war
    of 1812. He died about
    1819 in Illinois.

Ch.

1. Eliott Hopkins, b. Sept.
    12, 1774; m., Jan. 16 1815,

Julia Howell of Cincinnati,
O. Had six ch.

2. Benjamin Bronson Hopkins
    b. March 16, 1776; m.,
    Sept., 26, 1852, ——, and
    d. at Augusta, Ga. Had
    several ch.

3. Mary Hopkins, b. Dec. 2,
    1777; d., unm., in 1820 at
    Cincinnati, O.

4. Adelaide Hopkins, b. Mar.
    3, 1780; m. at Goshen, N.
    Y., where she d. Mar. 3,
    1846, leaving several ch.

5. Rebecca Hopkins, b. Jan.
    16, 1782; m. ——; d. April
    3, 1816, in Ontario co.,
    N. Y.

6. William Hector Hopkins,
    b. Nov. 12, 1784; m. ——,
    and d. in St. Louis, Mo.,
    leaving a large family.

7. Hannibal Mason Hopkins,
    b. Aug. 8, 1788; m. ——
    and settled at Goshen,
    N. Y.

8. Delinda Hopkins, b. Nov.
    25, 1792; m. ——, and d.,
    May 28, 1823, at Madison,
    Ga.

2. Mary Mason Eliott, b. July
    11, 1752, in Killingworth;
    m., about 1798, Dr. Chris-
    topher Ely, being his third
    wife.

3. Samuel Smithson Eliott, b
    July 2, 1753, in Killing
    worth; m., March 17, 1779,

Margaret Williams (b. May, 1753), dau. of Judge John Williams of Sharon. They settled at Sharon, where she d. Oct. 27, 1802.

Ch.

1. Samuel William Eliott, b. Mar. 31, 1781; m., Jan. 31, 1809, Sarah Canfield (b. Dec. 27, 1787, in Milford, Conn.) Settled at Northampton, N. Y., afterwards removing to Penfield, where he d. Aug. 30, 1830.. Had six sons and four dau.

2. William Worthington Eliott, b. April 21, ——, in Sharon; m., Jan. 1809, Eunice Thomas of Balston, N. Y. Settled at Northampton, N. Y., removing to Balston, and in 1836, to Niles, Mich., where he d., Oct. 13, 1839. Had three ch.

4. William Mason Eliott, b. June 26, 1755, in Killingworth. Graduated at Yale College, 1774; was a physician; m., at Saybrook, his 1st cousin, Ethelinda Ely (b. ——, 1764), dau. of Colonel John Ely and Sarah Worthington of Saybrook.

5. Aaron Eliott, b. Aug. 15, 1757.

6. Joseph Eliott, b. Nov. 9, 1760.

7. Benjamin Eliott,⎫ Twins, b.
⎬ Dec. 9,
8. Elizabeth Eliott,⎭ 1762.

27. SYBIL   born Nov. 9, 1723, in Stonington, Conn.; died Feb. 23, 1724.

CHILDREN BY HIS SECOND WIFE.

28. ELIZABETH,   born Feb. 27, 1728, in Saybrook, Conn. Was twice married, 1st, to Samuel Gale of Saybrook ; 2nd, Feb. 9, 1760, the Rev. Elnathan Chauncey of Durham, Conn.

Rev. Elnathan Chauncey died May 4, 1796, aged 71 years.

Mrs. Elizabeth Chauncey died Feb. 9, 1791.

CH. BY HER FIRST HUSBAND.

1. Asa Worthington Gale, b. about 1756; d. Aug. 14, 1772, at Cape Francois.

2. Benjamin Gale, b. about 1758. Was in the battle of Bunker Hill. Was drowned while returning to New York from the East Indies in 1796-7.

MRS. TEMPERANCE WORTHINGTON SMITH.

CH. BY SECOND HUSBAND.

1. Nathaniel William Chauncey, b. Sept. 12, 1761; d. Jan. 29, 1840.
2. Catharine Chauncey, b. Aug. 6, 1764; m., Mar. 14, 1790, Reuben Rose Fowler, of Madison, Conn., and d. Mar., 1841. Had several children, among them was Rev. William C. Fowler, Professor at Amherst College.
3. Elnathan Elihu Chauncey, b. March 15, 1767; d. April 8, 1773.
4. Worthington Gallup Chauncey, b. March 22, 1772. Lived at Durham, Conn.

29. SARAH, born April 3, 1730, in Saybrook, Conn.; died June 15, 1732.

30. TEMPERANCE, born April 15, 1732, in Saybrook Conn. Was twice married. 1st, Dr. Moses Gale of Goshen Orange Co., N. Y.; 2nd, May 31, 1758, to the Rev. Cotton Mather Smith of Sharon, Conn. (b. Oct. 15, 1730), son of Samuel Smith (one of the early settlers of Suffield, Conn.), and Jerusha, dau. of Atherton Mather. Samuel was the son of Ichabod, the son of Samuel, the son of Rev.

Henry Smith, who came from Norfolk and settled at Hingham, Mass., 1636. Rev. Cotton Mather Smith graduated at Yale College in 1751; was the second teacher of the Stockbridge Mission School, succeeding Rev. Gideon Hawley; and on Aug. 28, 1755, was ordained pastor of the church in Sharon, being the third pastor of the (then) Established Church in that place. An interesting tradition connected with the marriage of Temperance Worthington and Rev. Smith is, that while returning home from Goshen to Savbrook, on horseback, she was overtaken by a sudden storm near the boarding house of Rev. Smith in Sharon, and there obtained shelter from the rain. The acquaintance thus accidently formed led to matrimony.

Mrs. Temperance Smith died, June 26, 1800, in Albanv, N. Y., at the home of her son-in-law, the Hon. Jacob Radcliff, while on her return from Saratoga.

Rev. Smith died Nov. 27, 1806, at Sharon, Conn.

The following appeared in the "Home Maker," Vol. 2, No. 6 :

The provisions of Rev. Cotton Mather Smith's call to his first and only charge are peculiar and interesting.

Town Meeting, Jan., 1755. Voted, That a committee confer with Mr. Smith, and know which will be most acceptable to him, to have a larger settlement and a smaller salary, or a larger salary and a smaller settlement, and make report to this meeting.

Town Meeting, Jan 15, 1755.— Voted, That we will give to said Mr. Smith 420 ounces of silver, or equivalent in old tenor bills, for a settlement, to be paid in three years after settlement. * * * Voted, That we give to said Mr. Smith 220 Spanish dollars, or an equivalent in old tenor bills, for his yearly salary.

Mr. Smith's acceptance of the call contains this clause: "As it will come heavy upon some, perhaps, to pay salary and settlement together, I have thought of releasing part of the payment of the salary for a time, to be paid to me again. * * * The first year I will allow you out of the salary you have voted me, 40 dollars; the 2nd, 30 dollars; the 3rd year, 15; the 4th year, 20, to be repaid to me again; the 5th year, 20 more; the 6th year, 20 more; and the 25 dollars that remain, I am willing that the town shall keep 'em for their own use.

He discharged the duties of this pastorate for 52 years. He was distinguished for great eloquence, eminence in learning, piety and patriotism, and such gifts of heart and mind and person as endeared him indissolubly to his people. The smallpox breaking out in Sharon while he was still comparatively a young man, he and Mrs. Smith separated themselves from family and home, and labored diligently among their stricken flock until the pestilence subsided.

While at Ticonderoga with Gen. Schuyler, he fell dangerously ill, and "Madam" Smith, "being warned of God in a dream," undertook a journey of 160 miles by forest and stream to reach and nurse him.

The beautiful tale, as told by herself, and arranged and edited by her great great granddaughter, Miss Helen Evertson Smith, is given here as it appeared in the "Home Maker," Vol. 1. No. 1.

To my dear children :

I have been asked many times by you all to write an account of the strange and notable manner in which I was led of God to make the long and arduous journey from our home in Sharon, Connecticut, to Fort Ticonderoga, to the end of (under God) saving the life of your dear Father. Now that he has himself enjoined it upon me to do this as a testimony justly owed to that Divine Providence which has ever watched over, led and sustained us, I can no longer refuse.

For many years the oppressions of King George and his Parliament had been very great; far greater than we could or ought to bear. We knew ourselves to be of the same race and that we had the same birthright to a voice in our government as if we had chosen to remain in our old homes; yet by the Mother Country we were treated as subjected Aliens, as a conquered Nation. During the great French and Indian war it was our Militia Bands (composed of the best blood of the Colonies) which had saved them to Great Britain, yet we were allowed no representation in regard to our own proper affairs. In a large family where one child is treated better than another, an aggrieved feeling grows up among the less favored; so our hearts burned within us with indignation at the injustice of our treatment. As long ago as the time when your dear Father and I were married—seventeen years before the beginning of the war—this feeling was already very strong, and it grew and strengthened with every year. So at last when we heard of the fight at Lexington the news fell like a live coal upon gunpowder.

Never can I or any who were present forget the Sabbath morning on which the news was brought to us. Your Father had been preaching in the lively and spirited manner which is his wont, from Psalms vii., 6. "Arise, O Lord, in thine anger, lift up thyself because of the rage of mine enemies, and awake for me to the judgment thou hast commanded." And after the sermon, which had moved us all, we united in singing the hymn which at that time was a favorite one with us:

> "Let Tyrants shake their iron rod,
> And slavery clank her galling chains;
> We fear them not; we trust in God,
> New England's God forever reigns."

Before the close of the last line a messenger with jingling spurs strode down the aisle and up the high pulpit stairs, where he told his news to my husband, who proclaimed in clear, ringing tones that the die had been cast, that blood had been shed and there was now no choice between War and Slavery.

We all rose from our seats and could scarcely command ourselves to hear the benediction pronounced, as it was in commanding tones by one who felt that the Lord had commissioned him to bless His people. Outside of the Meeting House, on the very steps of the House of the Lord, full of righteous indignation and trust in the great Ruler of the Universe, one hundred men prepared to march immediately to the scene of action, while three hundred more already belonging to the Trained Bands promised to hold themselves in readiness to follow at short notice. But I must not dwell upon these things. You will find the whole story in history some day as you have already heard it many times from those who took part in it. My task is only to relate my own tale, which is too humble to be ever repeated for other ears than yours, yet which deserves to be remembered as a sure proof that God does not forget the humblest of those who trust in Him.

Your dear Father was among the very first to volunteer and received the honored post of Chaplain of the 4th Connecticut regiment, commanded by Col. Hinman, and ordered to march to Ticonderoga.

In common with many other well-qualified Pastors, my Husband had been in the habit of receiving into his family from time to time such young men as might wish, after leaving college, to fit themselves for the Gospel Ministry. At this time there were eight such students in our house. My Husband provided for them by engaging his beloved friend, the Rev. Dr. Bellamy of Bethlehem, to come and reside in his house, prosecute the education of the young Theological students, supply the Sharon pulpit and attend to other pastoral duties; a young friend of Dr. Bellamy's engaging to perform like brotherly service for him in his parish. As Dr. Bellamy had two students of his own he brought them with him, which, added to those already in our house, made my family to consist of twenty-two persons besides servants. In our present state of peace and plenty this does not seem so very great a burden; but at that time, when the exactions of the Mother Country had rendered it impossible to import anything to eat or wear and all had to be raised and manufactured at home, from bread-stuffs, rum and sugar, to the linen and woollen for our clothes and bedding, you may well imagine that my duties were not light. Though I can say for myself that I never complained

even in my inmost thoughts, for if I could even give up for the holy
cause of Liberty the Husband whom I loved so dearly that my constant fear was lest I should sin to idolatry, it would assuredly have
ill become me to repine at any inconvenience to myself. And besides,
to tell the truth, I had no leisure for murmuring. I rose with the
sun and all through the long days I had no time for aught but my
work. So much did it press upon me, that I could scarcely divert
my thoughts from its demands even during our family prayers, which
thing both amazed and displeased me, for during that hour, at least,
I should have been sending all my thoughts to Heaven in prayer for
the safety of my beloved Husband and the salvation of our hapless
Country; instead of which I was often wondering whether Polly had
remembered to set the sponge for the bread, or to put water on the
leech-tub, or to turn the cloth in the dyeing vat, or whether enough
wool had been carded for Betsey to start her spinning wheel in the
morning. or Billy had chopped light wood enough for the kindling,
or dry wood enough to heat the brick oven, or whether something
had not been forgotten of the thousand things that must be done
without fail or else there would be a disagreeable hitch in the housekeeping. So you may be sure that when I went to bed at night I
went to sleep and not to dream or to lie awake imagining all sorts
of disasters that might happen. There was generally enough that
had happened to keep my mind at work if I stayed awake, but that
I very seldom did. A perfectly healthy woman has good powers of
sleep. So you can see that what I am going to relate arose from no
unhealthy condition of mind or body.

The means of communication between us and General Schuyler's
Army were very scant at any time, and during the whole of August
and part of September, 1775, we had received no news at all, unless
you might so call the rumors which were constantly flying about.
On the third Sabbath in September Dr. Bellamy gave us a sound and
clear sermon in which God's watchful Providence over His People
was most beautifully depicted, and drew tears from the eyes of those
who were unused to weeping. And during the prayer meeting of the
evening the same thought was dwelt upon in a way showing that all
who spoke and prayed felt that our God is indeed a Father to all who
trust Him. So on that night I went to bed in a calmer and more
contented frame of mind than usual. I had, to be sure, been much
displeased to find that our supply of bread (through some wasteful
mismanagement of Polly's) had grown so small that the baking

would have to be done on Monday morning, which is not good housekeeping, for washing should always be done on Monday and the baking on Tuesday, but I had caused Polly to set a large sponge and made Billy provide plenty of firing, so that by getting up betimes in the morning, we could have the big oven heated and the baking out of the way by the time Billy and Jake should have gotten the clothes pounded out ready for boiling, so the two things should not interfere with each other. The last thought on my mind after committing my dear Husband and Country into our Maker's care for the night, was to charge my mind to rise even before daylight that I might be able to execute my plans.

How long I had been asleep I do not know, but judge that it must have been about two hours when I began to be conscious that my Husband's voice was calling me. I tried to rise and go to him, but could not move a muscle. Again I heard that dear voice that had always thrilled my heart, and its tones seemed to me weak and distressful. I could not rise, but after many struggles it seemed to me that I heard another Voice, saying in a low, sweet tone—

"Let her spirit go free. It is His command."

And in an instant I seemed to leave my body still sleeping on my bed—whose curtains were all drawn aside to admit air during the warm night—while my spirit, free and light but very anxious, seemed to be seeking to follow my Husband's call. For a moment I was undecided where to go, but again came the call, this time more clear, distinct and distressful than ever—

"My Wife, come to me! Come!"

Following the sound my spirit traversed long spaces of wood, marsh and water until I arrived at a great Lake. Here I found a boat waiting for me, and men who told me my Husband was very ill and had sent them to meet me or take me to him. I entered the boat without hesitation, and after some time in rowing, the boat touched the strand near stone walls, on which cannon were planted, and I was immediately conducted into a log house, where I found my beloved Husband, flushed and burning with fever, lying upon a mattrass of straw laid on a small camp-bedstead. He did not know me, but I heard an attendant say—

"She is come! Wonderful are thy ways, O Lord."

And I looked and saw that the speaker was one of our own church members—(Samuel Elmer, then Major of the Regiment) who was watching by my Husband's side. Then again I heard the sweet, clear Voice saying—"Take her back." I tried to resist, but ceased when the Voice said—

"You shall return, and your Husband's life shall be granted to the prayers of his Flock."

. I awoke. It was still in the depths of the silent September night. By my side slumbered my little Mary. On another bed within reach of my hand were Juliana and Betsey. They were both sitting up in bed. Juliana asked me—

"Mother, did you speak?"

"No, my daughter."

"But, mother," said Betsey, "I thought I heard you say—'His life shall be granted to the prayers of his Flock.'"

"No, my dears," I replied. "I did not say it." But I knew that they too had heard the Voice that had spoken to me. I bid them go to sleep again, and like obedient children they did so, and as soon as they were sound, I rose and knelt by the bed in the spot where my dear Husband and I always used to kneel, and I most earnestly prayed for the Lord's care and direction in the journey which I was to begin on the morrow.

When I rose from my knees, strengthened and heartened, I did not again seek my couch, but lighted a candle and sat down to write out instructions for the guidance of Juliana, who, young as she was, must try to take my place as head of the household during my absence. I tried to remember everything, and truly it seemed that both my Memory and Reason were mightily helped, for afterwards when I read over the paper, it appeared to me that I must have had previsions of just the instructions Juliana would need.

As early as three o'clock in the morning I called Nancy and Judy, Jake and young Billy, but would not allow old Billy to be disturbed; whereat the rest marvelled, seeing that I was not used to be more tender of him than of any of the other servants, but rather the less so, that he was my own slave that my Father had given to me upon my marriage. But I let them marvel, for truly it was no concern of theirs, and by five o'clock the bread was ready to be molded, the hickory coals were lying in a great, glowing mass on the oven's bottom, casting a brilliant light over its vaulted top, and sending such a heat into my face when I passed by the oven-mouth that it caused me to think then, as it always does, of Nebuchadnezzar's fiery furnace, seven times heated. . Young Billy was already pounding out the clothes, and over the fire Jake was hanging the great brass kettles of water for the washing, while Nancy and Judy had made ready the piles of smoking hot Johnny cake, the boiler of wheat-coffee (which was all we could get in those days, and a poor substitute it was for good Mocha), and the big platters of ham and eggs and plenty of good potatoes roasted in the ashes, which is the best way that potatoes can be cooked, in my opinion.

This was a full hour earlier than our usual breakfast, but it did not take long to assemble the Family to Prayers. It seemed that every one felt an unusual stir in the air that morning.

Before the prayer I had called Dr. Bellamy aside and requested his most earnest petitions for one who was that day to begin an arduous journey, and for one lying at the point of death, but more than this I would not then tell him. It seemed to me, though, that he was mightily helped in prayer that morning, for powerful indeed were his pleadings at the Throne of Grace, and when we rose from our knees all the family were moved, some of them even to tears, though they knew not why. It was not until we were all seated at the table that good Dr. Bellamy spoke—

"My sister," he said, "have you no communication to make to us? It seems to me that some heavy burden is lying upon you. Your face is very pale and you have the air of those who ate the Passover in silence and in haste, with staff in hand ready to depart."

"Truly is it so, Dr. Bellamy," I answered. "I have been warned of God in a dream that my revered and beloved Husband is nigh unto death at that Fort in the Wilderness, and I am this morning starting to join him."

For a moment there was not a sound. I should think that not even a breath was drawn around that table. Only Polly, who, by reason of her age, took great privileges to herself, put down the big plate of corn bread she was bringing fresh from the kitchen, and standing just behind my son Johnny's chair, raised her hands up as high as her red plaided turban, and rolling up her eyes so that only the whites showed like two ivory balls rolling in ink, ejaculated:

"Bress de Lawd! Bress de Lawd, Missy Temp'runce" (Polly, too, had been given me by my Father and could never remember to call me by any other than my childhood's name). "*Is* you done gone struck?"

Her manifest fright was in some sort a relief, for it made us all smile, though I have no doubt that others also thought that my senses were gone.

Dr. Bellamy was the next to speak, and began by remonstrating with me and even intimating that I was arrogating too much to myself when I thought that the Lord had condescended to grant visions to me. But I soon silenced him; first, by repeating my dream, and second by showing him pretty plainly that I was not beholden to him for his opinions or permission, but was going to set out directly we had breakfast.

Your dear Father's brother, Dr. Simeon Smith, had then lately bought a chaise (the only one at that time owned in western Connecticut), and when he left home to go with the troops he had told me to use it as I saw fit. So I had intended to drive the chaise myself, while old Billy should sit beside me and lead an extra horse. But Dr. Bellamy made me think better of this, saying that it was tempting Providence to venture forth in such a manner without at least two spare horses. So it was finally decided that the eldest student, Mr. Seth Swift (now and for many years pastor of the Congregational Church in Pittsfield, Mass.), should ride with me in the chaise leading a spare horse, and that old Billy should ride on horseback and lead a fourth horse, as far as Albany, and even beyond that if the roads should prove to be further practicable for wheels; and that then Mr. Swift and I should continue our journey on the best two horses, leaving Billy with the others to go back home or to remain and await our return as might then seem most judicious. Both of the led horses were saddled, and one saddle was provided with a Pillion, that we might both be able to continue on our way if reduced to even one horse.

It was hardly yet seven o'clock and the heavy dews of the morning were still sparkling like lately shed tears on the face of a smiling child, when we all assembled under the big Ash which had once been the Council Tree of the warlike Wegnagnock Indians, and now shaded the doorsteps of a Minister of God, who was perhaps as warlike as his predecessors here, though always and only for Righteousness sake.

This journey was indeed a terrible undertaking. About one hundred and sixty miles, and the last sixty through an unbroken Wilderness, but I felt no fear. I was only anxious to depart, and joined with all my heart, though silently, in the good old Connecticut hymn which Dr. Bellamy started to cheer our way.

"God led them through the Wilderness,
  His people, blessed of yore,
For us we trust He'll do no less,
  Rather, we'll hope for more.

"Transplanted Vines, He brought us here,
  He brought and will sustain,
If Sin alone we shun and fear,
  We cannot trust in vain.

"Let Satan rage and dangers rise,
  If God our strength uphold,
We'll turn our eyes unto the skies
  And trust like Them of old."

My heart was very full as we crossed the brook at the foot of the hill, its clear brown water sparkling over its gravelly bed and roaring beneath the fringe of drooping willows as loudly as if in the spring time, but not loudly enough to drown the Sacred Song pouring from the lips of Children and Friends.

Our way lay North by West through Shekomeco, striking the great Post Road on the boarders of the Hudson at Red Hook. We did not stop at Clermont as I should have done at another time, but pushed on that night to Johnstown, five miles beyond. Here we had to put up at a miserable Tavern, where it was impossible to get anything to eat save some Suppawn and fried Pork. But there was plainly no lack of verv bad Rum in the house, for the Roysterers of the Taproom kept up a clanking of pewter mugs and a cheering for King George for the greater part of the night. Near as it was to the patriotic homes of the Livingstons, it seemed that there were yet many who dared to declare themselves for the King, and continued so to do and even worse, until two years later, when Burgoyne's surrender taught them the wisdom of closing their unseemly mouths. At this time they thought themselves surely on the winning side, and it was Mr. Swift and I who had to close our mouths and not tell whither we were bound, lest we be hindered on our way.

The next morning, after an early breakfast of the same material as the previous supper, we headed for Albanv. All this part of our way was simple enough, I having been as far as Albany no less than three times, for I was ever fond of travel, and my old friend Catherine Livingston (now Widow of the late and Mother of the present Patroon Van Rennsalaer) had ever been very insistent that we should not allow the "Silver links of Friendship's chain to rust for the want of energy to take long journeys," as she was used to phrase it.

Much of the distance this day we were in full sight of the sweeping Hudson, burning with a sapphire glow between its dark emerald banks, and always were in view of the great dusk masses of the Catskills, seeming to belong to another world, so aloof are they in their splendid height and majestic loveliness, so veiled in mystery and silence as the dark piles of clouds rise from hidden valleys and gather round their frowning domes. I love the smiling, fruitful terraces of our own Yaghanic Hills, but better still do I love the grandeur and isolation and grim terrors of the mysterious mountains. The sight of them comforted me at every step, and sorry was I when they fell behind and no longer showed me a face of steadfast friendliness, and I do not wonder that King David of old was wont to lift up his eyes unto the Hills, for thence truly seemeth to come our Help.

Still, I was very anxious to get on as fast as possible. It is about ninety-five miles from Sharon to Albany, and with such good roads we ought perhaps to have been able to get on five miles beyond Albany by the night of the second day, but neither of us knew anything of the way beyond that place, and besides I thought it better to stop over night with my friend Mrs. Van Rennsalaer and take counsel with her.

I found her as ever, loving and hospitable, though much troubled at the perilous condition of our Country, and yet a little inclined to make a jest of my "attempting to follow a dream through the Wilderness." But I heeded not this, knowing in my heart that my dream was no common one, but a Vision sent of God. Besides, my Grandfather had commanded a regiment of Cromwell's Ironsides and I was too much his descendant to be frightened out of a righteous thing by words of Ridicule, even from one so skilled in the use of that weapon as was Catherine. A few months later when she had fled from Albany with her young son (now the Patroon, General Stephen Van Rennsalaer) and had taken refuge in our house, fearing for the safety of her son who had so much property that he would have been a valuable prize to the British, she told me how she had been convicted by my steadfast demeanor at that time, and how it always gave her strength to believe in the goodness of God, as she had never before believed in it, to see how firm and strong was my Faith. But in truth it might better have been called Knowledge than Faith, for the

Great Apostle has defined Faith to be the evidence of things not seen, and I had *seen*. Though only in a vision of the night, yet I had seen, and it was not Faith but Knowledge that bore me on my way.

By the advice of Mrs. Van Rennsalaer, Mr. Swift and I proceeded in the Chaise drawn by one of her own fresh horses, while one of her servants and old Billy rode the worst two of mine and led the best two as far as Schuylersville, which made the end of our third day's trip, for though it was not quite thirty miles, the roads not being so good as from Red Hook to Albany, our progress was slower. At Schuylersville we found the settlement which the sagacious and patriotic General Philip Schuyler had caused to be planted at the period when the exactions of our Tyrants first became too grievous to be endured, in order that there might be made some of the things which we could no longer import from the Mother Country.

Here we found mechanics of every class and hundreds of them, for here had General Schuyler built saw-mills and smithies, and mills for spinning and weaving wool and flax. Also he had many men and women engaged in the culture of flax.

Here, too, was his country-seat, at which hospitable home Mr. Swift and I met a warm welcome not only on account of the letter which I bore from Mrs. Van Rennsalaer, but also because my Husband as Chaplain of Colonel Hinman's regiment had used his influence with the men to soften the bitterness of feeling which so many of them entertained toward "the Dutchman," as they were wont somewhat contemptuously to style General Schuyler. The latter is a man of the purest patriotism and of much capacity, but he was then unused to the state of things in our Colonies of New England, whereby a man of the best birth and breeding may yet be a mechanic or a tradesman by reason of the poverty of the land and of the fact that so many of us had been obliged to relinquish all our estates when for Conscience' sake we left the Mother Country. On the contrary such of the settlers from Holland as were of good family were able to bring their worldly goods with them to the new land, and by reason of the fertility of the soil and their advantageous trade with the Indians were never obliged to resort to handicrafts for a livelihood. My Husband has many a time told us of the surprise of General Schuyler to find that one of our privates whom he knew to be but a carpenter, was at the same time a man of much influence in his native town, being the son of a Colonial Magistrate. He could never be brought to see that while we in Connecticut were all so

much on a social equality, it was yet an equality on a high plane;
while on the other side it was very difficult for our men (so many of
whom, though poor, had received the best education that the country afforded) not to feel themselves superior "to a parcel of stupid
Dutchmen" (thus discourteously, I grieve to say, were they often
referred to), many of whom spoke but imperfect English and almost
none of whom had received a collegiate training. My Husband had
all along been striving to bring about a better understanding between the troops of Connecticut and New York and had thus gained
and still retains the active friendship of General Schuyler. Mrs.
Schuyler was cognizant of much of this, and thus her welcome and
assistance were secured.

On the morning of Thursday we left roads and civilization behind
us and started to enter the Wilderness by means of a Trail to Fort
Edward. This had been traversed so often that we were in no danger of losing our way, though the woods were very thick and dark
and the underbrush greatly annoyed our poor horses. Mr. Swift
had taken the strongest of them and the saddle with the pillion to
be ready for use in case of necessity, while I followed on the next best
of our horses. Behind my saddle across the back of my horse was a
large bag of feed for the animals, and from the pommel of my saddle
hung as large a packet of edibles for ourselves as could well be car-
ried, made up by Mrs. Schuyler's own kind hands. As Mr. Swift
rode on before me I could not help laughing right out at the grotesque figure he cut with a large roll of blankets strapped fast to
the pillion behind him, and leaving only his head and shoulders to
appear above them, while his legs dangled out over the well-stuffed
saddle bags in a most uncomfortable looking fashion. In front of
him was carefully tied another large packet containing Restoratives
and Cordials, for good Mrs. Schuyler was a notable provider for all
medicaments for the sick, and though I had brought some of my
own also, yet would I not decline hers, knowing there might be sore
need.

By agreement with Mrs. Van Rennsalaer, her horse and the poorest
one of mine, together with the chaise, were to be sent back to her
house in charge of her servant, while Billy rode our third horse and
was laden in a similar manner to Mr. Swift, though being behind me
I did not have so good a view of his plight. I have my suspicions
that my own was grotesque enough, for during the earlier part of

our way I several times heard from Billy a half stifled chuckling, indicative of mirth chastened by a proper respect.

It was only fifteen miles from Schuyler'sville to Fort Edwards, yet, the sun was already past noon when we reached it. Being armed by a letter from Mrs. Schuyler, we here met a hospitable welcome from young Lieutenant Philip Livingston (the same who afterwards married Margaret Kane) and a good dinner of ham an eggs and potatoes, for Fort Edward was not so far from civilization as to be so destitute as we later found Fort Ticonderoga to be.

The young officer urged us to remain because at best we could hope to get but little farther that night, but I was too anxious. I felt that I could not delay an unnecessary moment. So, as soon as the horses had eaten we resumed our way, this time being provided with two Indian guides. I felt a little distrustful about this, but Lieutenant Livingston assured me of their faithfulness and I was aware that if any one knew upon whom among the Indians reliance could or could not be placed, it should be one of the Livingston family, who have been trained purposely to acquire that useful knowledge, some one of them being always habituated to live in the very midst of the Savages to learn their ways and languages, and to gain an influence over them; and this is one of the wise things that have contributed to make that noble and talented family at once so rich and so powerful in our country.

So I commended our way to God and went on trustfully, but our progress was very slow. In spite of the long drought we found that in the midst of these dense and lofty pine and cedar forests there were many spots where there was danger of getting mired and so we had to make long turns, sometimes almost doubling upon our tracks for long distances, and always having to move very slowly, by reason both of the heavy nature of the way for our good horses, and of the caution necessary to get through the underbrush and beneath the low growing branches of the younger trees, without having our eyes torn out by branches and twigs flung into the faces of those in the rear, by the recoil from the one who had first passed through them. With all our care Billy, in following me, had received a severe blow from a branch which escaped from my hand as I was trying to hold it until he could take it in his hand.

Night seems to come on very early in the woods. It was but rarely that we could catch through the trees the yellow glow of the sunset, and deep darkness settled down upon us before we had accomplished more than ten miles. Having reached a small clearing where many fires had evidently been made before ours, it was decided to pitch our camp for the night.

The guides had brought axes, and while Mr. Swift and Billy were attending to the horses, and I was unpacking the blankets and provisions, they were cutting down fine young cedar trees and gathering as many dry pine branches as they could find. When they had made a great pile of these small trees and with their trunks directed inward to a point, and their light branches outward and filled in the interstices with the dry pine branches, the elder Indian from a powder horn sprinkled a very thin thread of gunpowder just under the outer edge of the great fantastic pile which made a heart of darkness in a gloom of lesser dark. Then from the flint of his musket he struck a spark and in an instant the flame had flashed all around the pile and caught to the fine dry branches, and soon all the light pine was blazing and kindling the heavy green wood of the fragrant cedar, as the flame of God's love may surround and finally enkindle our hardened hearts. The heart of darkness was now become a centre of flame in a circle of shadow. The ruddy high streaming light from the pine mingled with the thick fragrant smoke from the green cedar, brightening and coloring it as the sun brightens and colors the rolling clouds, and flashed and gleamed over the ground brown and slippery with pine needles, and upon the dense mass of surounding evergreens which seemed to guard us like the walls of a temple.

With two of the blankets and a few poles the men made a rude tent for me in which over a thick bed of pine needles they spread another blanket for a couch, for themselves were content each to roll himself in a blanket and lie down facing the flame; only Mr. Swift did not lie down, for he feared that hostile Savages might be attracted by our fire. For my part I feared neither the Indians nor the wolves which howled around us. Such was the confidence in the vision which God had vouchsafed to me, that I felt sure that neither prowling Savage nor roaming Wolf would be allowed to assault us, and I fell asleep as calmly as if the beasts of the Forest were no more to be dreaded than are the Frogs which fill the long summer nights with their booming.

Towards morning I waked and insisted on Mr. Swift's getting some sleep, while I watched; for, in despite of all my confidence in God, I did not feel like trusting this duty to the Guides, and I knew that old Billy would fall asleep if a Tomahawk were flashing over his head.

So I sat by the fire, or walked around it, musket in hand, and watched the high blazing pillar of fire growing lower and lower, while star after star came forth from the darkness, showing pale and mysterious on the deep black desert of sky, and then fading away again as Dawn approached, and turned the sky from blackness to a pale grayness gradually flushed into a rosy pink, and then glorified it with the golden glow of a new morning shedding hope and joy and beauty over the purple hills, and brightening even the dense gloom of the solemn woods.

All were early astir, for though the distance from our camp to the little Settlement at the head of Lake Champlain was only about twenty miles as the bee flies, it would be made much longer by the circuitous path which wood, ravine, marsh and water would compel us to take. If, indeed, that might be called a path which few save the Red Man of the Forest had traversed until within the past few months.

Shortly after breaking camp we noticed gatherings of clouds into those full, softly rounded masses which children call "Thunderheads," delicately gray on their lower sides and changing into uncertain purples and faint pinks and snowy whites, as the sun shone on their fleecy curves. As the day wore on these scattered groups of clouds collected into greater ones, and exchanged their light and glory of shifting color for gloomy deeps of gray and purple, and the whole Heaven became overcast.

We pressed our horses on as fast as possible, but had not accomplished half our distance when the sky became black and threatening, flashes of lightning darted across the Heavens, and thunders rolled in a fury of warning, while yet the air all around us was so silent and motionless that even the ever busy insects were hushed as with terror at the lurid light like that of fire shining through fog, which filled the atmosphere and made the more distant trees look dim and ghostly in its glare.

Then in the pine-tree tops the wind began its solemn whispers, changing them rapidly into shrieks as of agony as it descended and filled the air with riven branches and beat the stately trees before it, till they bent and swayed like waving plumes or snapped like clay pipe stems, while the deep, harmonious thunder tones shook the Earth and rolled through the Forest in wild and marvellous Music. Our terrified horses cowered and whinned a piteous appeal to us for the help we could not give. Crows, hawks and small song birds together sought the densest thickets for shelter. The gloom around us deepened till it became black like the woods that enclosed our camp the previous night, and the lurid flashes of the lightning only served to show us our helplessness.

Then the rain began. Not in scattering drops leading up to a heavy shower, but in sheets as if we were under the great Waterfall which the Guides had told us was but about five miles away,* and

*Glen's Falls.

the dry ground beneath our horses' feet was converted into a shallow lake, and glares of Lightning flashed so burningly across our eyes that we could no longer see. We could only hear the angry thunder's incessant roar and feel the drenching downpour of a rain so cold that it penetrated our clothes like icy daggers. And then our horses cowered with fear and fled we knew not where, for a Bolt had split in twain a gigantic tree not far away, and our horses ran as if Fiend-ridden deeper and deeper into the heart of the horrid gloom, we powerless to do ought save to hang to their necks, all our boasted Human Intelligence being absorbed by the one effort to keep our seats and hold our breaths. Yet all the while I knew no fear. I knew that I was fulfilling a mission appointed to me, and my heart was serene in its high hope and confidence.

At last the wind sank, the lightnings become less frequent and vivid, the thunder roll receded and became soft and almost tender, like the rich, subdued harmonies of the Organ I heard in old Boston Cathedral when in my girlhood I visited England with my Father, and our blinded eyes became once more able to see, though they ached for days thereafter, and the horses dropped from their wild, terrified running to a gentle pace, and the glorious sun shone out warm and bright over great trees still trembling from their fight for life and shining as bedecked with diamonds. Again the World was new and the crows sped away with hearty *caw-caws* as if the miracle of Transfiguration had been of their doing, while the little birds fled in screaming terror from the hawks which so lately had cowered by their sides in the fraternity of a common danger.

Where were we? Where were our Guides? Neither question could we answer. In the depths of this diamond flashing forest we were still helpless as prisoners in a Donjonkeep. Yet I did not fear. "Let us rest here," I said, "our Guides will follow our wild trail and bring us back to the path." And in the midst of the flashing, quivering, glorified solitude, we lifted up our voices and sang the solemn song of Thanksgiving which David raised, when in the Wilderness God had delivered him from the hand of Saul. And even while we sang there came to our ears a faint Halloa! which we answered, and ere long appeared our two faithful Guides, who turned us upon our right way again, and finally in much bodily discomfort but great peace of mind we reached the collection of huts at the foot of Lake Champlain, now known as Whitehall, where we were most hospitably received, fed and sheltered.

Arrived here—I shame to say it—my Faith hitherto so sustaining began to falter, for here I had confidently expected to find in waiting the boat I had seen in my dream. But none was there, and during that night I told myself a thousand times that after all I was but a Visionary, and that my beloved Husband would censure me for having imagined ourselves to be of so much consequence that I should be warned of God in a dream like Joseph of old. And in the morning I watched and waited with a sinking heart until well on to Noon, when I discerned a long boat with a sail and also with Oarsmen pulling down the glittering, placid Lake, and then I bent my knees and thanked my God with a full heart the while that I bewailed my faithlessness, and I was not at all surprised when dear Mr. Isaac Chamberlain (now Deacon Chamberlain) got out of the boat and came toward me, and with uplifted hands and trembling voice exclaimed—

"Now have I indeed seen the wonderful ways of God!"

Sailing and rowing up the long Lake, beaming between forest-crowned hills, over which the vivid crimson and gold of early Autumn were already mingling with the deep green and purple glooms of late Summer, I heard the story of the way in which my beloved Husband had fallen a victim to the deadly fever of the Camp, by his tireless ministrations to the Sick, and how during the previous night rousing from a heavy stupor he had spoken in a way so authoritative that they dared not disobey, and told his watchers that in the morning they must man a Bateau and go down the Lake to the Settlement, that there I was waiting to come to him; and how General Schuyler had said that they could go, for though it must be the delirium of fever, yet it was possible that news and supplies might be at the Settlement, and it could do no harm to go down.

Toward the sun, setting as a blessed Sabbath peace was settling over the world, our Bateau touched the rocky shore and I was led to the rude log cabin in which your dear Father lay, attended by the

very man of my dream—Major Elmer—who as he saw me raised his-
hands and exclaimed (just a I had heard him in my dream) "**Won-**
derful! wonderful are thy ways, O God !'"

My beloved Husband did not know my voice, but having been
Divinely led so far I could but trust all would yet be well. And so it
was, and when your dear Father came to himself, he was not surprised to find me by his side, but only pleased and happy as he might.
have been had he been expecting me, as, indeed, he had been. He afterwards told me that on the night of my wonderful dream he had
prayed for my coming and called aloud for me in a Voice that roused
the Watch, and that then he had received a comforting Assurance
that his prayers were answered, and though all about him had lost
hope, he had no fear for me or for himself.

Thus had God led me, and thus I found my Husband at Death's-
very door, and thus did God keep the promise made to me in my
dream, that I might be blessed to save a life so useful to his Family
and to his Flock. This, my Children, I have written out to the
end that you may tell of God's goodness to your Children and your
Children's Children to the latest generation. T. W. S."

The old homestead is still oc
cupied by the descendants of
the family.

" The house was built by Genoese
architect and workmen, brought.
across the sea for that purpose.
They kept secret their method of
mixing the cement which holds the
stones together. It is as hard now
as marble, and the rigors and
damps of over one hundred New
England winters have not disinti-
grated a morsel.

It is a stately home for a stately
race, and a history that has not a
blot. Upon the walls of the sitting-
room are the portraits of the brave
pastor and his faithful wife. He
was painted for and at the order of

his parishioners, "who insisted
that he should be painted in the act
of preaching. It is a pity, for he
was really a handsome man, and
possessed great dignity of manner."
Echoing "the pity of it!" we turn
to the placid visage framed by the
mob-cap, and seek in the gentle,
serious eyes of Temperance (Worthington) Smith traces of the fire that
enabled her to overbear erudite Dr.
Bellamy's remonstrances, when he
even intimoted that she was arro-
gant in believing "that the Lord
had condescended to grant visions
to her." The clear cut face of their
son, Governor John Cotton Smith,
is between those of the grand old
couple."--From the "Home Maker,"
Vol. 2, No. 6.

Children of Temperance by her
first husband.

1. Temperance Gale and per-
    haps one other.
    Children by second husband

1. Elizabeth Smith, b. June 29,
    1750, in Sharon, Conn.; m.
    Dr. Lemuel Wheeler of Red
    Hook, N. Y., son of ———
    Wheeler and Anna Gros-
    venor.

    Mrs. Elizabeth Wheeler
    died in Jan., 1788.

Ch.

1. Eliza Maria Wheeler, b. —, 1784; d —, 1859; m. John Alfred Davenport of New York. Six children.
2. Mary Wheeler, b. Jan. 5, 1786; m. Hubert Van Wagener, March 20, 1808, and d. Aug. 13, 1864. Eight children.

2. Juliana Smith, b. Feb. 12, 1761, in Sharon, Conn.; m., 1782, Hon. Jacob Radcliff of Albany, N. Y. (b. ——, 1763, in Rhinebeck, N. Y.), son of William Radcliff and Sarah Kip; was one of the Judges of the Supreme Court of New York state. He died ——, 1840, in Troy, N. Y.

Mrs. Juliana Radcliff died June 25, 1823.

Ch.

1. William Smith Radcliff, b. ——, 1793; d. ——, 1821.
2. John Cotton Radcliff left home when 21 years old and was never heard of afterwards.
3. Maria Clara Radcliff, b. —— 1792; d. ——, 1875.
4. Charles Radcliff.
5. Julia Radcliff.

3. Thomas Mather Smith, b. Jan. 21, 1763; d. April 18, 1782.

4. John Cotton Smith, b. Feb. 12, 1763, in Sharon, Conn.

"The son of Cotton Mather Smith and the beautiful daughter of Rev. William Worthington of Saybrook, John Cotton Smith, was a striking figure in a day when there were giants in the land. A handsome person, features classically beautiful; natural gracefulness, ready wit and culture, a model of the Christian gentleman."— From the "Home Maker," Vol. 2, No. 6.

He was a member of the Connecticut Council, twice speaker of the Connecticut House of Representatives; three times elected to Congress; Judge of the Connecticut Superior Court; Lieutenant-Governor and Governor from 1812 to 1817, and the last Governor under the charter of Charles II. M., Oct. 29, 1786, Margaret Evertson (b., 1765, in Amenia, N.Y.), dau. of Jacob and Margaret Bloom Evertson, and had one child,

William Mather Smith (b.
Aug. 6, 1788, d. March,
1864), who m. Helen, dau.
of Gilbert Robert Living-
ston. They had three sons,
one of whom, Dr. Robert
Worthington Smith, m. Gertrude L'Estrange Bolden,
and had three children.

Gilbert Livingston Smith.
Helen Evertson Smith.
Gertrude Smith.
Governor Smith died Dec.
7, 1845.

5. Lucretia Smith, b Jan. 20,
1767, in Sharon, Conn.; d.
——, 1773.

6. Mary Smith, b. Feb. 16,
1769, in Sharon, Conn; m.
Rev. Daniel Smith of Stam-
ford, Conn. (b. 1789, d.
1823), son of Noah Smith
and Anna Kent, and d. Dec.
10, 1801.

Ch.

1. Thomas Mather Smith.
2. Julia Smith, who m. Milo
M. North, M. D.

31. SARAH,   baptized May 19, 1734, in Saybrook,
m., July 12, 1759, Colonel and
Doctor John Ely of Saybrook,
who was then in his twentieth

year. She was considered one
of the most beautiful women of
her day. The Elys settled in
Lyme, Conn., about 1660, and
the family has ever since been
one of influence, many of its
branches being among the sub-
stantial citizens of New York ;
among them was Major Smith
Ely. " In 1775 Dr. John Ely was
the father of seven children, the
most eminent physician in the
county, and wealth flowed in
abundantly. There was every
enticement to hold him in his
elegant, prosperous and happy
home, but with patriotic ardor
he promptly left all to aid the
Revolution. He was then 38
years old. He first mustered
and commanded a militia company. The next year, with the
rank of Colonel, he commanded at Fort Trumbull over a
regiment he had raised by his
own exertions and equipped
with his own money. To do
this he sold one of his farms.
After supplying perfectly the
needs of his soldiers, the remainder of the money in gold
and silver, tied in a silk hand-
kerchief, he brought and poured

into his wife's lap, saying :
" Here, Sarah, is all that is left
of the Griswold farm." She,
like a true mother of the
Revolution, replied with a smile,
" It is the price of liberty."

Dr. John Ely d. Oct. 3, 1800,
aged 63 years.

CHILDREN.

1. Worthington Ely, b. ——.
1760, in Saybrook, Conn.
" He was a man of such
marked ability and such
distinguished characteristics
that he deserves honorable
mention in the annals of the
family. His tall,
graceful figure was remarkable for an air of great
elegance and superiority;
his features were finely
moulded; his eye large, dark
and soft, yet full of the fire
of genius. His intellectual
and moral traits were in
harmony with these fine
physical attributes, and his
manners were so pleasing
that they charmed all who
came within the sphere of
their influence." He graduated at Yale College, and at

nineteen years of age, with
a few others, fitted out
a ship at their own expense,
and, having manned her,
sailed against the English,
hoping by that means to ac-
complish the exchange of
his father, Col. John Ely.
They were successful in
capturing an English force,
but Col. Ely's exchange was
not effected until three years
later.   At twenty-eight he
married Prudence Bushnell.
A few years later he went
south to where the yellow
fever was then raging.   For
many weeks he devoted himself, night and day, to the
care of the sick, until he was
at last stricken down himself. He was obliged to part
with his faithful servant to
pay for medicines and his
expenses home. Soon after
his return to his family they
removed to Coeymans, a
small town four miles west
of the Hudson river, in
Albany co., N. Y., where he
died.

His grand-dau, Charlotte
Augusta, dau. of Jonathan

Southwick of New York city, m. Coventry Waddell, eldest son of Henry and Eliza Dauberry Waddell of New York city, who was U. S. Marshall under President Jackson, Financial Agent of the State Department under Secretaries Edw. Livingstone and John Forsyth, and subsequently official and general assignee in bankruptcy for New York city.

2. Elizabeth Ely, b. ——, 1762; m., July 29, 1784, Rev. Samuel Goodrich (b. Jan. 12, 1763; d. Apr. 19, 1835, in Berlin, Germany), son of Elizur Goodrich and Katharine Chauncey, and brother of Chauncey Goodrich, who was U. S. Senator and Lieut. Gov. of Conn.

Mrs. Elizabeth Goodrich d., Mar. 3, 1837, at Berlin.

Elizur Goodrich (b. Oct. 18, 1734), was son of David of Wethersfield, Conn., and Hepzibah Boardman.

David, b. Dec. 8, 1694, was son of David and Hannah Wright of Wethersfield, Conn.

David, b. May 4, 1667,
was son of Ensign William
Goodrich, one of the first
settlers of Wethersfield,
Conn., and Sarah Marvin
his wife, who were m. Oct.
4, 1648, at Hartford, Conn.
Wm. Goodrich d. in 1676.

Ch. of Samuel and Elizabeth
(Ely) Goodrich.

1. Sarah Worthington Goodrich, b. Aug. 7, 1785; m.,
   1st, Amos Cooke; 2nd,
   Hon. Frederick Wolcott.
2. Elizabeth Goodrich, b. Apr.
   26, 1787; m. Rev. Noah
   Coe.
3. Abigail Goodrich, b. Nov.
   29, 1788; m. Rev. Samuel
   Whittlesey.
4. Charles Augustus Goodrich,
   b. Aug. 19, 1790; m. Sarah
   Upson.
5. Catharine Goodrich, b. Dec.
   4, 1791; m. Daniel Dunbar
   of Berlin.
6. Samuel Griswold Goodrich,
   b. Aug. 19, 1793, in Ridgefield, Conn.; m., 1st, Adaline Bradley; 2nd, Mary
   Boot. Was a publisher in
   Hartford, Conn., and Boston, and a writer under the
   name of Peter Parley. He
   d. May 9, 1860, in New
   York city. His son, Frank

Boot Goodrich, b. Dec. 14, 1826, in Boston, grad. H. C., 1845, was for several years Paris correspondent of the *N. Y. Times*, writing under the name of Dick Tinto.

7. Elihu Chauncey Goodrich, b. Nov. 18, 1795; d. June 9, 1797.

8. Mary Ann Goodrich, b. May 29, 1799; m. Hon. N. B. Smith of Woodbury.

9. Emily Chauncey Goodrich, b. Nov. 25, 1801; d. Oct. 22, 1803.

10. Emily Chauncey Goodrich, b. Nov. 13, 1805; m. Rev. Darius Mead.

3. Ethelinda Ely, b.-——, 1764; m., ——, William Mason Eliott (b. June 26, 1755, in Killingworth), her first cousin, son of Aaron Eliott and Mary Worthington, and great - great - grandson of John Eliott, "the Apostle to the Indians."

4. Annie Arnold Ely, bap. July 13, 1766.

5. Lucretia Ely, bap. Feb. 7, 1768; d. Feb. 12, 1769.

6. Lucretia Ely, bap. April 18 1770.

7. Temperahce Ely, bap. Oct. 10, 1772.

8. Edward Ely, bap. Jan. 6, 1777.

32. MEHITABLE,   born Sept. 11, 1736, in Saybrook, Conn.; m., Jan. 16, 1760, Michael Hopkins of Saybrook. They are supposed to have removed to Guilford.

Mrs. Mehitable Hopkins died in 1770, leaving surviving ch.:

1. Augustus Hopkins.
2. George Hopkins.
3. Silvia Hopkins.
4. Belinda Hopkins.

†33. WILLIAM,   born Nov. 21, 1740, in Saybrook, Conn.

7.

DANIEL WORTHINGTON of Colchester, Conn., married, Jan. 3, 1720, Elizabeth (b. Nov. 13, 1702), dau. of Deacon Samuel Loomis, Jr., of same town.

Daniel Worthington died March 1, 1784.
Mrs. Elizabeth Worthington died Dec. 3, 1789.

Children.

34. ELIZABETH,   born July 24, 1721; m., Dec. 19, 1743, Nehemiah Daniels of Hebron, Conn.

Children.

1. Rhoda Daniels, b. April 17, 1744.
2.
3.
4.
5.
6.
7.
8. Jonathan Daniels, b June 1, 1760.
9. Amasa Daniels, b. Sept. 19, 1762.

†35. ELIAS,   born Oct. 31, 1722.

36. ASA,   born June 16, 1724; died Sept. 30, 1751. Unmarried. In 1745 he was witness to a quit claim deed of the Indian reservation of Norwich, Conn., from the decendants of Owaneco and other principal Mohegans, in favor of the English claimants, for the sum of £137. This was the last aboriginal claim to land in Norwich, and amounted to 300 acres, more or less.

37. SIBYL,   born April 19, 1727. Was twice married. 1st, Nov. 8, 1750, to Deacon Elijah Smith (b. in 1723 in Hatfield, Mass.), son of John Smith of So. Hadley, Mass and Elizabeth Hoovy, by whom

she had all of her children.
Deacon Smith died April 21
1770, and she m., 2nd, in 1771
Reuben Smith (b. in 1723),
cousin to her first husband. He
died in July, 1798. Elijah Smith
served as Captain in the French
war, 1756, under Gen. Wm. Johnson, in the regiment of Col.
Ephraim Williams. Was deacon
in the church of Belchertown,
Mass. "He was a man," says
Rev. Mr. Forward, in the
Church records, "of sound
judgment, ready utterance,
pleasing deportment and ardent
piety." After the death of her
2nd husband, Mrs. Sibyl Smith
lived with his children in So.
Hadley until the winter of 1806,
and then with her son, Jacob,
in Hadley, until her death on
May 26, 1827, in her 101st
year. She was a remarkable
woman, not only on account of
her age, but upon the retention
of her faculties to the last. On
her one hundredth birthday she
attended church and listened to
a centennial sermon preached
by Dr. Woodbridge of Hadley.

Joseph Smith, grandfather of
Elijah, first husband of Sibyl

Worthington, removed from Wethersfield, Conn., to Hadley, Mass., about 1659. He was son of Joseph from England (who settled in Hartford in 1651). Had four sons who lived to maturity.

1. Joseph.
2. John, b. 1686.
3. Jonathan.
4. Benjamin.

2. John, the father of Elijah, settled in Hadley, and d. in 1777, aged 91. Had children:

1. John.
2. Abner, father of Rev. Eli Smith of Derby, Conn.
3. Daniel.
4. Joseph, father of Rev. Eli Smith of Hollis.
5. Rev. Amasa.
6. Rev. Dr. John of Bangor, Me.
7. Elijah, who m. Sibyl Worthington.

Ch. by 1st Husband.

1. Asa Smith, b. May 7, 1752; m., in 1782, Submit Severance, and died at Halifax Conn., Feb. 13, 1835.

Ch.

1. Elijah Smith, b. March 1, 1783.
2. Jesse Smith b. May 22, 1785.

3. Clarissa Smith, b. Feb. 26, 1788.
4. Asa Smith, b. Aug. 9, 1790; d. Sept. 10, 1810.
5. Miranda Smith, b. Sept. 27, 1792.
6. Sibyl Smith, b. Feb. 2, 1795.
7. Jareb Smith, b. March, 9, 1797.
8. Theophilus Smith, b. Feb. 17, 1800, in Halifax, Conn· Grad. Y. C. 1824; m., June 27, 1831, Hannah B. St. John. Was ordained pastor in New Canaan, Conn., Aug. 31, 1831, and d. Aug. 29, 1853.
9. Tirzeh Smith, b. Dec. 17 1802; d. Jan. 27, 1803.

2. Sibyl Smith, b. Aug. 26, 1754; m., Jan. 27, 1774, Deacon Joseph Bardwell of Belchertown and So. Had ley, Conn., and d. Nov. 23, 1829.

Ch.

1. Hadassa Bardwell, b. Dec. 11, 1774; m. Spencer Clark of Worthington, Mass.
2. Electa Bardwell, b. Jan. 9, 1776; m. Jonathan Lyman of Goshen, Mass., son of Sarah Worthington and Josiah Lyman.
3. Josiah Bardwell, b. July 12, 1778; d. March 22, 1845.
4. Experience Bardwell, b.

——; m. —— Lyman of Chester.

5. Asenath Bardwell, b. ——; m. Daniel Hubbard.
6. Violet Bardwell, b. ——; m. Asahel Billings.
7. Theodolia, b. ——, 1791; m. Ira Parsons of Pittsfield, Mass., and d. July 19, 1842.
8. Joseph Bardwell.
9. Alonso Bardwell.

3. Sarah Worthington Smith, b. April 2, 1756; m., Dec. 18, 1777, Elijah Bardwell of Belchertown and Goshen, Mass.

Ch.

1. Rhoda Bardwell, bap. May 9, 1778; m. Wm. Fisher.
2. Sophia Bardwell, bap. Sep. 3, 1780; m. Reuben Dresser.
3. Laura Bardwell, bap. July 14, 1782; m. Calvin Cushman.
4. Anna Bardwell. Elijah Bardwell.
5. Rev. Horatio Bardwell of Oxford, Mass., and missionary to India. Died May 5, 1866.
7. Selah Bardwell.
8. Sarah Bardwell, m. Rev. William Richards of the Indian Mission.
9. Aurelia Bardwell, m. Phoenis Narrarnore.

10. Phoenis Bardwell, d. at 12
years of age.

4. Elijah Smith, b. Dec. 9,
1758; m. Mary Stebbins,
and d. Sept. 7, 1843, at
Greenfield, Mass.

Ch.

1. Robert Smith, b. Sept. 8,
1787.
2. Polly Smith, b. June 18,
1789.
3. Patty Smith, b. March 1,
1793.
4. Orin Smith, b. June 14, 1797.
5. Belinda Smith, b. Dec. 2,
1806.
Five others who died young.

5. Elizabeth Smith, b. Jan. 31,
1761; m., April 23, 1778,
John Cole, and d. July, 1827
at Belchertown, Mass.

6. Rev. Ethan Smith, b. Dec.
15, 1762, grad. Dartmouth
College 1790. He served in
the War of the Revolution,
being at West Point at the
time of Arnold's treason;
was settled successively over
the Congregational churches
of Hopkinson, N. H., Poult-
ney, Vt., and Hanover, Mass.
He published many books,

among which were: "Dissertation on the Prophecies," "View of the Trinity." "Lectures on Baptism." His presence in the pulpit is thus well described:

"All was still as death while the sexton escorted the pastor to the high pulpit. There he stood in powdered periwig, the massive rolls hanging down his shoulders, and in a black robe almost concealing the black silk stockings and the bright shoe buckles. He preached until the sands ran out of the hour glass; and if he sometimes took the second glass, no one found fault, for in those days, before the daily newspaper was thought of, the intellectual feast of the week was served in the church on the Lord's day."

Rev. Mr. Smith married Bathsheba Sanford (b. Feb. 14, 1771, in Gt. Barrington, Mass.), dau. of Rev. David Sanford, who was settled for forty years over the Congregational church of Medway, Mass., and was chaplain in the War of the Revolution; and Bathsheba Ingersoll. Rev. Ethan Smith died Aug. 29, 1849, in Boylston, Mass.

Ch.

1. Myron Smith, b Jan. 10, 1794, d. 1818.
2. Lyndon Arnold Smith, b. Nov. 11, 1795; grad. D.C., 1817; married, Nov. 20, 1823, Francis L. Griffin dau. of Rev. Edw. D. Griffin, D.D., Pres. of Williams College. Mr. Smith was a physician in Newark, N. J.; d. 1866.

Ch.

1. Malvina Smith.
2. Edward D. G. Smith.
3. Frances Louisa Smith.
4. Lyndon Arnold Smith.
5. Sanford Huntington Smith.
6. Myron Winslow Smith.

3. Rev. Stephen Sanford Smith, b. Apr. 14, 1797, was for many years a pastor of the Cong. ch. in Warren, Mass.; m., in 1823, Lucretia Bishop.

Ch.

1. Emily Smith.
2. Maria Louisa Smith.
3. David Sanford Smith.
4. Henry Martyn Smith.
5. Cornelia Stevens Smith.
6. Elizabeth Smith.
7. George Smith.
8. Harriet Eliza Smith.

9. Frederick Worthington Smith.

4. Laura Smith, b. June 14, 1799; d ——, 1800.

5. Rev. Carlos Smith, D. D., b. July, 1801; d.——, 1875; grad. U. C., 1822, was pastor of the Cong. ch. in Paines-ville, O., and Akron, O., where he died; m. Susan Saxton.

Ch.

1. Julia Louisa Smith.
2. Harriet S. Smith.
3. Charles Smith.
4. Sarah P. Smith.
5. Harriet S., Smith, 2nd.
6. Ellen Smith.
7. Eliza Smith.
8. Malvina Smith.
9. Ethan Sanford Smith.
10. Grace Fletcher Smith.
11. Grace, Smith, 2nd.

6. Grace Fletcher Smith, b. May 23, 1803, d. 1840; m. Aug. 23, 1827, Rev. J. H. Martyn of N. Y. city, who grad. Middlebury College, 1825; d. 1868.

Ch.

1. Edward Payson, b. June 27, 1828; d.——, 1828.
2. Sarah Louisa, b. Feb. 11, 1830; m., Oct. 14, 1852, R. W. Wright of New Haven, Conn., who grad. Y. C., 1842. The author of "Life, Its

True Genesis." his last
and principal work.

Ch.

1. Grace Livingston.
2. Robert Worthington
3. Robula Virginia.
3. Henry Smith, b. July,
1832, d.——, 1834.
4. Charles Henry, b. Aug.
24, 1836, d. ——, 1873.
5. Sanford Smith, b. July
23, 1839.

7. Sárah Towne Smith, born
Aug. 15, 1805; d.——, 1879;
m., March, 1841, Rev. J. H.
Martyn of N. Y. city.

"She was a woman of
rare culture and refinement,
a brilliant conversational
ist, a graceful writer, and
as thoroughly versed in lit-
erature as in matters of
Church history."
Among her works are:
"Woman of the Bible,"
"The Crescent and the
Cross," "The Huguenots
in France."

Ch.

1. Wm. Carlos Martyn.
2. Malvina Martyn.
3. Frank Lancing Martyn
4. Herbert Sedgwick Mar-
tyn.

8. Harriet Smith, b. Sept. 12,
1807; m., Aug. 23, 1830,

Rev. Wm. H. Sanford, who grad. H. U. and d. in Worcester, Mass., in 1879.

Ch.

1. Myron, b. July 12, 1831.
2. Elizabeth, b. Oct. 22, 1833.
3. William, b. Sept. 18, 1856.
4. George Lyndon, b. Jan. 17, 1838.
5. Charles Ethan, b. July 27, 1840.
6. Frank Dwight, b. Aug. 30, 1848.

9. Ellen Chase Smith, b. Dec. 3, 1812; d.——, 1843; m., in 1838, Charles B. Sedgwick, a lawyer of Syracuse N. Y.

Ch.

1. Ellen, b. ——, 1841.
2. Charles B., b.——, 1843.

7. Deacon Jacob Smith, b. Dec. 15, 1764; married Martha Lyman, and died April 5, 1832.

Ch.

1. Elizabeth Smith, b. Jan. 26, 1798; m. Rev. Wm. Hervey of the Indian mission, and sailed for Bombay Aug. 2 1830, where she d. May 3, 1831.
2. Sibyl Worthington Smith

b.——, 1800; m.; ——, 1825,
Reuben Dresser.
3. Elijah Smith, b. ——, 1802.
4. Esther Smith, b. Aug. 17,
1805; m. John Dunbar and
went to the Pawnes as mis
sionary.
5. Martha Smith, b.——, 1809;
m. Rev. Orlando G. Hub-
bard of Leominster, Mass.
6. Henry Smith, b ——, 1813;
d. ——, 1823.
7. Miranda Smith, b. Aug. 24,
1816; m. Rev. P. Belden of
. Amherst, Mass., and d.
Sept. 29, 1848.

8. William Smith, b. Nov. 15,
1766. Lived at Scipio, N.
Y., until 1825; m. Mary
Foster.
9 Joseph Smith, b.——. Lived
at Scipio; m. there, in 1828,
Polly Capen.

Mrs. Sibyl Worthington
Smith lived to see her descendants of the fifth generation, and died May 26,
1827, at the age of 101
years. All her children lived
until the youngest was 56
years old.

†38. SAMUEL, born Feb. 16, 1728 or 9.
39. RHODA, born Sept. 25, 1730; m., Oct. 15,
1734, Thomas Smith of Hadley,

Mass., brother of Reuben, who was the 2nd husband of Sibyl Worthington Smith Mrs. Rhoda Smith died in 1831 or 2, over 100 years of age.

CHILDREN.

1. Rhoda Smith, b. Feb. 8, 1755.
2. Lydia Smith, b. Feb. 27 1757; m., Nov. 10, 1779, Seth Smith, and d. Aug. 23. 1828. Mr. Smith d. June 30, 1828.

   Ch.

   1. Ebenezer Smith, b. Aug. 4, 1781; d. June 15, 1782.
   2. Ebenezer Smith, 2nd, b. Jan. 21, 1783; d. Jan. 22, 1783.
   3. Rev. Seth Smith, b. July 4, 1785; grad. Y. C. 1803; m. Nov. 29, 1816, Margaret Porter, and d. Jan. 30, 1849.
      They lived at Genoa, N. Y. Had 9 ch.
   4. Ephraim Smith, b. June 17, 1786; d. Jan. 8, 1788.
   5. Ephraim Smith, 2nd, b. Oct. 8, 1788; m., Jan. 29, 1812, Ruth Smith, who d. April 27, 1857.
      He d. Nov. 7, 1869, at So. Hadley.
   6. Elijah Smith, b. Oct. 24,

1791; m., Dec. 3, 1817,
Maria Smith, and d. June
20, 1861.

7. Rev. Worthington Smith,
D. D., b. Oct. 11, 1793;
grad. W. C. 1816; m., July
1, 1823, Mary Ann Little.
He was President of Ver-
mont University . 1844–
1855, and d. Feb. 13, 1856.

8. Lydia Smith, b. March 13,
1795; m., July 3, 1826,
Wm. Owen Gadcomb, and
d. Feb. 13, 1856, at St.
Albans, Vt.

3. Daniel Smith, b. Oct. 26,
1759; m. Lucy Cook of
Williamstown, Mass.

4. Thomas Smith, b. Dec. 3,
1761; m. Catherine ———.
They were of Hadley, Mass.

Ch.

1. Mehitable Smith, b. Dec.
24, 1785.

2. Eunice Smith, b. June 12,
1787; d. same day.

3. Roswell Smith, b. June 24,
1788; d. July 31, 1802.

4. Stephen Smith, b. Jan. 3,
1790.

5. Susanna Smith, b. Oct. 16,
1791.

6. Patty Smith, b. Dec. 15,
1795; d. April 18, 1797.

7. Christopher Smith, b. June
9, 1798.

8. Salome Smith, b. July 1, 1800; d. Aug. 19, 1812.

5. Ephraim Smith, b. Sept. 27, 1764.
6. Mehitable Smith, bap. Feb. 1, 1767; d. Sept., 1775.
7. Loomis Smith, bap. Aug. 17, 1769; d. Sept. 14, 1779.

40. MEHITABLE, born Feb. 10, 1732; d. June 27, 1742.
41. DANIEL, born Aug. 12, 1733, in Colchester, Conn.
42. SARAH, born Nov. 27, 1734; married, Jan. 9, 1759, Major Josiah Lyman of Belchertown and Goshen, Mass. He was the first male child born in Belchertown to live to adult age. Was baptized March 25, 1736, by President Edwards, and died Nov. 18, 1822, at Goshen, Mass.

Mrs. Sarah Lyman died Feb. 19, 1799.

CHILDREN.

1. Deacon Aaron Lyman, b. Oct. 1, 1760; m., Jan. 9, 1788, Electa Graves, and died Aug. 14, 1845, at Charlemont, N. H. She d. Aug. 14, 1848.

They lived at Charlemont N. H., and had ch.

Ch.

1. Josiah Lyman, b. Dec. 12,
   1788; m., May 26, 1819,
   Jerviah A. Loop, and d.
   March 11, 1848. No ch.
2. Eunice Lyman, b. Oct. 21,
   1790; d. Nov. 25, 1826.
3. Sophia Lyman, b. Oct. 27
   1792; d. April 16, 1811.
4. Almira Lyman, b. Sept. 30,
   1794; d. May 4, 1828.
5. Susanna Lyman, b. Sept.
   15, 1796; m., March 6,
   1827, Thomas Carter, and
   d. [Sept. 20, 1869. Had 1
   son, Aaron.
6. Emily Lyman, b. Oct. 14,
   1798; d. April 19, 1822.
7. Margaret Lyman, b. Nov.
   22, 1800; m., Aug. 19,
   1827, Josiah Ballard. Had
   2 ch.
9. Electa Lyman, b. March 28,
   1805; m., Oct. 25, 1831,
   James M. Claghorn, Erie,
   N. Y. Had 3 ch.
10. Myron Lyman, b. May 5,
    1807; d. Oct. 5, 1808.
11. Frederick Augustus Lyman,
    b. June 25, 1809; d. July 8,
    1809.
12. Lynden Graves Lyman, b.
    June 14, 1810; m., 1st, July
    22, 1844, Mary W. Chester,
    who d. Oct. 16, 1847; 2nd,
    Jan. 12, 1859, Jane Robb,
    and d. Sept. 4, 1871, at
    Newark, N. J. 7 Ch.
13. Augustus LeBaron Lyman,

b. June 20, 1813; d. March 8, 1815.

2. Sophia Lyman, b. Jan. 1, 1763; m., in 1757, Amasa Smith of Belchertown.

3. Giles Lyman, b. May 2, 1765; m., Nov. 11, 1785, Mary Hubbard, and d. May 14, 1848, at Fowlersville, N. Y.

Ch.

1. Mary Lyman, b. July 30, 1796; d. July 31, 1796.
2. Lucy Lyman, b. Aug. 1, 1797; m., in 1846, Ebenezer G. Hubbard. who d. Feb. 19, 1868, at Middletown, Conn. She d. Aug. 31, 1866. No ch.
3. Maria Augustus Lyman, b. Nov. 11, 1798; d. Sept. 4, 1801.
4. Elihu Hubbard Lyman, b. Aug. 19, 1800; m. Martha Collins of Lyon, Mich. 2 ch.
5. Rev. Giles Lyman, b. March 16, 1802; grad. Amherst College 1827; m., Dec. 14, 1835, Louise Whitney of Marlborough, N. H.
6. Frederick Lyman, b. June 30, 1804; d. Aug. 28, 1808.
7. Henry Lyman, b. March 30, 1806; d. Aug. 12, 1806.
8. Mary Lyman, b. Nov. 17, 1800; d. March ——, 1850.

9. Sophia Augusta Lyman, b. Dec. 25, 1811; m., May 15, 1834, Wm. Fullerton, M.D., of Chillicothe, O. Had 10 ch.

4. Deacon Jonathan Lyman, b. March 20, 1767; m. Electa Bardwell (b. Jan. 9, 1776 · grand dau. of Sibyl Worthington and Elijah Smith). Lived at Granby, Mass., and d. Sept. 27, 1846. Had no ch.

5. Augustus Lyman, b. May 26, 1769; m., Nov. 6, 1795, Eunice Arms. Lived at Deerfield, Mass., and d. Oct. 14, 1829.

Mrs. Eunice Lyman d. April 14, 1859. Had 6 ch.

†43. JACOB,   born Feb. 3, 1736.

44. MARY,   born Aug. 2, 1737; married, Nov. 24, 1761, Orlando Root of Belcher town, Mass., son of Hezekiah Root, who was one of the first settlers of North Hampton Mass.

Mrs. Mary Root d., in Sept., 1829, in Belchertown.

Mr. Orlando Root d. in 1805 in Belchertown.

CHILDREN.

1. Aseneth Root, b. in ●1762;

m., in 1788, Wm. Towne of
Granville, N. Y. Had 3 ch.

2. Julia Root, b. 1764; m.
Mark Stacy of Belchertown,
and d. 1850.

Ch.

1. Ira Stacy
2. Arba Stacy.
3. Alonson Stacy.
4. Hannah Stacy, m. Israel
Towne.
5. Dimmis Stacy, m. Mark
Hinckley.
6. Julia Stacy, m. Luther
Morse of Boston, Mass.

3. Mary Root, b. 1766 ; m., in
1816, Amasa Cowles of
Belchertown, and d. in 1835.
No ch.

4. Hannah Root, b. 1768; m.
John Miller of Williamsburg,
Mass. Had 3 ch.

5. Dimmis Root, b. March 9,
1771; m., Jan. 5, 1792
Abner Hunt of Williams
burg, and d. Nov. 29, 1856.
Mr. Hunt d. Sept. 12,1847
at Williamsburg.

6. Rhoda Root, b. 1773; m.
Josiah Walker of Illinois.

7. Amanda Root, b. 1775; m.,
in 1800, Amos Washburn

and d. in 1864 at Williamsburg.

8. Orlando Root, b. Jan. 10,
1777; m. Elizabeth, dau. of
Joseph Ramsdell, and d.
March 12, 1823.

Mrs. Root d. Dec. 19, 1852,
aged 74 years.

9. Elihu Root, b. July 5, 1779;
m., Nov. 21, 1803, Levinah
Fay. Lived at Belchertown,
Mass., and d. Jan. 23, 1863,
at Belchertown.

Mrs. Root d. Dec. 18, 1860,
aged 77.

45. TABITHA,   born Nov. 25, 1728, married, Nov.
9, 1758, John Skinner, Jr., of
North Bolton, Conn. (b. Feb.
28, 1728 or 9), son of Dea. John
Skinner and Elizabeth Hitchcock of Colchester, Conn. Mrs.
Tabitha Skinner d. in 1829.

CHILDREN.

1. John Skinner, b. June 6, 1760.

46. ABIGAIL,   born March 10, 1740; m. Benjamin
Mather, Lyme, Conn. (b. Sept.
19, 1732). She was his 2nd
wife. Mrs. Abigail Mather d.
about 1817. Mr. Mather d. at
Whately, Mass.

47. AMY,   born April 12, 1741; m., 1st, April 8,
1752, Noah Sexton of South-

ampton; 2nd, in 1787, Captain
James Walker of Belchertown,
Mass. In 1832 she was the sole
survivor of this large family.

CH. BY 2ND HUSBAND.

1. James Walker.
2. Silas Walker, father of Dr.
   Charles Walker of Northampton, Mass.
3. Hezekiah Walker.
4. Jason Walker.
5. Nathaniel Walker.

48. MEHITABLE,   born July 9, 1742; m., April 12, 1764,
Dea. Aaron Skinner of Shelburne
Mass., and died Aug. 16, 1816.
Mr. Skinner died Aug. 6, 1826.
at Shelburne, to which place
they had removed in 1773.

CHILDREN.

1. Aaron Skinner, b. Jan. 13,
   1765; m., Jan. 14, 1796,
   Charity Nims.

Ch.

1. Aaron Skinner, b. Dec. 29,
   1796. Removed to Bran-
   don, Mich.
2. Charity Skinner, b. April
   17, 1798, in Shelburne,
   Mass.; unm.
3. David Skinner, b. March 9,
   1800; d. Oct. 20, 1820.
4. Eunice Skinner, b. June 8,
   1802; d. Sept. 19, 1842.

5. Fanny Skinner, b. Feb. 4, 1804; m. Lysander Bard well, and d. in May, 1876 at N. Y. city.
6. Electa Skinner, b. April 10, 1806; m. Hiram Holmes, and d. Sept. 19, 1842, at Williamsburg, Mass.
7. Hannah Skinner, b. Feb. 16, 1808.
8. Lydia Skinner, b. Oct. 5, 1810; m. Otway O. Bardwell, and lived at Manteno, Ill.

2. Mehitable Skinner, b. Sept. 13, 1767.
3. Asa Skinner, b. May, 1769; d. —, 1843.
4. Eunice Skinner, b. Feb. 23, 1771; d. July 28, 1803.
5. Appleton Skinner, b. Jan. 5, 1773; m. Rachel Childs, who d. May 19, 1843, aged 64. He d. March 13, 1844, at Shelburne, Mass.
6. Elias Skinner, b. Feb. 4, 1776; d. July 28, 1777.
7. Dr. Elias Skinner, b. Aug. 21, 1778; m. —— Atherton, and moved West. He d. Sept. 25, 1828, at Geneseo, N. Y.
8. Electa Skinner, b. March 23, 1780; d. Oct. 3, 1821.
9. Justin Skinner, b. Dec. 22

1781; m. Betsey Winter, and
removed to Western New
York in 1818.

10. Joel Skinner, b. June 26,
1785; d. Sept. 24, 1785.

49. WILLIAM, born Oct. 20, 1743; died March 4,
1744.

†50. WILLIAM, 2ND, born Jan 29, 1745.

51. AMASA, born April 16, 1746; d. Aug. 4, 1753-4.

52. INFANT, died without name.

10.

ELIJAH WORTHINGTON of Colchester, Connecticut, married,
Oct. 4, 1733, Mary Welles of same town, and died Oct. 13,
1764, at Colchester, aged 54 years.

CHILDREN.

†53. ELIJAH, born, Jan. 1, 1736.

54. MARY, baptized June 24, 1739; married,
April 19, 1759, John Hopson of
Colchester, Conn. (b. Jan. 29,
1734), son of Capt. John Hopson (b. Nov. 12, 1707, in Colchester), and Lydia Kellogg.

Mrs. Mary Hopson died July
30, 1797.

Had 5 children of whom no
record can be found.

55. JUDITH, born Jan. 22, 1742, in Colchester;
married, Jan. 11, 1759, John
Bulkeley (b. Aug. 23, 1738,
in Colchester), son of Gershom,

son of Rev. John, son of Rev. Gershom, son of Rev. Peter the Puritan, and Abigail Robbins of Colchester. In Neal's History of the Puritans, is the following ·

" But notwithstanding the prohibition, numbers went to New England this summer [1635] and amongst others, the Rev. Peter Bulkeley, B. D., fellow of St. John's College, Cambridge. He was the son of Dr. Edward of Bedfordshire and succeeded him at Woodhill and Odell, in that county "

CHILDREN.

1. John Bulkeley, b. Oct. 7, 1759; m. Theodore Foote.
2. William Bulkeley, b. Aug. 30, 1761; m., Dec. 18, 1788, Mary Champion and had ch.

   1. Infant, d. April —, 1790.
   2. Henry Bulkeley, b. June 16, 1791; m. and lived in Middle Haddam, Conn.
   3. Epaphraditas Bulkeley, b. June 16, 1791, twin to Henry; d. Jan. 26, 1807.
   4. Mary Bulkeley, b. July 13, 1793; m. Chas. Hurd of Middle Haddam, Conn. No ch.

3. Gershom Bulkeley, b. Oct. 3,
    1763; m. Mrs. Mary (Day)
    Noble, and removed to Will-
    iamstown, Mass.

Ch.

1. George Bulkeley, a lawyer,
    lived in Kinderhook, N. Y.
2. William Bulkeley lived in
    Kinderhook, N. Y., and had
    ch., Elizabeth and William.
3. Gershom Bulkeley.
4. Harriet Bulkeley, d. unm.
5. Judith Bulkeley, m. Platt
    Talcott of Lanesboro,Mass.
6. Mary Bulkeley, d. unm.
7. Martha Bulkeley, m. Mr.
    Buel.

4. Elijah Bulkeley, b. Jan. 29,
    1766; m., April 22, 1787,
    Pamela Loomis, and d. July
    31, 1842.

Ch.

1. John Worthington Bulke-
    ley, b. Jan. 22, 1788 ; d.
    March 12, 1850, unm.
4. Richard Bulkeley, b. Dec.
    26, 1789; m. Dec. 23,1813,
    Aurel Chapman. Had 2 ch.
3. Celinda Bulkeley, b. Aug.
    23, 1793; m., 1st, Alanson
    Porter of Williamstown,
    Mass.; 2nd, Russell Chap-
    man of Colchester, Conn.,
    and d. Dec. 1, 1867. No ch.

4. Emeline W. Bulkeley, b. Sept. 12, 1806; m., Oct. 5, 1823, Pomeroy Hall (b. May 8, 1796; d. July 9, 1865), of Colchester, Conn. Had 11 ch.
5. Clarissa Pamela Bulkeley, b. May 8, 1809; m. John T. Bulkeley (b. Oct. 3, 1801), of Colchester, Conn. Had 5 ch.
6. Sophia Maria Bulkeley, b. Nov. 15, 1811; m. Jonathan Chapel. No ch.

5. Abigail Bulkeley, b. Dec. 30, 1769; m., Dec. 6, 1789, Roger Taintor.

Ch.

1. Clarissa Taintor, b. Sept. 19, 1790; d. Sept. 27, 1794.
2. John A. Taintor, b. April 22, 1800; m. Delia Crook; had 2 ch.

6. Joshua Robbins Bulkeley, b. Nov. 2, 1771; m., Sept. 7, 1793, Sally Taintor. Lived and died in Williamstown Mass.

Ch.

1. Clarissa Bulkeley, m. Job Pierson.
2. Mary Bulkeley, m. Parker Hall.

3. John Bulkeley lived at Williamstown; unm.
4. Abbv Bulkeley.

7. Mary Bulkeley, b. Feb. 2, 1774; m. Aaron Buckland. No ch.
8. Judith Bulkelev, b. Jan. 30, 1775; m. Solomon Taintor.

Ch.
1. Bulkeley Taintor, Brookfield, Mass.
2. Henry G. Taintor, Hampton, Conn.

9. Gurdon Bulkeley, b. March 15, 1777; m., 1st., Nov. 22, 1798, Fanny Wright, who d. Dec. 24, 1819; 2nd, Sept 10, 1820, Nancy Porter, who d. July 7, 1859.

Mr. Bulkeley d. June 13, 1845, the last of his 8 brothers and sisters.

Ch. by 1st Wife.
1. Harriet Amelia Bulkeley, b. Sept. 1, 1799; m., May 24, 1826, Dr. Alvon Wheeler, and d. Oct. 24, 1875. 6 ch.
2. Albert Rodney Bulkeley, b. Oct. 14, 1802; m., April 1832, Delia Catharine Brown, who d. Nov. 9, 1848. No ch.

3. Leander Wright Bulkeley,
   b. Oct. 2, 1805; d. July 28,
   1820.
4. Hiram Worthington Bulkeley, b. March 30, 1807;
   m., Dec. 10, 1834, Mary
   Jane Oliphant, and d. ——,
   1890, at Cleveland, Ohio.
   Had 11 ch.
5. Sophia Adaline Bulkeley, b.
   Oct.20,1808; m.,Sept.1830
   Rev. Benj. Franklin Hoxsey,
   and d. April 4, 1832. 1 ch·
6. Francis Emeline Bulkeley, b.
   July 31, 1810; m., Aug. 3,
   1830, Rev. George Clinton
   Wood, who d. Jan. 5,1879.
7. Gurdon Henry Bulkeley, b.
   March 27,1812; m.,Dec.4,
   1834, Susan Eliza Brown,
   and d. Feb. 6, 1879, at
   Cleveland, O.
8. Aristarchus Bulkeley, b.
   May 3,1813; m.,1st,Mar.
   27, 1834, Mary Matilda
   Chamberlain. who d. Feb.
   16, 1836; m., 2nd, Dec. 24,
   1838, Mary E. Harrison,
   and d. March 11, 1872.
9. Clarissa Bulkeley, b. Jan.
   25, 1816; m., Sept. 14,
   1841, Hurlburt F.Fairchild.
10. Ralph Bulkeley, b. April 9,
    1817; m., April —, 1857,
    Mercy Briggs.
11. Dan Alonzo Bulkeley, b.
    Nov. 12, 1819; m., Nov.
    28, 1843, Marietta Town-

send, and lived at Williamstown, Mass. Had 3 ch.

Ch. by 2nd Wife.

12. Lucius Edwards Bulkeley,
    ɔ. Jan. 17, 1824; m., May
    17, 1852, Marv King Tut-
    hill. Had 1 son.

10. Gad Bulkelev, b. Feb. 20,
    1779; m. Orra Barstow,
    and lived at Canterbury,
    Conn.

Ch.

1. Adaline Bulklev, m. Jared
   Warner Fitch.
2. John Worthington Bulkeley, b. in 1811; m., 1st, Adelaide Hilliard; 2nd, Eliza
   Tracy; 3rd, Mrs. Helen
   Reynolds.
3. Samuel Barstow Bulkeley,
   b. Jan. 21, 1813; m., Sept.
   30, 1839, Mary Elizabeth
   Roath, and lived in Nor
   wich, Conn. Had 2 dau.
4. Simon Spalding Bulkley, b.

11. Lydia Bulkelev, b. April 25
    1781; m., 1st, John Worth-
    ington (bap. Feb. 12, 1772,
    in Colchester, Conn.; d. June
    5, 1806), son of John Worth-
    ington and Abigail Wright
    of Colchester; 2nd, Dr. Wm.
    Mason.

		12. Dan Bulkeley, b. March 20, 1784; m. Phebe Burnett.
		13. Harriet Bulkeley, b. Jan. 22. 1787; m. Samuel Mosely.
†56.	JOHN,	born Feb. 17, 1744.
†57. GAD,	twins,	born June 11, 1749.
†58. DAN,		

13.

JONATHAN WORTHINGTON, 2nd, of Agawam, Mass., married Mary Purchase, and died at Agawam.

CHILDREN.

†59.	JONATHAN, 3rd,	born, March 31, 1744, in Agawam.
60.	ELEANOR,	born Oct. 27, 1746; d. July 22, 1749.
61.	AMY,	born July 6, 1749, in Agawam; married, Dec. 10, 1772, Lieut. Jube Leonard (b. March 12, 1747). son of Benjamin Leonard and Thankful ———, and settled at Agawam.

Mrs. Amy Leonard died April 26, 1813, at Agawam.

Mr. Leonard died Sept. 22, 1820, at Agawam.

CHILDREN.

1. Amy Leonard, b June 27, 1774; m. Eli Bodurtha (b. April 4, 1771; d. April 22, 1806), son of Samuel Bodurtha and Sibyl Rising.

2. Jube Leonard, b. Feb. 11, 1776; m. Sophia Coofer.

3. Numa Leonard, b. March 25, 1778. Lived and died at Rome, N. Y.

4. Thankful Leonard, b. Sept. 5, 1780; d. Sept. 10, 1810.

5. Arah Leonard, b. Mav 10, 1783.

6. Benjamin Leonard, b. Aug. 11, 1785; m. Jane Barker.

7. Alfred Leonard, b. Dec. 24, 1788; d. July 8, 1812.

8. Calvin Leonard, b. —, 1792; d. March 30, 1840.

†62. JOHN, born July 25, 1751, in Agawam.

63. ELEANOR, born July 23, 1754; married Aug 15, 1771, Stephen Bodurtha (b. March 22, 1746, in Agawam), son of Jonathan Bodurtha and Joanna Frost.

Mr. Bodurtha died Jan. 22 1803.

Mrs. Eleanor Bodurtha died April 7, 1820.

CHILDREN.

1. Clarissa Bodurtha, b. March 3, 1773; d. April 2, 1774.

2. Jonathan Bodurtha, b. Jan. 7, 1775, in Agawam; m., 1st, Feb. 26, 1796, Sylvia

Day; 2nd, Mary Hannum, and d. Sept. 2, 1842.

Ch. by 1st Wife.

1. Harriet Bodurtha.
2. Sylvia Bodurtha, m. Colonel Chatfield of Waterbury, Ct.
3. Eleanor Bodurtha, b. Feb. 6, 1810, in Agawam; m., Oct. 19, 1836, Simeon Pomeroy of Agawam, who died March 23, 1879, at Rochester, N. Y. Had 3 ch.
4. William Bodurtha, b. Nov. 24, 1803; m., Nov. 26, 1826, Sibyl L. Stocking (b. Oct. 24, 1806, d. Sept. 17, 1886,) and d. April 26, 1863. Had 3 ch.

3. Persis Bodurtha, b. Oct. 14, 1776, in Agawam; m., Nov. 9, 1797, John Rockwell, and d. Feb. 7, 1810.

Ch.

1. Betsey Rockwell, b. ——, 1799, in Agawam; d. Feb. 6, 1853.
2. Frank Rockwell, b. ——, 1800, in Agawam; d. Nov. 8, 1819, Springfield, Mass.
3. Lucy Rockwell, d. in 1815, in Agawam, unm.
4. Cynthia Rockwell, d. in 1839, in N. Y. City.

5. Sophia Rockwell, d. in 1849, Pittsfield, Mass.
6. Washington Rockwell, b May, 1809; d. Feb. 24, 1810.

4. Walter Bodurtha, b. April 29, 1779, in Agawam; m Lucretia Henry of Chester, Mass., and died in 1815 or 16.

Mrs. Lucretia Bodurtha, died August 28, 1889, in Springfield, Mass.

Ch.

1. Almira Bodurtha, b.———, 1804; m., first, about 1833, J. P. Caldwell, who d. in 1841. M., second, Noah Safford of Springfield, Vt., and d. Dec. 10, 1886, at Springfield, Vt.
2. Jael Eliza Bodurtha, d. February, 1882.
3. Lucretia H. Bodurtha, b. Aug. 23, 1806, in Chester, Mass.; m., May, 1829, George W. Porter of Ware, Mass. (b. July 25, 1800, d. May, 1879), and d. Aug. 28, 1889, at Springfield Vt. Had 6 ch.
4. Stephen H. Bodurtha, b. July 10, 1812.

5. Stephen Bodurtha, b. Nov. 28, 1782, in Agawam; m.,

October 28, 1824, Hannah
Kent (born July 25, 1791,
in Schenectady, N. Y.), dau.
of Bela Kent and Lucretia
Remington.

Stephen Bodurtha d. July
29, 1858.

Mrs. Bodurtha, d. May 5,
1876.

Ch.

1. Charles Leonard Bodurtha,
   b. Jan. 15, 1826; d. Feb. 3,
   1841.
2. Cornelia Clementine Bodurtha, b. Feb. 29, 1828;
   d. Dec. 2, 1886.
3. Hannah Maria Bodurtha,
   b. May 25, 1831, unm.
4. Edward Kent Bodurtha, b.
   June 9, 1833.

6. Harvey Bodurtha, b. July
   2, 1784, in Agawam; m.,
   May ,27, 1811, Dorothy
   Taylor (b. May 10, 1788, d.
   July 3, 1855), and died
   March 26, 1849, in Pitts
   field, Mass.

Ch.

1. Amanda Bodurtha, b. Feb.
   23, 1812; d. Oct. 15, 1842,
   unm., and was buried at
   Pittsfield.
2. Harvey Lawrence Bodurtha,
   b. May 16, 1813; m., first,
   Nov. 6, 1838, at Chatham,

N. Y., Lovinia Holmes.
Had one son. Mrs. Lovinia
Holmes d. July 21, 1842,
and Mr. Holmes m., second,
May 5, 1857, Mary Haight,
and had one son.

3. Daniel Bodurtha, b. Jan. 9,
1815; m., Sept. 22, 1842,
at Berlin, N. Y., Deborah
Hall, who d. April 19, 1844.
Daniel Bodurtha d. Feb. 12,
1867, at Hudson, N. Y.
Both were buried in Pittsfield, Mass. Left one son.

4. Sarah Taylor Bodurtha, b.
Jan. 10, 1817; m., July 5,
1837, Henry Merriman, at
Pittsfield, Mass., and d.
May 13, 1851, at Bing-
hampton. Buried at Hins-
dale, Mass. Had 2 ch.

5. Fannie Sophia Bodurtha,
b. June 29, 1823; m., Sept.
4, 1850, Albert R. Holmes,
and d. July 21, 1851, in
Hudson, N. Y., buried at
Pittsfield. Had one dau.

6. Elizabeth Bodurtha, b. Feb
6, 1814; d. May 26, 1860.
Springfield, Mass., buried in
Pittsfield. Was unm.

7. Marietta Bodurtha, b. Apr.
15, 1821; m., Sept. 6, 1843,
at Pittsfield. Henry Tracy,
and died June 30, 1869, at
Peru, Ind. No ch.

8. Pamela Stevins Bodurtha,
b. Oct. 15, 1826; m., Nov.
27, 1845, at Pittsfield,

George Davis, and d. July
18,ˑ 1879, Richmond, Va.
Had 2 ch.

7. Alden Bodurtha, b. Jan. 18,
1786, in Agawam ; m.
Sophia Russell (b. 1790,
Springfield, Mass., d. Aug.
2, 1958), and d. Dec. 30,
1864.

Ch.

1. Sophia Bodurtha, b. Sept.
26,1818; d. Oct. ——,1861.
2. David Bodurtha, b. Sept.
15, 1819; lives (1890) in
Blandford, Mass.
3. Walter Bodurtha, b. July 1,
1822; lives (1890) in Mar
celine, Mo.
4. Lucy Maria Bodurtha, b.
May 2,1826; m. Mr. Fowler
of Hartford, Conn.

8. Jerre Bodurtha, b. July 31,
1788, in Agawam ; m., first,
in 1811, Lovina, daughter
of Wm. Brown and Hannah
Lucas, who d. March 10,
1821; m., second, in 1824,
Sally Hough ; m., third,
Nancy Brent.

Mr. Bodurtha d. in 1860.

Ch. by 1st Wife.

1. Eleanor Bodurtha, b. in
1817; m., in 1842, Oliver

Ripley, son of John B. Ripley and Elizabeth his wife.

2. Jene Almon Bodurtha, b. April 7, 1820; m., first, in 1845, Sarah Ewings; m., second, Sarah Gibbs. Had a dau.

Ch. by 2nd Wife.

3. Sarah Bodurtha, b. ———, 1826; m., in 1851, Judson Nye, son of Wm. Nye and Ann Burdick, and d. in 1863.
4. Daniel Y. Bodurtha, b. July 4, 1828; m. Mary Smith, and died Aug. 14, 1881.
5. Lucy Bodurtha.
6. Eri. Bodurtha.
7. Royal Bodurtha.

Ch. bv 3rd Wife.

8. William Davis Bodurtha.
9. Mary Elizabeth Bodurtha.
10. George Bodurtha.
11. Alvina Bodurtha.

9. Daniel Bodurtha, b. March 30, 1791, in Agawam; died about 1819, in Maryland, unm.

10. Fannie Bodurtha, b. Feb. 20, 1794, at Agawam; m., Nov. 6, 1817, Daniel Munger (b. Aug. 30, 1795, in So. Brimfield, Mass., d. Oct. 21, 1876, Grass Lake, Mich.), son of Daniel Munger and

Elizabeth Worthington, and d. March 15, 1822.

Ch.

1. Norman W. Munger, b. Oct. 15, 1818, in W. Springfield; m. Mahalah Polly, at Homer, N. Y., and d. May 23, 1850, Le Rov, N. Y. No ch.

2. Fannie B. Munger, b. July 5, 1821, in Amherst, Mass.; m., October 2, 1845, at Le Roy, Reuben Glass, and d. March 5, 1874. Had 1 dau.

11. Alpheus Bodurtha, b. Feb. 21, 1796; d. June 30. 1797.

64. HULDAH, born Aug 23, 1756, married, July 10, 1774, Isaac Cooley. She was probably his second wife, as he is recorded in Springfield, Mass., as married in 1767. Mrs. Huldah Cooley died June 5, 1782, aged 26 years. Isaac Cooley married for his third wife, April 10, 1783, Abigail Gotty, who d. March 8, 1834, aged 70 years.

Mr. Cooley died March 4, 1824, aged 79 years.

CHILDREN OF ISAAC COOLEY
AND HIS WIFE HULDAH.

1. Isaac Cooley, b. June 13, 1775, d. same year.

2. Huldah Cooley, b. Nov. 11, 1777.

3. Eunice Cooley, b. Oct. 27, 1778.

4. Lucinda Cooley, b. Oct. 30, 1780; m. Elias Russell, of Springfield, Mass., who d. April, 1821.

   Mrs. Russell d. May, 1817.

Ch.

1. Flavia Russell.
2. Betsey Russell.
3. Rodney Russell, b. —, 1808.
4. Mable Russell, b.   , 1810.
5. James Russell, b. —, 1812.
6. Lucinda Russell, b. —— 27, 1814.
7. Edwin Russell, died young.

CHILDREN OF ISAAC COOLEY
AND ABIGAIL GOTTY.

1. Isaac Cooley, b. Feb. 21, 1784; m. and removed to Springfield, Penn.

2. Jesse Cooley, b. Aug. 22, 1789.

3. Abigail Cooley, b. Aug. 20, 1791.

4. Amanda Cooley, b. July 19, 1795.

5. Mary Cooley, b. July 23 1797; m. Oliver Sexton. Had 12 ch.

6. Lurancy Cooley, b. Dec. 27 1800.

65. SETH,   born Aug. 18, 1760. Was killed by Indians, in an ambuscade, near Fort Stanwix (now Rome, N. Y.), during the Revolutionary war.

66. MARGARET,   born Sept. 30, 1763.

67. EUNICE,   born Sept. 30, 1763, twin to Margaret; married Major Gad Warriner (b. Jan. 29, 1762, in West Springfield, Mass.), son of Hezakiah Warriner and Persis Hitchcock.

Mrs. Eunice Warriner died May 23, 1820, and Mr. Warriner married for 2nd wife Miss Phelps. No ch. bv 2nd wife.

Mr. Warriner died May 19 1842.

CHILDREN.

1. Tabitha Warriner, b. Feb. 10, 1785, in West Springfield; m., April 4, 1811 Seth Adams, son of Seth Adams and Elizabeth Lane.

Mr. Seth Adams d. June 12, 1833.

Mrs. Tabitha Adams d. Dec. 9, 1841

Ch.

1, Ralph Adams, b. Dec. 20, 1812; m., March 26, 1840,·

Francis Leonard (b. ——,
1820). Had 1 dau., Phil-
ura, who married Rev.
G. O. King of Cleveland, O.

2. Renel Warriner, b. Jan. 12,
1787, in W. Springfield; m.,
Anna Chaffee (b. May, 29
1793, in Enfield, Ct.), dau.
of Wm. Chaffee and Mary
Whipple.

Mr. Renel Warriner d. June
19, 1854.

Mrs. Warriner d. Jan. 29
1882.

Ch.

1. Adeline Antoinette Warriner, b. Jan. 18, 1815; m.
Nov. 27, 1841, Barnabus
Norton Cooley, and d. Feb.
3, 1885.

2. Samuel Dexter Warriner, b.
Feb. 11, 1817; m., Dec.
29, 1869, Mary E. Lepard.

3. Renel Warriner, b. March
2, 1819, d. young.

4. Infant son, b. Feb. 11, 1821,
died in infancy.

5. Anna Augusta Warriner,
b. April 8, 1822; m., Sept.
4, 1845, Monroe Bates, and
d. Feb. 11, 1873.

6. Laura Warriner, b. June 8,
1824; d. when about 3
years old.

7. Philura Amelia Warriner,
b. July 28, 1826; unm.

8. Rev. Edward Augusta Warriner, b. Feb. 18, 1829; m., Louisa Voorhes, and lived at Montrose, Pa. Had 4 sons and 1 dau.
9. Martha Miranda Warriner, b. March 2, 1832, m., July 21, 1857, Rev. S. C. Dutcher

3. Harriet Warriner, b. March 15, 1789, W. Springfield, Mass; m., Nov. 28, 1815, Marvin Kirkland of Worcester, Mass. (b. May 9, 1788, d. April 15, 1860), son of Jabez Kirkland and Eunice Burnham

Mrs. Harriet Warriner d. Nov. 14, 1873.

Ch.

1. Bela Burnham Kirkland, b. July 28, 1816; d. Sept. 13, 1887.
2. Albinus Theodorus Kirkland, b. April 25, 1819; m., Nov., 1845, Mary E. Spencer, and d. Dec. 15, 1884. They lived in New Haven, Ct.
3. Eunice Ann Kirkland, b. March 6, 1821; m., May 18, 1843, Corbin O. Wood of Worcester, Mass.
4. Sarah Caroline Kirkland, b. May 5, 1823, d. Feb. 9, 1844.

5. John Augustus Kirkland, b,
   July 15, 1825; d. Sept. 6,
   1827.
6. Edward Kirkland, b. Oct.
   27, 1828.
7. Edwin Kirkland, twin to
   Edward, b. Oct. 27, 1828;
   m., in 1850, Jane A. Osborne. Lived in New
   Haven, Ct.
8. Rachel Warriner Kirkland,
   b. Jan. 25, 1831; d. Feb. 9,
   1831.

4. Phyluria Warriner, b. Feb. 9,
   1791, W. Springfield, Mass.;
   m., Sept. 20, 1821, in Agawam, Anson Bingham of
   Forestville, Ct. (b. Oct. 16,
   1788), son of Itharnac
   Bingham and Hannah ———.
   Mrs. Phyluria Bingham
   d. Aug. 3, 1838.
   Mr. Anson Bingham d.
   Feb. 28, 1863.

   Ch.

   1. Anson Bingham, b. March
      12, 1828; m., Nov. 30,
      1848, Margaret Graves,
      who d. Dec. 16, 1887. Had
      3 ch.

5. Rachel Warriner, b. Sept.
   20, 1793, in W. Springfield;
   m., 1st., Joel Worthington,

son of Stephen Worthington and Lydia Rogers, 2nd., Joshua Howse.

Ch. by 1st Husband.

1. William Worthington, b. July 5, 1813, in Enfield, Ct.; removed to Rockford, Ill., in 1838; m., first, Oct. 27, 1844, Maria Baker, who died Oct. 2, 1846. Had one ch. M., 2nd., Aug. 3, 1847, Eliza Kellogg of Clarendon, O., and d. April 11, 1886, at Rockford. Had 7 ch.

2. Rev. Henry Worthington, b. ——, 1815, in Springfield, Mass.; m., 1st., in 1839, Jane Mills, 2nd., in 1862, Mary Clower, and d. July 10, 1881, at Dowangiac, Mich. 4 ch.

6. Orpha Warriner, b. Dec. 26, 1798; m., April 6, 1824, David Worthington of Suffield, Ct. (b. July 5, 179*i*, in W. Springfield, Mass.), son of David Worthington and Mary Rogers.

Mrs. Orpha Worthington d. Jan. 5, 1871.

Mr. David Worthington d. Aug 20, 1883.

Ch.

1. Orpha Warriner Worthington, b. Jan. 6, 1826; m., Sept. 12, 1844, Joseph Creighton Hastings (b. Oct. 5, 1822, Suffield, Ct.), son of Wm. Hastings and Lydia Remington, who d. Nov. 12, 1866, at Suffield. Had 2 ch.
2. Harriet Ann Worthington, b. Nov. 15, 1829, in Agawam; d. March 28, 183/.

7. Gad Warriner, b. May 13, 1801; d. in infancy.
8. Gad H. Warriner, b. Sept. 3, 1803, in W. Springfield; m., 1st., Nov. 2, 1827, Abigail Carpenter (b. Nov. 5, 1807, in Suffield, Ct.), dau. of Israel Carpenter, and Abigail Rumnell, who d. July 25, 1840, and Mr. Warriner m., 2nd., April 2, 1844, Fanny C. Morley (b. Sept. 16, 1824), by whom he had no ch.

Mrs. Fanny Warriner d. March 8, 1855.

Mr. Gad H. Warriner d. Sept. 11, 1879.

Ch. by 1st Wife.

1. Sarah Eunice Warriner, b. Dec. 25, 1829; m., July 25,

1846, Rosewell Clark Ramsdell of Hartford, Ct. (b. June 11, 1825). Had 8 ch.
2. Orpha Electa Warriner, b. Jan. 11, 1831. Living (1890) at Springfield, Mass.
3. Lucy Maria Warriner, b. Aug. 16, 1832; m. John R. Turner of New Haven, Ct.
4. Abigail Jane Warriner, b. Oct. 13, 1834; m. George F. Cornwall of Buffalo, N.Y.

15.

WILLIAM WORTHINGTON of Agawam, Mass., until 1774. Married, about March 21, 1743, Sarah Rogers, who died December 17, 1804.

CHILDREN.

68. WILLIAM, born Nov. 19, 1744; died Dec. 13 1750.

69. SARAH, born Dec. 26, 1746; died Dec. 28, 1746.

70. SARAH, born Aug. 10, 1748; m., Nov. 22, 1770, Gideon Allen of Suffield, Ct. She was his 2nd wife, his 1st being Mary Worthington, who died April 18, 1766, leaving one son, Gideon Allen, b. April 8, 1766.

Mr. Gideon Allen died March 11, 1810.

CHILDREN OF SARAH AND GIDEON ALLEN.

1. Mary Allen.

2. Jonathan Allen.
3. Jonathan Allen.
4. Sarah Allen.
5. Loval W. Allen.
6. Admira Allen.

71. ELIZABETH, born Feb. 9, 1750; m., about 1775, Daniel Munger of Agawam, Mass. (b. April 17, 1748), son of Elnathan Munger and —— Thompson. They removed from Agawam, about 1827, to Pumpkin Hill, near North Byron, N. Y.

Mrs. Elizabeth Munger died May 13, 1829, at Byron.

Mr. Munger died Dec. 21, 1835, at Byron.

Both are buried there. The old stone marking their resting-place, now replaced by a new one, was inscribed: "The sweet remembrance of the just shall flourish though they sleep in dust. To the memory of Eliza beth, wife of Deacon Daniel Munger, who died May 13, 1829, aged 78 yrs."

CHILDREN.

1. Desdemona Munger, b. 1779; m., about 1800, Levi Adams, son of Seth Adams and -—— Taylor.

Mrs. Munger d. April,
1857, at Warsaw, N. Y.

Ch.

1. Franklin Munger, b. ——,
   1801.
2. Miner Munger, b. —, 1803;
   d. unm.
3. Desdemona Adams Munger,
   b. ——, 1805; m. Daniel
   Lee. Lived in Michigan.
4. Elvin Munger, b. —. 1807;
   m., —— Griswold.
5. Loren Munger, b. —, 1809;
   d. unm.
6. Hiram Munger, b. —,1811;
   m., 1st, Marietta Hodge;
   2nd, Salvina Hodge.
7. Elizabeth Worthington
   Munger, b. April 1, 1813;
   m., Oct. 9, 1837, Chauncey
   C. Buxton. She is living
   (1890) at Angelica, N. Y.
   Had 8 ch.

2. Gaius Munger, b. April 5,
   1781; m., May 8, 1804,
   Abigail Button (b. July 16,
   1783; d. 1868, at Rochester,
   N. Y.).

   Mr. Munger d. July, 1858,
   at Canandaigua, N. Y.

   Ch.

   1. Merrick Munger, b. Feb.
      16, 1806.
   2. Nancy Munger, b. Sept. 30,
      1808.

3. Lyman Munger, b. Sept. 22, 1811. Living (1890) Galva, Ill.
4. Sophia Munger, b. Oct. 25, 1814; m., Dec., 1834, John Chamberlain, who d. 1848. Had 3 ch.
5. Bennett Munger, b. Oct. 25, 1817.
6. Abigail Munger, b. Nov., 1819; m., —— Hills, and living (1890) at Hyde Park, Ill.
7. Olive Munger, b. April, 1822.
8. Jane Munger, ⎰born Jan. 16,
9. Julia Munger, ⎱ 1826.

3. Dr. Aaron W. Munger, b. Aug. 14, 1785; m., 1st June, 1812, Lucy Edson, who d. Sept. 14, 1821; 2nd. Sally Zeomans, who d. about 1888.

Dr. Munger d. Dec. 25, 1834.

Ch. by 1st Wife.

1. Lucy Maria Munger, b. May 24, 1813.
2. Sylvester Edson Munger, b. February 20, 1815; d. March 1, 1873, leaving a dau. Carrie, and 1 son.

Ch. by 2nd Wife.

3. James Worthington Mun-

ger; lives (1890) Carbon-
dale, Pa.
4. Sarah Munger; died young.

4. Dr. James Harvey Munger,
b. Dec. 18, 1788; m., Oct.
22, 1815, Sarah Southgate
(b. Jan. 11, 1796: d. Sept.
30, 1870, at Rochester, N.Y.;
buried at Albion, N. Y.).
Dr. Munger d. Aug. 23,
1834, Byron, N. Y.

Ch.

1. James F. Munger, b. June
14, 1817; d. Oct. 14, 1823.
2. Lyman Franklin Munger,
b. May, 13, 1822; m., Nov.
7, 1844, Herter, dau. of
Samuel Munger and Herter
B. Holmes.
Mrs. Munger d. July 20,
1888, at Rochester, N. Y.
Had 3 ch.
3. Mary Southgate Munger,
b. Feb. 18, 1826; d. Dec.
11, 1833.

72.	WILLIAM,	born July 22, 1755, in Springfield.
73.	EUNICE,	born Jan. 25, 1757, in Springfield.
†74.	Stephen,	born Oct. 16, 1758, in Springfield.
†75.	ELIPHALET,	born —— —, 1759,? in Springfield.
76.	FREDERICK,	born Dec. 19, 1761, in Springfield.
†77.	HEMAN,	born April 3, 1764, in Springfield.

21`

HON. JOHN WORTHINGTON, LL.D., of Springfield, Mass. An eminent lawyer. Was graduated at Y.C., 1740. In 1774 was a member of the legislature of Mass., and opposed the measures of the "Friends of Liberty." His name was in the same year included in the list of the Mandamus Councillors, but he declined the appointment. He was high sheriff previous to the American Revolution.

Col. John Worthington, one of the most prominent and noteworthy men who ever lived in the town [Springfield], was a native of the place. He was educated at Yale college, where he was graduated in 1740, and remained as tutor for three years, read law about a year with Gen. Lyman of Suffield, Ct., and commenced practice in 1744 in his native town. He was a man of great influence in the town, and of wide practice in his profession. He was king's attorney, or public prosecutor, for Old Hampshire county, and was held in as high esteem by the colonial authorities as by his fellow-townsmen. The following copy of a letter, now in possession of Josiah Hooker, Esq., of Springfield, in the hand-writing of Gov. Hutchinson, will show how highly he was esteemed by the latter. It will be remembered that the letter was written while Bernard was governor—in fact, during the year in which he was recalled and the administration left in the hands of Hutchinson·

BOSTON, 28th Febr., 1769.

DEAR SIR:—In conversation with the Governor, a few days ago, about the Attorney-General's place, which will be vacant in a short time, it was agreed that I should write to you and propose to you to accept of it, provided a salary not less than £200 sterling a year should be annexed to it. I could not give any great encouragement to the Governor, because it is necessary an Attorney-General should live at or near Boston, and I know your attachment to that foggy, unhealthy air from the Connecticut River, which, if you do not remove, will shorten your days; but, as it is possible, I thought it best to make the proposal. If you can bring yourself to be willing, the Governor will immediately represent to Lord Hillsborough the advantage the Publick will receive from it, and will try to .obtain 300 instead of 200 a year. I will add my little interest, though I doubt not his recommendation would be sufficient. If the attempt for a salary should fail, it cannot be expected you should take the place, though I fancy there is more in it than is generally known, or Sewall would not be so fond of it. It will not be discovered by me, and I should think, not by the Governor, that such a proposal had been made to you. I shall be glad to receive an answer as soon as you have deliberated.

I am Yours Sincerely,

THOS. HUTCHINSON.

To the Honorable John Worthington, Esq., Springfield.

This plan was never consummated, but the consideration which Col. Worthington received from the government was doubtless the cause of a leaning to toryism which subsequently made him unpopular with the patriotic masses. He evidently endeavored to act neutral, but his sympathies had been made too apparent by his action in the legislature. It is a forcible commentary on the spirit of the times that this man, so long honored and revered, suffered the humiliation of being forced inside a ring of Whigs in the open air, in his own town, and there made to kneel, and ask forgiveness for his toryism. From the time of the interruption of the courts, in 1774, Col. Worthington retired from practice, but lived to the good old age of 80 years. His law library is now in the possession and office of Josiah Hooker, Esq., who inherited it through his father, Judge Hooker, a student and nephew of Worthington. It was one of the best law libraries of its times   Colonel Worthington occupied an important military position as well as legal. After the military division of the county into two regiments, he was chosen the commander of the Southern regiment, and was ever afterwards known as Colonel Worthington. He was a man of liberal attainments, and, as an advocate, nervous, brilliant and effective, possessing withal a good degree of that "popular talent" which gave him influence and fame. .   Worthington was a scholar and a gentleman, accustomed to the usages of polite society.

Of the ten townships sold at Auction in Boston on the 2nd of June, 1762, the present town of Worthington (Mass.) occupies the territory of No. 3. The township was sold to Aaron Willard for £1,860.

Subsequently, but at what time it does not appear, the township passed into the possession of Col. John Worthington of Springfield, and Major Barnard of Deerfield. The settlement was commenced in 1764, and was so rapid that, in 1768, the town was incorporated with the name of Worthington, in honor of Col. Worthington, one of its proprietors, whose liberality to the settlers, in building for them a church and a grist mill, at his own expense, and in assigning generous lots for ministerial and school purposes, well earned the distinction.—['History of Western Massachusetts,' J. G. Holland.]

He was twice married, 1st, January 10, 1759, to Hannah (bap. Jan. 29, 1731; d. Nov. 25, 1766), dau. of Rev. Samuel Hopkins, who grad. Y. C., 1718, was second pastor of the first church (Congregational) in West Springfield, Mass., and Esther, his wife, who was sister of Rev. Jonathan Edwards, and dau. of Rev. Timothy Edwards, the first pastor of the Second Congregational church of East Windsor, Ct. Married, 2nd, Dec. 7, 1768, Mary Chester Stoddard (b. Nov. 27, 1732 · d. July 12, 1812), daughter of Major John Stoddard of Northampton, Mass., and Prudence Chester, and grand-daughter of Rev. Solomon Stoddard, the first minister of Northampton, Mass.

Hon. John Worthington died April 25, 1800.

Mrs. Mary Worthington died July 12, 1812.

The ancestors of Hannah Hopkins are traced to John of Hartford, Ct., her great-great-grandfather, who was one of the first settlers of Hartford. He m. Jane——, who, after his death, m. Nathaniel Ward of Hadley, Mass.

John Hopkins died in 1654. Had 2 ch.

      I. Stephen, b. about 1634.

      II. Bethia, b. about 1635.

I. Stephen of Hartford, m. Dorcas Bronson dau. of John Bronson of Farmington, Ct., and d. Oct., 1689. She d. May 13, 1697. Had 6 ch.

III. John. IV. Stephen. V. Ebenezer, who m. Mary Butler. VI. Joseph. VII. Dorcas, who m. Jonathan Webster. VIII. Mary, who m. Samuel Sedgewick of Hartford in 1689.

III. John Hopkins of Waterbury, Ct., m., in 1683, Hannah ——, who d. May 30, 1730. He died Nov. 4, 1732. Had 10 ch. Their sixth child, Rev. Samuel Hopkins, b. Dec. 27, 1693, m., June 28, 1727, Esther Edwards, granddaughter of Richard of Hartford, Ct., and great–granddaughter of William of Hartford, who came from England with his mother, Mrs. Ann Edwards, and her 2nd husband, James Cole, and was one of the first settlers of Hartford. The ancestors of Mary Chester, 2nd wife of Hon. John Worthington, are traced to Leonard Chester, who came from England and m., about 1634, May —— (dau. of Nicholas Sharpe?). Their eldest son John, b, Aug. 3, 1635, in Watertown, Mass.; m., Feb., 1653, Sarah Welles, dau. of Thos. Welles, one of the first settlers of Hartfort, Ct., and of Wethersfield, and 4th governor of the colony of Connecticut. John, eldest son of Capt. John Chester and Sarah Welles, b. June 10, 1656; m., Nov. 25, 1686, Hannah Talcott, dau. of Hon. Samuel Talcott of Wethersfield.

Prudence, sixth dau. of John and Hannah Chester, b. March 4, 1699; m., Dec. 13, 1713, Col. John Stoddard of North. ampton, Mass.

CH. OF JOHN WORTHINGTON AND HIS 1ST WIFE.

78. MARY,   born March 7, 1760; married in, 1790, Jonathan Bliss, who grad. H C. 1763. They settled in the Province of New Brunswick, N. S., and afterwards went to England, where he died. Their

grandson, J. Worthington Bliss, is a rector in the Church of England, now residing at Betteshanger rectory, Sandwich, England.

CHILDREN.

1. John Worthington Bliss.
2. Lewis Bliss.
3. William B. Bliss.
4. Henry Bliss. Was a lawyer in London.

79. HANNAH, born June 17, 1761; m., 1791, Thomas Dwight of Springfield, Mass.; grad. H. C. 1778, and d. Jan. 2, 1819, aged 60 years.

"Behold, He taketh away, who can hinder Him, who will say unto Him, What dost Thou?" Springfield burying ground.

She died July 10, 1833.

CHILDREN.

1. Mary Stoddard Dwight, b. Jan. 26, 1792; m., Dec. 18, 1818, John Howard, and d. July 20, 1836.

Ch.

1. Hannah Worthington Howard, b. Aug. 12, 1821; m., April 18, 1844, Wm. H. Swift.

2. Margaret Howard, b. May
   11, 1823.
3. Francis Ames Howard, b.
   April 20, 1825.
4. Eliza Wetmore Howard
   b. May 3, 1826.

2. John Worthington Dwight,
   b. Oct. 31, 1793; d. Feb.
   12, 1836.
3. Elizabeth Buckminster
   Dwight, b. Feb. 18, 1801;
   m., June 1, 1824, Charles
   Howard.

Ch.

1. Lucinda Orne Howard. b.
   March 8 1825.
2. Thomas Dwight Howard,
   b. Dec. 25, 1826.
3. Elizabeth Bridge Howard
   b. Dec. 17, 1828.
4. Sophia Worthington Howard, b. Jan. 26, 1831.
5. Catharine Lathrop How-
   ard, Feb. 24, 1833.
6. Mary Dwight Howard, b.
   Oct. 12, 1835.
7. Sarah Bancroft Howard,
   b. Sept. 13, 1838.
8. Emily Williams Howard,
   b. Dec. 21, 1840.
9. Amelia Peabody Howard,
   b. June 4, 1843, d. Jan. 21,
   1844·
10. John Howard, b. June 28,
    1845; d. Aug. 27, 1845.

80. JOHN,   born August 10, 1762; d. Aug. 30, 1763.

81. JOHN,   born Sept. 2, 1763; d. Nov. 10, 1765.

82. FRANCIS,   born October 29, 1764; m , July 15, 1792, Fisher Ames (b. April 9, 1758 in Dedham), 3rd son of Dr. Nathaniel Ames and his 2nd wife, Deborah, daughter of Jeremiah Fisher of Dedham, Mass.

The Ames family are descended from one Richard of Bruton, Somerset, England. His son William, b. October 6, 1605, in Bruton, and settled in Braintree, Mass, 1640 or earlier; there his eldest son John was b., May 24, 1647, who removed about 1672, to West Bridgewater. Capt. Nathaniel Ames, 2nd son of John, b. Oct. 9, 1677; d., in 1736, at Bridgewater. His son, Dr. Nathaniel Ames (b. July 22, 1708, in Bridgewater), in 1732 removed to Dedham, Mass.; m., Sept. 14, 1735, Mary, dau. of Capt. Joshua Fisher of Dedham. She d. Nov. 11, 1737, and Dr. Ames m. his 2nd wife, Deborah Fisher, October 30, 1740, and died at Dedham July 11, 1764.

Hon Fisher Ames was one of the most brilliant men of this country; admitted to Harvard at the age of 12 years, grad. 1774. He began life as an attorney-at-law in Dedham, from which he was soon diverted to a wider and more congenial field. His name and fame as an orator and statesman have become a part of American history. He was a delegate to the state convention on adopting the Federal Constitution, 1788. First representative in congress for Suffolk district. President-eleet of Harvard in 1804, which honor he declined.

He d. July 4, 1808. In the cemeterv of Dedham a plain monument of marble marks the spot where his remains are deposited, bearing the simple inscription

"Fisher Ames."

Mrs. Francis Ames died Aug. 8, 1837.

CHILDREN.

1. John Worthington Ames, b. October 22, 1793; d. October 1, 1833, unmarried. Grad. H. C. 1813. Was a lawver

in Dedham, representative
to the General Court, 1832,
and president of the Dedham
bank.

2. Nathaniel Ames, b. May 17,
   1796; d. Jan. 18, 1835.
3. Hannah Ames, b. March 1,
   1799; d. Aug. 23, 1829.
4. William Ames, b. October 3,
   1800.
5. Jeremiah Fisher Ames, b.
   October 9, 1803; d. unm.,
   Jan. 23, 1829, at Dedham.
   Grad. H. C. 1822. Was a
   physician at Providence,
   R. I.
6. Seth Ames, b. April 19,
   1805. Grad. H. C. 1825.
   Was a lawyer in Lowell,
   Mass. Senator from Middle
   sex. M. Margaret, daughter of Gamaliel Bradford of
   Charleston, Mass.
7. Richard Ames, b. June 16,
   1807.

83. SOPHIA, born Dec. 5, 1765; m., Sept. 25, 1799,
John Williams (b. Sept. 11,
1762), grad. Y. C. 1781, son of
Ezekiel Williams of Wethers
field, Ct., and Prudence, dau.
of Col. John Stoddard and
Prudence Chester of Northampton, Mass., who was sister

to Mary, 2nd wife of Hon. John
Worthington.

Mrs. Sophia Williams died
May 15, 1813.

Mr. Williams married, for his
2nd wife, Jan. 1, 1817, Mary
Dyer of Windham, Ct., widow
of Rev. Ebenezer Silliman of
Amsterdam, N. Y., and d. Dec.
19, 1840.

CH. OF JOHN AND SOPHIA
WILLIAMS.

1. John Worthington Williams,
   b. Sept. 28, 1802; d. Oct.
   4, 1802.
2. John Worthington Williams,
   b. Nov. 17, 1803.
3. Hannah Hopkins Williams,
   b. Feb. 3, 1805.
4. Ezekiel Salter Williams, b.
   Nov. 11, 1806; d. Jan., 1816.

CH. OF JOHN AND MARY
(SILLIMAN) WILLIAMS.

1. Thomas Scott Williams, b.
   Nov. 20, 1818.
2. Esther Sophia Williams, b.
   May 19, 1820.
3. Mary Dyer Williams, b. Feb.
   10, 1822.
4. Henry Silliman Williams, b.
   June 2, 1824.

CHILDREN BY 2ND WIFE.

84. JOHN,   born April 22, 1770; d. Aug. 11, 1770.

23.

SAMUEL WORTHINGTON of Springfield, Mass., married Sarah ————.

Mr. Samuel Worthington died Dec. 3, 1760, at Springfield.

CHILDREN.

85. LYDIA,   born Dec. 9, 1747; m., May 9, 1782, Edward Boylston, and d. Dec. 26, 1813.

86. TEMPERANCE, born May 29, 1748; d. at Ex-Gov. Strong's in 1820, unmarried.

†87. SAMUEL,   born Dec. 29, 1749, Springfield, Mass.

88. ANNA,   born about 1751; m., Dec. 10, 1772, Judah Leonard.

89. SABRAH,   born April 4, 1753; m., April 23, 1774 Benoni Dewey, and died May 6, 1835.

90. TIMOTHY   born ————, 1755.

91. MAY,   born ————, 1757; m., June 8, 1780, William Cooley.

92. LUCRETIA,   born Dec. 27, 1758; d. Dec. 5, 1759.

93. LUCRETIA,   born Oct. 29, 1760; died in infancy.

33

WILLIAM WORTHINGTON married Elizabeth Lyndes, and died at Hudson, N. Y.   Had no children.

FOURTH GENERATION.

35.

COLONEL ELIAS WORTHINGTON of Colchester, Ct., married, Sept. 30, 1744, Rhoda Chamberlain, dau. of Wm. Chamber lain of same town and Sarah Day? who married Jan. 14, 1710-1.

Colonel Worthington died Sept. 23, 1811, aged 89.

CHILDREN.

94.	LYDIA	born April 15, 1745 ; d. June 8, 1758.
†95.	ELIAS,	born Dec. 25, 1749.
96.	RHODA,	born Nov. 7, 1751 ; d June 8 1758.
†97.	JOEL,	born April 21, 1753.
†98.	ASA,	born Oct. 11, 1755.
99.	ELIZABETH,	born Aug. 14, 1757.
100.	LYDIA,	born Oct. 22, 1761 ; m., Jan. 23, 1777, Asa Newton of Colchester, Conn.

CHILDREN.

1. Elias Worthington Newton b. Nov. 16, 1780; m., April 25, 1803, Judith Worthington, who d. Nov. 2, 1856. They lived at Middletown, Conn., where he d. Oct. 26, 1851.

Ch.

1. Francis Caroline Newton, b. April 27, 1804; m. Cornelius Shepard, and d. Dec. 25, 1835, in New York.

2. Emeline Judith Newton, b. March 16, 1806; m. Wm. Boardman, and d. in 1863 in Middletown, Conn.
3. Elizabeth Worthington Newton, b. Nov. 7, 1808; m., Sept. 13, 1828, Lyman G. Morgan of Perry, N. ʼ
4. Lydia Louise Newton, b. May 9, 1811; m. Daniel Camp, who d. in 1877. She d. in 1866 in Middletown, Conn.
5. Laura Marion Newton, b. Feb. 18, 1813; m. —— Tucker.
6. Charles Worthington New ton, b. Feb. 18, 1815; m. —— Bacon, and d. in 1877.
7. Mary Louisa Newton, b. June 22, 1817; d. in 1872, unm.

2. Asa Newton, b. Oct. 3. 1782 · m. Abby Fox, and d. in 1836 at Colchester.

Ch.

1. William Henry Newton, b. —, 1815, in Cleveland, O.
2. Mary Sophia Newton, b.—, 1819, in Cleveland, O.
3. Rhoda Newton, b. Jan. 28, 1785; m., 1st, April 30, 1807, William Matson of Lyme, Conn.; 2nd, Rev. Ly man Strong, and d. Dec. 18, 1843.
   Hon. Wm. N. Matson of

Hartford, Conn., was a son by 1st husband.

4. Lydia Newton, b. Jan. 21, 1788; m. John S. Ransom, who d. Dec. 22, 1871, in Salem, Conn. She d. Nov. 17, 1828.

5. Sally Newton, b. April 2, 1791; m. Justin Williams, and d. in 1827.

6. Deacon Israel Newton, b. Feb. 11, 1794; m. Harriet Turner, and d. June, 1869, at Colchester. Had 6 ch.

7. Louisa Newton, b. Jan. 23, 1796, and d. unm.

8. Rev. Joel Worthington Newton, b. May —, 1799; grad. Y. C. 1818; was chaplain in U. S. navy; m. Azubah Ruggles, and d. Oct. 29, 1865.

9. Laura Maria Newton, b. Feb. 15, 1802; d. young.

†101. DANIEL   born Feb. 9, 1766.

38.

SAMUEL WORTHINGTON of Shelburne, Mass., married, Dec. 26, 1749, Elizabeth Welles of same town (b. April 9, 1730). They moved to Belchertown and returned to Shelburne in 1787, where Mr. Samuel Worthington died in 1790.

CHILDREN.

102. DAVID,   born May 19, 1750; d. July 29, 1754

103. ASA,   born June 23, 1752; d. Aug. 18, 1754

†104. DAVID,   born July 19, 1755, at Shelburne.
105. TEMPERANCE,   born Nov. 1, 1756; m., 1798, Shubal
                      Atherton of Shelburne.   They
                      moved to Norwich, Conn.

CHILDREN.

1. Nabbie Atherton.
2. Adoniah Atherton.
3. Temperance Atherton.
4. Mina Atherton
5. Lucy Atherton.
6. Filinda Atherton.
7. Pierce Atherton.
8. Shubal Atherton.

106. MOLLY,   born ——; married Asa Nims.

CHILDREN.

1. Elihu Nims.
2. Betsy Nims.
3. Polly Nims.
4. Samuel Nims.
5. Asa Nims.
6. Lucinda Nims; m. Asa Barnard.
7. Worthington Nims; m. Betsey Barnard, sister to Asa. They lived near Sandusky, O., where Mrs. Molly Nims died, aged 80.

41.

DANIEL WORTHINGTON of Williamstown, Vt., married, in 1772, Margaret Parsons of Palmer, Mass. (b. about 1740), daughter of Benjamin Parsons and Martha Bliss, who were married Aug. 15, 1723.

Daniel Worthington was a native of Colchester, Conn.; removed to Belchertown, Mass., in 1753, where he joined the church; was a soldier in the French war, and served under Capt. Nathaniel Dwight in the relief of Fort William Henry in 1757.

He died April, 1830, at Woodstock, Vt.

CHILDREN.

†107.	AMASA,	born May 9, 1773.
†108.	DANIEL,	born March 1, 1775.
109.	ELIJAH,	born Oct. 22, 1776; d. in infancy.
110.	MARTHA?	born Aug. —, 1782; d. Sept. 19, 1782.
111.	ELIZABETH,	born May 22, 1784; d. May 24, 1784.
112.	SON,	born Aug. 24, 1785; d. Oct. 24, 1785.
113.	SON,	born Oct. 4, 1786; d. same day.

43.

JACOB WORTHINGTON of Colchester, Conn., married, May 29, 1760, Mary Burchard (b. Dec. 15, 1732), daughter of John Burchard of Norwich, Conn.

Mr. Worthington died Sept. 25, 1763.

CHILDREN.

114.	MARY,	born July 10, 1761; m., 1780, Dr. Asahel Wright of Windsor Hill, Mass. (b. Feb. 26, 1757). She died Jan. 18, 1807, at Winsted, Conn., and Dr. Wright m. 2nd, her cousin, Mrs. Lydia Worth ington Dutton (b. Jan. 29,

1775), daughter of William Worthington and Sarah Welles, and widow of William Dutton of Boston, Mass.

Dr. Wright died Feb. 16, 1834.

Mrs. Lydia Wright died Oct. 19, 1838, at Knoxville, Tenn.

CH. OF ASAHEL AND
MARY WRIGHT.

1. Asahel Wright, b. March 27 1782; was a lawyer; died Dec. 2, 1830.
2. Rev. Worthington Wright, b. June 16, 1785, in Windsor, Mass.; m., 1st, April 21, 1811, Chloe Swift (b. May, 1795, in Warren, Conn.; d. June 29, 1816); 2nd, July 31, 1817, Orlinda Munson (b. April 17, 1796, in Nor wich, Mass.); d. June 4, 1825; 3rd, Nov. 29, 1825, Mrs. Catharine S. Russell (b. Sept. 13, 1795, in Saratoga, N. Y.), dau. of James Greene and Hulda Fiske.

Mrs. Russell Wright died May 27, 1867.

Rev. Mr. Wright died Oct. 28, 1873.

Ch. by 1st Wife.

1. Rev. Edwin Swift Wright,
    b. March 31, 1815; m., July
    27, 1848, Lucia Eliza Dut-
    ton (b. Sept. 11, 1827), and
    d. Nov. 28, 1888.

Ch. by 2nd Wife.

2. Worthington Munson
    Wright, b. Nov. 4, 1819;
    d. Nov. 12, 1827.
3. Mary Elizabeth Wright, b.
    May 28, 1822; d. July 2,
    1854.

Ch. by 3rd Wife.

4. Katharine Frances Wright,
    b. June 7, 1835; m. James
    O. Putnam of Buffalo, N. Y.

3. Dr. Orrin Wright, b. Dec.
    17, 1787, in Windsor; re-
    moved to Pittsfield, Mass.,
    and practiced medicine there
    until his death, July 28,
    1836. He m., 1st, Dec. 25,
    1818, in Pittsfield, Frances
    Jeannette Gold, dau. of Thos.
    Gold and Martha Marsh.
    She d. Dec. 9, 1826, and Dr.
    Wright m., 2nd, Jan. 1, 1833,
    in Pittsfield, Mrs. Frances
    Pease (b. in England). She
    survived her husband many
    years, living in German-
    town, Pa., with her son,

Oliver Pease, and dau., Mrs.
Livingston Erringer, ch. by
her 1st husband.

Ch. by 1st Wife.

1. Charles Gold Wright, b. Jan.
   11, 1820; m., in 1846 in N.
   Orleans, La., Celina ——,
   and d. there about 1865.
   Had 2 ch.
2. Frances Jeannette Wright, b.
   July 24, 1821; m., April 27,
   1846, in Rochester, N. Y.,
   George Franklin Danforth,
   son of Isaac Danforth of Boston, lawyer and later judge
   of the Court of Appeals of
   N. Y. State. Had 6 ch.

3. Thomas Wright, b. May 20,
   1823; d. about 1850 in
   Mexico.
4. Dr. Uriel Wright, b. May 13,
   1790; lived at Mt. Pleasant, Pa., and d. Sept. 30,
   1866.
5. Dr. Erastus Wright, b. May
   18, 1794; lived at Salem,
   Pa.; d. 1858 or 9. Had ch.
6. Mary Wright, b. June 29
   1796; d. July 29, 1878; unm.
7. Eliza Wright, b. April 20,
   1798; m. —— Crocker of
   Troy, N. Y., and d. Sept. 10,
   1839. Had several ch.

8. Dr. Clark Wright, b. Dec. 20,
    1799; m., and had several
    ch.
9. Philo Wright, b. May 3
    1801; m., Sept. 27, 1826,
    Harriet Wells, who d. May
    27, 1870. Mr. Wright d.
    Sept. 17, 1867.

Ch.

1. Harriet A. Wright, b. July
    20, 1827.
2. Julia Wright, b. Aug. 18
    1829; d. —, 1834.
3. Clark Wright, b. Oct. 12,
    1831; d. —, 1834.
4. Mary Jane Wright, b. Sept.
    12, 1833.
5. Julia A. Wright, b. Sept. 2,
    1835.
6. Henry Clark Wright, b. Oct.
    —, 1837.
7. Edward Clark, b. Oct —;
    1839.
8. Martha Wright, b. Sept. 5
    1843; d. Aug. 14, 1864.

10. Dr. Julius Cæsar Wright, b.
    Nov. 9, 1802, in Newtown,
    L. I.; m. Elizabeth Ann
    Powell, who d. July 12,
    1870. He d. Jan. 26, 1874.

Ch.

1. George Powell Wright, b.
    Aug. 20, 1837; d. July 26,
    1876.

2. Charles Wright, b. April 11,
   1841.
3. Edward Clark Wright, b.
   Feb. 22, 1843.
4. Mary Wright, b. Aug. 21,
   1846.
5. Julia Worthington Wright,
   b. Nov. 11, 1848.
6. Fannie Wright, b. Feb. 23,
   1851.
7. Albert Wright, b. March 12,
   1853.

50.

WILLIAM WORTHINGTON of Colchester, Ct., removed to
Pittsfield, Mass.; married, July 5, 1770, Sarah Welles (b. May
14, 1747), dau. of Israel Wyatt Welles (b. Dec. 17, 1714, in
Colchester, son of Noah and Sarah Wyatt Welles), and Sarah
Pratt of Colchester.

Mr. William Worthington died Jan. 1, 1825, at Pittsfield,
Mass.

Mrs. Sarah Worthington died Aug. 5, 1822, at Pittsfield,
Mass.

CHILDREN.

115. ISRAEL,   born March 20, 1771; died Feb. 9
                      1775.

116. HENRY,   born May 27, 1773; died Feb. 20,
                      1777.

117. LYDIA,   born Jan. 29, 1775; m., 1st, about
                      1795, William Dutton of Boston,
                      Mass. (b. Oct. 28, 1773, in Had
                      dam, Conn.), son of Amasa Dut
                      ton (b. Jan. 28, 1754), and
                      Mary Rogers (b. June, 1771).

He was for many years editor of the Boston *Transcript* and died about Dec., 1813, Geneseo, N. Y.

M. 2nd, in Worthington, Mass., Dr. Asahel Wright of Windsor Hill, Mass. (Feb. 26, 1757). She was his 2nd wife. Dr. Wright m., 1st, in 1780, Mary Worthington (b. July 10, 1761), daughter of Jacob Worthington and Mary Burchard, and cousin to Lydia. Dr. Wright died Feb. 16, 1834.

Mrs. Lydia Worthington Dutton Wright d. Oct. 19, 1838, at Knoxville, Tenn.

CH. BY 1ST HUSBAND.

1. Henry Worthington Dutton, b. April 17, 1796, in Lebanon, Conn.; m., June 1, 1825, in Boston, Ann Spear (b. Nov. 14, 1793; d. Nov. 28, 1874.

Mr. Dutton died April 15 1875, in Boston.

Ch.

1. Elizabeth Spear Dutton, b. March 28, 1826; d. Dec. 14, 1868; unm.
2. Lydia Worthington Dutton, b. Aug. 17, 1827; unm.

3. Martha Gilbert Dutton, b.
   Nov. 15, 1828; m., Oct. 3,
   1849, W. Tracy Eustis of
   Boston.
4. Julia Wright Dutton, b.
   Aug. 5, 1830; d. April 22,
   1864; unm.
5. Ann Edwards Dutton, b.
   June 2, 1832; m., Nov. 14
   1860, Samuel Brandell.
6. William Henry Dutton, b
   Aug. 17, 1835; m., July 1,
   1864, M. E. Gane.
7. Mary Maria Dutton, b.
   Feb. 21, 1837; unm.

2. Mary Ann Dutton, b. ——,
   1798; m., about 1820, Daniel
   O. Holbrook of Windsor,
   Ct., afterwards of Attica,
   N. Y. She d. Oct. 13, 1870.

Ch.

1. Henry Josephus Holbrook;
   m. Mattie Norton, Utica,
   N. Y.
2. William Owen Holbrook;
   m. No ch.
3. Lydia Selina Holbrook, b.
   Aug. 21, 1826; m. Leonidas
   Doty.
4. Edwin Augustus Holbrook;
   m. Elizabeth Tweedy.
5. Francis Elliott Holbrook;
   d. in Utica, N. Y.
6. Henry Eugene Holbrook;
   d. in infancy.

3. William Dutton, b. about
1801; d. Oct. 29, 1824, in
Boston, Mass.; unm.
4. Elizabeth Dutton, b. Sept. 9
1803, Lebanon, Ct.; d. Sept.
1, 1874, unm.

CH. BY 2ND HUSBAND.

1. Clarissa G. Wright, b. Jan.
24, 1808; d. May 11, 1811.
2. Julia Wright, b. Jan. 16,
1812; d. Sept. 2, 1820.
3. Sarah Maria Wright, b. July
29, 1814; m., Feb. 19, 1835,
Rev. Henry Herrick (b.
March 5, 1803), son of Rev.
Claudius Herrick and Han
nah Pierpont.
   Rev. Henry Herrick grad.
Y. C., 1822.
   Rev. and Mrs. Sarah Her
rick are living (1890) in
Woodstock, Ct.

Ch.

1. Henry Herrick, b. April 20,
1838, in Knoxville, Tenn.;
d. Oct. 12, 1838.
2. Lydia Worthington Her-
rick, b. Jan. 15, 1841; m.,
1st, July 25, 1862, Rev.
Thaddeus H. Brown, grad.
Y. C., 1860, who d. Oct. 19,
1868 ; m., 2nd, Oct. 5, 1887,

George Gould of Andover.
Had 2 ch. by 1st wife.

3. Charles Claudius Herrick,
   b. June 23, 1843; m., May
   20, 1868, Julia A. Peck of
   New Haven, Ct.

4. Rev. Edward Pierpont
   Herrick, b. Feb. 12,
   1846; m., May 25, 1871,
   Amelia G. Wheeler of New
   Haven, Ct.

5. George Lucius Herrick, b.
   March 28, 1848; m., Sept.
   13, 1877, Elmira G. Thomas
   of New York.

6. Sarah Maria Herrick, b.
   Aug. 15, 1850.

7. Lewis Herrick, b. Nov. 6,
   1852; d. in infancy.

8. Anna Caroline Herrick, b.
   Feb. 15, 1855.

9. William Wright Herrick, b.
   Feb. 23. 1857; m., March
   29, 1882, Emma A. Yost of
   N. Y. city.

118. SARAH,   born Dec. 2, 1776, in Colchester, Ct.,
married Ira West of Pittsfield,
Mass.

Mrs. Sarah West died July 10,
1862, in E. Boston; buried in
Springfield, Mass.

Mr. West died Aug. —.

Ch.

1. William West, b. ——, 1810,
   in Pittsfield, Mass.; lived in
   Cincinnati, Ohio, in 1840.

2. Sarah Ann West, b. ——,
1813, in Pittsfield, Mass;
m. Rev. Hubbard Beebe, and
d. 1887.

Rev. Mr. Beebe died 1885.

Children.

1. Mary Beebe; m. —— Bunce.
2. William Beebe.
3. Charlotte Beebe; m. ——
Bellamy.
4. Charles Beebe.
And four others who died
in infancy.

3. Samuel West, b. ——, 1816,
in Pittsfield; lived in E.
Boston, Mass.; m., 1849,
Lydia Banks (b. 1816),
dau. of William and Lydia
Banks, who d. 1860.

Ch.

1. Charles A. West, b. ——,
1850.
2. Millie Etta West, b. ——,
1857.

119. CAROLINE SELINA, born Sept. 14, 1779, in Colchester
Ct.; married, Feb. 6, 1806, in
Peru, Mass., Asa Pierce of Hins-
dale, Mass. (b. March 25, 1779),
son of Ebenezer Pierce and
Eunice Loomis of Peru, Mass.

Mr. Pierce d. Sept. 1, 1819.

Mrs. Caroline Pierce died July
23, 1862, in Hinsdale.

CHILDREN.

1. Martha Caroline Pierce, b. Jan. 30, 1809, in Hinsdale; m., March 12, 1834, Frederick Curtis, and d. April 23, 1876, in Hinsdale.

   Mr. Curtis d. Feb. 3, 1889 in Pittsfield, aged 92.

Ch.

1. Worthington Weeden Curtis, b. Dec. 12, 1835, in Hinsdale; m., June 2, 1870, Margaret Roach, and d. June 27, 1876. No ch.
2. Sarah Squires Curtis, b. March 2, 1837, in Hinsdale; lives (1890) in Worcester, Mass.; unm.
3. Clinton Wells Curtis, b. Dec. 17, 1838, in Hinsdale; m., Nov. 21, 1877, at Indianola, Iowa, Louise Edith Noble (b. May 22, ——, in Indianola), dau. of B. F. Noble and Mary Armstrong.

   Mrs. Curtis d. Dec. 16, 1884, in Denver, Col.

   No. ch.
4. Arthur Frederick Curtis, b. April 11, 1842, in Hinsdale; lives at Worcester, Mass. (1890), unm.
5. Franklin Pierce Curtis, b. May 2, 1849, in Hinsdale; d. Jan. 1, 1872; unm.

2. Warren Pierce, b. Nov. 25,
1811, in Hinsdale; m., 1st,
May 14, 1837, Climena
Morgan of Hinsdale (b. Oct.
21, 1813; d. Feb. 6, 1834);
m., 2nd., June 26, 1838,
Abigail Wright of Hinsdale
(b. March 1, 1813, in Hinsdale), dau. of Samuel Wright
and Betsey Watkins.

Mrs. Abigail Pierce d. July
22, 1880.

Mr. Pierce d. Aug. 19,
1881, at Vergennes, Vt.

Ch.

1. Wyatt W. Pierce, b. April
11, 1840, in Hinsdale; m.,
Sept. 20, 1865, Adelaide
Rose (b. Dec. 19, 1843, in
Vergennes, Vt.). Had 5 ch.

3. Juliet Pierce, b. March 2
1813; d. 1817.
4. Harriet Pierce, b. Feb. 22,
1815; m., Dec. 18, 1862,
Levi Phillips of Albany, N.
Y., who d. Jan. 5, 1866.
No ch.
5. Elbridge Pierce, b. Aug. 26,
1816, in Hinsdale; m., Jan.
1, 1841, Electa Rockwell.

He was a physician in

Holyoke, Mass., and d. Aug. 7, 1862, at Fortress Monroe.

Ch.

1. Francis F. Pierce, b. Oct. 8 1843; d. June 19, 1856.
2. Alice Pierce, b. March 18, 1845.
3. Electa Pierce, b. Dec. 29 1848; d. Aug. 7, 1849.

6. Francis Pierce, b. May 15, 1818, in Hinsdale, died in Oregon, Texas, in 1875.

His eldest son was thirteen years old when his father died.

Ch.

1. Edward Pierce.
2. Frederick Pierce.
3. Arthur Pierce.
4. Carrie Pierce.

7. Franklin Pierce, twin to Francis; d. in infancy.
8. Rev. Asa C. Pierce, b. July 17, 1819, in Hinsdale; m., Oct. 25, 1855, Mary Wilson of Brooklyn, N. Y. He was a Congregational minister in Brookfield, Conn., and d. there Dec. 2, 1888.

Ch.

1. Wilson H. Pierce, b. Oct. 12, 1857; m. May 7, 1889.

2. Elbridge W. Pierce, b. June 18, 1862; physician in Meriden, Conn; unm. (1890).

9. Caroline Pierce, twin to Asa, d. in infancy.

120. THEODOSIA, born Oct. 13, 1782, in Colchester; married, Dec. 16, 1806, John Sanford of Sommers, Conn. (b. March 20, 1782, in Litchfield, Conn).

Mrs. Theodosia Sanford died April 13, 1847, in Marcellus, New York.

Mr. Sanford died Oct. 6, 1862, at Marcellus, New York.

CHILDREN.

1. Marietta Sanford, b. March 9, 1809; m., April 22, 1829, Hugh L. Humphreys of Philadelphia, Pa., who d. Aug. 11, 1878. No ch.
2. Maria Antoinette Sanford, b. Nov. 17, 1811; d. June 19, 1820, in New York city.
3. Albert Worthington Sanford, b. Aug. 22, 1814; m., 1st, in 1844, Cornelia Pitcher of Little Rock, Ark., who d. in 1845; m., 2nd, June 25, 1857, in New York city,

Helen Waldo, who d. Feb. 19, 1881.

Ch. by 2nd Wife.

1. Mary Sanford, b. April 10, 1858; unm. (1890).
2. Clara W. Sanford, b. April 23, 1865.
4. Theodore Sanford, b. Nov. 14, 1822; d. Dec. 7, 1860. in New York city; unm.

†121. WILLIAM   born July 24, 1784, in Colchester or Belchertown.

†122. FRANCIS,   born Nov. 29, 1787, in Colchester.

123. ORRA   born June 24, 1790, in Colchester; m., Oct. 8, 1818, in Hinsdale, Mass., Bezaleil Sanford of Somerset, b. July 7, 1786, in Litchfield, Conn.), brother of John, who married Theodosia Worthington. In 1828 they settled in Cincinnati, O., and in 1840 removed to Davenport, Iowa.

Mr. Sanford served in the War of 1812, and many years after received for his service a warrant for 120 acres of land, which he located in the, then, wilderness of Iowa.

Mrs. Orra Sanford died Dec. 2, 1862, at Davenport.

Mr. Sanford died Jan. 15, 1873, at Davenport.

CHILDREN.

1. Ariana Worthington Sanford, b. Dec. 13, 1819, in New York city; m., in 1845, Charles Leslie of Davenport, Iowa. Had 4 ch.

2. Maria Antoinette Sanford, b. Dec. 23, 1821, in New York city; m., March 15, 1842, Alfred Sanders of Davenport, who d. April 25, 1865.

Ch.

1. Edwin Sanders, b. March 6, 1843; d. July 28, 1843.

2. Julia Elma Sanders, b. July 27, 1844.

3. George Clinton Sanders, b. Jan. 3, 1847; m., March 15, 1873, Louisa S. Christie, and d. April 10, 1883. Had 2 ch.

4. Ella Worthington Sanders b. Dec. 22, 1849, m., May 25, 1871, Almon Keeler Raft of Davenport. Had 3 ch.

5. Caroline Elizabeth Sanders, b. March 2, 1853.

6. Anna Leslie Sanders, b. March 3, 1857, d. Oct. 17, 1860.

3. DeWitt Clinton Sanford, b. July 28, 1824, in New York city; m. Elizabeth Slayback of Cincinnati, O.

Ch.

1. Roe Whitaker Sanford, b.—,
   1870, New Orleans; d. Jan.
   10, 1875, St. Louis.

4. Walter Homer Sanford, b.
   Oct. 21, 1831, in Cincinnati,
   O.; d. June 24, 1832.

53.

CAPTAIN ELIJAH WORTHINGTON of Colchester, Conn., married, April 29, 1756, Anna (b. March 23, 1739), dau. of Rev. Joseph Lovet—Episcopal clergyman—and Anna Holmes.

Captain Worthington died July 15, 1797, in Colchester.

Mrs. Anna Worthington died March 19, 1814, in Colchester.

CHILDREN.

124. ELIZABETH, born Jan. 15, 1757, in Colchester; m., March 17, 1782, Israel Foot of Marlborough, son of Israel Foot. She was his 2nd wife.

Mrs. Elizabeth Foot died April 6, 1795.

CHILDREN.

1. Israel Foot, b. Jan. 19, 1783.
2. Elijah Foot, b. Sept. 14 1784; m., Feb. 15, 1811, Lois Worthington (b. Oct. 1, 1785), dau. of Joel Worthington and Eunice New ton. They removed to Delaware county, O., and Mrs. Lois Foot died Dec. 26, 1818.

3. Elizabeth Foot, b. May 2, 1786; m. John Hollister of Glastonbury, Conn. Resided in Hamilton, O.
4. Erastus Foot, b. Feb. 28, 1788; unm.
5. Justin Foot, b. April 1, 1790; unm; lived in Natchez. Miss.
6. A son, b. Nov. 9, 1800; d. in infancy.

125. MOLLY   born Oct. 16, 1758; d. Nov. 10, 1758.
†126. ERASTUS,   born May 8, 1761.
†127. ELIJAH,   born Dec. 6, 1765.
†128. JOSEPH,   born 1768, in Colchester, Ct.
†129. JUSTIN,   born July 29, 1770, in Colchester, Ct.
130. ANNA,   born Jan. 24, 1775, in Colchester, Ct.;
                      m., Jan. 17, 1796, Charles Day of Colchester, Ct. (b. July 14, 1763, in Colchester), son of Isaac Day and his wife (Mrs.) Dorothy Bigelow of Colchester. Mr. Day died Aug. 29, 1836.

CHILDREN.

1. Nancy Day, b. Jan. 25, 1797; d. Feb. 6, 1797
2. Charles Frederick Day, b. Jan. 12, 1798; lived at Colchester; was unm.
3. Elijah Worthington Day, b. Sept. 17, 1799; m., July 20, 1834, Annie Baillie, (b.

1793, in Edinburgh, Scotland). They lived at Port Tobacco, Md.

Mrs. Annie Day d. May 17, 1845.

Ch.

1. John Baillie Day, b. June 17, 1835; d. Oct. 11, 1837.

4. Anna Lovet Day, b. July 31, 1801.
5. Albert Day, b. March 16, 1803; d. March 28, 1803.
6. Eliza Maria Day, b. Sept. 21, 1804.
7. Justin Edwin Day, b. Oct. 7, 1806; m., Nov. 10, 1835, Eliza Maria Ransom of Colchester. They lived at Colchester.

Ch.

1. Francis Ann Day, b. Jan. 28, 1837.
2. Elijah Worthington Day, b. Nov. 25, 1840.

8. Isaac Henry Day, b. Nov. 10, 1808; m., Oct. 10, 1842, Sarah Ellis Williams of Chatham (b. June 10, 1817). They lived at Colchester.

Ch.

1. Ann Eliza Day, b. April 29, 1844.

2. Sparrow William Day, b.
Feb. 22, 1846.

9. Erastus Day, b. Nov. 13
1810 , m., Sept. 15, 1846,
Miranda Matilda West, dau.
of Rev. Joel West of Chatham.

Ch.

1. Mary Day, b. Aug 24, 1837.
10. Artemas Day, b. Dec. 11
1812.
11. John Day, b. May 16, 1815;
d. Dec. 12, 1825.
12. Guy Bigelow Day, b. July
21, 1818, in Colchester, Ct.;
grad. Y. C., 1845, theological department 1848; .m.,
1st, Oct. 1, 1849, Mary A.
Lewis; 2nd, Aug. 11, 1853,
Mary Barnes, dau. of Dr. J.
S. Barnes.

†131. ARTEMAS,   born Dec. 11, 1777, in Colchester, Ct.

56.

JOHN WORTHINGTON of Colchester, Ct., married, Jan. 4
1770, Abigail Wright (b June 25, 1746), dau. of Dudley Wright
of Colchester.

· Mr. John Worthington died April 10, 1783.
Mrs. Abigail Worthington died Sept. 28, 1795.

There is on record at Colchester the following :

"Know all men by these presents that I, Abigail Worthington of Colchester, New London County, being possessed of a certain Negro man, named Eliphalet, thirty years of age in April last, in good health and free from any bodily infirmities; in consideration of his good services heretofore performed, do emancipate and set free him, the Eliphalet, and do hereby discharge him from any further services or demand I have upon him. In witness, I have hereunto set my hand and seal this 4th day of November, 1794.

Witness, DUDLEY WRIGHT. } ABIGAIL WORTHINGTON.
JOHN K. WATROUS. }

CHILDREN.

†132.	DUDLEY	born Aug. 18, 1770, Colchester.
†133.	JOHN,	born Feb. 12, 1772, Colchester.
†134.	RALPH,	born June 4, 1778, Colchester.
†135.	GEORGE,	born Jan. 11, 1781, Colchester.
†136.	ELIJAH,	born ——, 1782, Colchester.
137.	ABIGAIL,	born ——; married —— Watrous.

57.

GAD WORTHINGTON of Colchester, Conn , married Sept. 25 1774, Rebecca Robbins of Colchester.

Mrs. Rebecca Worthington died Sept. 21 1821.

CHILDREN.

138.	JOSHUA,	born Aug. 20, 1775.
139.	WILLIAM ROBBINS, born ——	

58.

CAPTAIN DAN WORTHINGTON of Colchester, Conn., afterwards of Lenox, Mass., where the house still remains that he and his son, Dr. Robert, occupied; adjoining it is the house where Dr. Charles Worthington lived.

Capt. Dan. Worthington married, Nov. 10, 1771, Lois
Foote (b. April 20, 1752), dau. of Charles Foote of Colchester.
Capt. Worthington died Oct. 24, 1821, at Lenox, Mass.
Mrs. Lois Worthington died Feb. 22, 1840, at Lenox, Mass.
They are both buried in the old burying ground on the hill,
and every Decoration day finds the captain's grave marked by
a flag and wreath of laurel.

CHILDREN.

140.	MARY,	born Dec. 3, 1772; d. July 14, 1854, at Lenox, Mass.; unm.
†141.	DAN,	born Sept. 22, 1774; lost at sea.
142.	JERUSHA,	born June 26, 1776; d. March 28, 1853, at Lenox, Mass.; unm.
†143.	CHARLES,	born Aug. 17, 1778, in Colchester.
144.	JUDITH,	born June 30, 1780; m., April 25, 1803, Elias W. Newton, of Colchester and afterward of Middletown. Conn.

Mr. Newton died Oct. 26, 1851.
Mrs. Judith Newton died Nov.
, 1856.

CHILDREN.

1. Francis Caroline Newton, b. April 27, 1804.
2. Judith Emeline Newton, b. March 16, 1806; d. March 10, 186ɔ.
3. Elizabeth Newton, b. Nov. 7, 1808.
4. Lvdia Louise Newton, b. May 9, 1811.

5. Laura Moriah Newton, b. April 17, 1813.

6. Charles Worthington Newton, b. Feb. 18, 1816; d. — 1857.

7. Mary Louise Newton, b. June 20, 1818; d. March 26. 1870.

145. BETSY,   born April 14, 1782; m., March —, 1810, Samuel Kellogg of Colchester, son of John.

Mr. Samuel Kellogg died Dec. 12, 1862.

Mrs. Betsy Kellogg died Jan. 30, 1866. Had no children.

146. JOHN,   born May 2, 1784; died Nov. 1, 1849, unmarried. He was the first treasurer of the railroad between New York and Philadelphia, which position he held for thirty years, until his death.

†147. GAD,   born May 28, 1786, at Colchester.

†148. GUY,   born April 5, 1788, at Colchester.

†149. ROBERT,   born Sept. 29, 1791, at Colchester.

150. LAURA,   born Aug. 14, 1793; d. Oct. 21, 1859 unmarried.

151. LOUISE,   born Dec. 9, 1795; d. Oct. 16, 1822.

59.

JONATHAN WORTHINGTON 3RD of Agawam, Mass., received, upon the division of the land in West Springfield (now Agawam), Mass., lot number 1, which was east of Darby

Brook to the main road, also number 21, which was south of
number 1. He afterwards purchased, from the Indians, a
piece of land one mile square, situated in the south part of the
town. His grandson, Henry, now lives on the same land, and
part of it has been held by the family ever since. Mr. Worthington married, 1st, Jan. 11, 1770, Mary Burbank (b. in 1750),
who died May 10, 1794. Married, 2nd, June 5, 1795, Mrs. Svbil
Cotton, who died March 29, 1803. Married, 3rd, Feb. 26,
1804, Lovina Chapin.

Mr. Worthington died Aug. 14, 1809, at Agawam, Mass.

CHILDREN BY 1ST WIFE.

152. LUCY,   born Aug. 26, 1872; married, Nov.
25, 1787, Captain Eli Ball of
Agawam (b. April 2, 1764), son
of Moses Ball.

Mrs. Lucy Ball died April 20,
1838, at Agawam.

Mr. Ball died May 26, 1844,
at Agawam.

CHILDREN.

1. Norman Ball, b. Jan. 2,
1788; m. Mrs. Betsey Leonard, widow of Alfred Leonard, and dau. of Lewis
Warriner and Elizabeth
Remington.

Norman Ball d. Nov. 30
1862.

Ch.

1. Alfred,Leonard Ball, b. Sept.
11, 1815. Lived at Springfield, Mass., unm.

2. Cynthia Ball, b. Feb. 23,
   1817; m., Dec. 27, 1843,
   Wm. Chapman Clark of
   Worcester, Mass.

   Mr. Clark m., 1st, May
   8, 1834, Mary Worthington, dau. of Ambrose Worthington and Ruth Chapin,
   by whom he had two sons,
   James Worthington and
   Wm. Watrous Clark.

   Had 2 ch. by his 2nd wife,
   Cynthia.
3. Elizabeth Ball, b. Jan. 31,
   1819; m. Dexter Winter of
   Springfield, Mass.
4. Norman Ball, Jr., b. Sept.
   16, 1821. Lives (1890) at
   Lewisburgh, Pa.
5. Meshach Warriner Ball, b.
   July 6, 1825.
6. Lucy Jane Ball, b. Dec. 1,
   1829; m. Joseph Creighton
   Hastings.

2. Eli Ball, Jr., b. Jan. 3, 1790;
   m., Dec. 6, 1821, Orpha L.
   Leonard of Agawam (b.
   March 17, 1793), who d.
   Sept. 29, 1878.

   Mr. Eli Ball, Jr., d. Sept.
   28, 1849.

Ch.

1. Margaret Ball, b. Sept. 7,
   1823; d. June 28, 1852.
2. Francis Ball, b. May 27,
   1825; d. Aug. 6, 1874.

3. Charlotte J. Ball, b. Feb. 8, 1827.
4. William H. Ball, b. April 11, 1829. Lives (1890) at Yonkers, N. Y.
5. Henry C. Ball, b. Sept. 5, 1831; d. Sept. 13, 1883.

3. Cynthia Ball, b. Nov. 10, 1791; was drowned Dec. 10, 1807.
4. Lucy Ball, b. Sept 22, 1793; m., Jan. 1, 1816, Wm. Dewey of Mass., and d. Dec. 2, 1860.
5. Benjamin Ball, b. May 5, 1795, at Westfield, Mass.; died Feb. 19, 1838; unm.
6. Francis Ball, b. April 14, 1797; m. Charlotte Jordan and lived in Milton, Pa. He d. Feb. 26, 1840.
ι. Elizabeth Ball, b. Feb. 12, 1799; m. Warren Chapin of W. Springfield, Mass., and died Aug. 9, 1866.

Ch.

1. Judson Chapin, b——.

8. William Ball, b. Nov. 12, 1801; m. Nancy Jenks. Lived in Springfield, Mass. He d. July 10, 1867.
9. Dezier Ball, b. Jan. 11, 1804; m. Palmer Gallup, and d.

April 20, 1838, at Agawam.
Had 4 ch.

10. Margaret Ball, b. Jan. 29 1806; d. 1808.

11. Cynthia Ball, 2nd, b. Jan. 18, 1808; d. Nov., 1810.

12. Adeline Ball, b. Dec. 4, 1809; m. Joseph Russell of Springfield, Mass., and d. in 1861-2. Had 3 ch.

13. Seymour Ball, b. Aug. 12, 1812; was married; died in 1836. No ch.

14. Samuel Ball, b. July 22, 1814; removed to Milwaukee, Wis., and d. March 24, 1890.

153.	AMOS,	born Oct. 19, 1774, at Agawam, Mass.
†154.	AMBROSE,	born April 16, 1777, at Agawam, Mass.
†155.	JONATHAN, 4TH,	born Sept. 2, 1779, at Agawam, Mass.
156.	MARY,	born July 15, 1782, at Agawam, Mass.; married, Oct. 21, 1802, Roderick Morley.

CHILDREN.

1. Fanny W. Morley, m. Milton Hoar of Munson, Ma., who changed his name to Woodford.

2. Emeline Morley, m. Albert

Remington of Suffield, Conn. Had 3 ch.

3. Susan Morley, m. Aaron Phelps of Suffield, Conn. Had 3 eh.

4. Roderick Morley, married and settled at Palmer, Mass.

ɔ. Mary Morley, m. James Lewis and settled at Suffield, Conn.

6. Lucy Ball Morley.

15ɩ. MARGARET,   born Oct. 30, 1784; m., Jan. 6, 1805 Samuel Smith of Groton, Conn., (b. June 9, 1772), son of Captain Samuel Smith and Abigail Woodmansee. They lived at Suffield, Conn., where both died.

Mr. Samuel Smith died Oct. 4, 1828.

Mrs. Margaret Smith died April 25, 1829.

CHILDREN.

1. Samuel Smith, b. Oct. 1, 1806, in Suffield, Conn.; m., Feb. 8, 1842, Susan M. Kil born, and d. April 8, 1878, at Winsted, Conn.

2. Jonathan Worthington Smith, b. March 9, 1808, in Suffield, Conn.; was for a number of years conductor on the Long Island Railroad;

m., 1st, Jan. 30, 1832, Marv Ann Comes; m., 2nd, Jan. 10, 1841, Elizabeth Anson. Jonathan Smith d. Oct. 4, 1857.

3. Margaret Smith, b. Dec. 8, 1809, in W. Springfield Mass.; m., Oct. 27, 1831, Marvin Hastings.

   Mrs. Smith d. June 2, 1837, in Suffield.

4. Benjamin Franklin Smith, b. Dec. 11, 1811, in W. Springfield; m., in 1833, Mary Ann Loomis.

   Mr. Smith d. Feb. 3, 1839, in Suffield.

5. Mary Smith, b. Nov. 1, 1813, in W. Springfield; d. Nov. 16, 1843, in Suffield.

6. Addison Smith, b. Mav 9, 1816, in Suffield; m., in 1845, at New York, Eliza Middle ton.

7. Eli Smith, b. Dec. 15, 1818, in Suffield; d. Nov. 26, 1821.

8. Fanny Smith, b. June 14, 1821, in Suffield; d. April 6, 1827.

9. Lucy Smith, b. March 10, 1823, in Suffield; d. Sept. 15, 1825.

10. Emeline Smith, b. Aug. 15, 1825.

158. SETH,   born Jan. 5, 1790; d. at 4 yrs. of age.

159. FANNY,   born Aug. 18, 1787; married, April 17, 1823, Benjamin Austin of Kirkland, Ohio.

CHILDREN.

1. Charlotte Austin, b. about 1825, and died unmarried.

62.

JOHN WORTHINGTON of Agawam, Mass., married three times; 1st, Jan. 20, 1774, Eunice Ferre (b. Sept. 6, 1752, at Springfield, Mass.; d. May 16, 1780), dau. of Aaron Ferre and Eunice Chapin; 2nd, Polly Leonard; 3rd, Sept. 30, 1794, Betsey Pettee.

Mr. John Worthington died April 15, 1815, at Agawam.

CHILDREN BY 1ST WIFE.

†160. DAVID,   born June 12, 1774.
†161. JOHN,   born Nov. 3, 1775.
162. EUNICE   born about 1776, at Ludlow Mass.; married, Feb. 1, 1797, Nathaniel Williston.

CHILDREN.

1. David Worthington Williston, b. April 24, 1800.
2. William Williston, b. Oct. 17, 1808.
3. Celina Williston, b. —— · d Aug. 10, 1810.

†163. AARON,   born May 13, 1780, W. Springfield, Mass.

CHILDREN BY 2ND WIFE.

164. POLLY,   born ——.
165. BETSEY,   born July 28, 1795, at Agawam, Mass.; married, Oct. 19, 1823, Nehemiah W. Smith (b. Dec. 13, 1798). They settled in Lyons, N. Y., where their children were born, and where Mr. Smith died Dec. 11, 1857, and Mrs. Betsey Smith died April 8, 1864.

CHILDREN.

1. Ira N. Smith, b. Dec. 8, 1824; d. Feb. 2, 1825.
2. Mary Elizabeth Smith, b. Feb. 15, 1826; d. Jan. 1 1847.
3. Susan Jane Smith, b. Jan. 7, 1830; d. Dec. 29, 1846.
4. John T. Smith, b. Nov. 18, 1831; d. Jan. 6, 1834.

†166. SETH,   born Oct. 12, 1796, W. Springfield, Mass.
167. HULDAH,   born ——, 1798; d. in infancy at Oxford, Conn.
†168. THOMAS,   born 1800.
169. ABBIE,   born Jan.——, 1802; d. May 16, 1803.
†170. HARVEY,   born March 4, 1804, at Agawam, Mass.

171. MARY   born April 11, 1806, at Agawam,
Mass.; m., Nov. 23, 1825, Judah
Ellis (b. Aug. 26, 1791). They
removed from Agawam to
Lyons, N. Y., where Mr. Ellis died
May 17, 1839, and Mrs. Mary
Ellis married, 2nd, June 19,
1841, Beekman Mead of Lyons,
who died Nov. 23, 1866.

Mrs. Mary Ellis Mead d. Nov.
23, 1878, at Lyons.

CHILDREN.

1. Laura Elizabeth Ellis, b.
July 22, 1826; d. Sept., 26
1854.
2. Jane Ann Ellis, b. Aug. 3,
1828; d. Aug. 24, 1831.
3. John Lyman Ellis, b. Feb.
27, 1831; m., Aug. 23, 1854,
Hannah M. Stone, and d.
Dec. 14, 1876, in Bangor,
Mich.

Ch.

1. Laura Elizabeth Ellis, b.
Oct. 18, 1856; m., Aug. 14,
1877, Frank W. Bidwell of
Wyoming Ter. Have 1 ch.

4. James Amassy Ellis b. July
24, 1834; m., July 4, 1857,
Frances H. Nelson (b. June
8, 1835; d. May 5, 1867).
Mr. Ellis d. June 11, 1871.

Ch.

1. Mary Diana Ellis, b. Sept. 17, 1860; m., Oct. 17, 187/, Augustus W. Vosteen.

5. Edwin Alfred Ellis, b. Nov. 1, 1836; d. Nov. 8, 1837.

6. Adelbert Judah Ellis, b. April 28, 1839; d. Aug. 25, 1860.

†172. ALFRED, born Feb. 23, 1809, at Agawam.

†173. LEWIS, born ——, 1812, at Agawam.

74.

STEPHEN WORTHINGTON of W. Springfield, Mass., gave intention of marriage, Nov. 24, 1781, to Lydia Rogers.

Mr. Stephen Worthington died —— 1827 ?

Mrs. Lydia Worthington died Jan. 8, 1828.

CHILDREN.

†174. SYLVESTER, born ——.

175. LYDIA, born ——; m. William Smith of Springfield.

†176. THEODORE, born Sept. 17, 1794.

†177. JOEL, born ——.

1.78. JOSHUA, born ——.

179. WILLIAM, born ——.

180. FLORILLA, born ——; died unm.

181. JOSEPH, born ——, 1798; died Dec. 3, 1799.

75.

ELIPHALET WORTHINGTON of Stoughton Mass., until about 1820, when they removed to Springfield, Mass., and later to

New Haven, Conn. Married Meletiah Packard of Stoughton widow of a Mr. Bliss.

Mr. Worthington died ——, 1823.

Mrs. Meletiah Worthington died ——, 1848, aged 75.

CHILDREN.

182. SARAH,   born Sept. 15, 1799, in Stoughton, Mass.; married, 1st, Stillman Porter Morse, in about 1820; 2nd, Phineas Terrill, about 1822.

Mr. Terrill died in 1829, and his widow married, 3rd, in 1831, William Hutton (b. in New York), son of John Hutton. Mr. William Hutton died about 1880. Mrs. Sarah Hutton died Sept. 3, 1885.

CHILDREN BY 1ST HUSBAND.

1. Hannah Morse, b. April 27 1821, in Stoughton, Mass.; married Jan. 1, 1843, Jeremiah Greenfield Wilbur (b. Sept. 28, 1813, in Delhi, N. Y.), son of William Benjamin Wilbur and Marcy Greenfield. Mr. Jeremiah Wilbur died Feb. 3, 1877.

Ch.

1. William Hutton Wilbur, b. March —, 1844.

2. Susan Jane Wilbur, b. Aug. 23, 1847.
3. Amelia Augusta Wilbur, b. April 15, 1850.
4. Charles Edgar Wilbur, b. Oct. 8, 1853; Prof. of Greek and Belles Lettres at Adrian college, Adrian, Mich.
5. Juliet Wilbur, b. Aug. 16, 1856.
6. Mary Alice Wilbur, b. April 13, 1859.
7. Frederick Oliver Wilbur, b. Feb. 21, 1862; d. Aug. 9, 1890.
8. Fanny Maria Wilbur, b. Aug. 29, 1864.

CHILDREN BY 2ND HUSBAND.

There were three who died in infancy.

4. Allen T. Terrill, b. April 2, 1825, in New Haven, Conn.; married, April 7, 1847 Phebe Ann Robinson (b. Aug. 11, 1831, in Manorville, L. I.), dau. of John and Naomi Robinson.

Ch.

1. Sarah E. Turrill, b. Nov. 30, 1848.
2. Eva A. Terrill, b. Sept. 27, 1850.
3. Clarissa A. Terrill, b. Nov. 19, 1852.

4. Serena Amelia Terrill, b. Oct. 26, 1855; d. Dec. 10, 1855.

5. Ada Alice Terrill, b. Feb. 13, 1857.

6. Mary A. Terrill, b. Jan. 18, 1859.

7. Edith Bell Terrill, b. Oct. 4, 1863; d. Feb. 11, 1865.

8. Allen G. Terrill, b. March 27, 1866.

9. John R. Terrill, b. Dec. 19, 1867.

10. Charles Ransom Terrill, b. Feb. 20, 1870; d. July 16, 1872.

11. Adele M. Terrill, b. Dec. 20 1872.

CHILDREN BY 3RD HUSBAND.

1. William Hutton, b. —, 1833, in N. Y. city.

2. George B. Hutton, b.   , 1835, in N. Y. city.

3. Thomas J. Hutton, b.   , 1837, in N. Y. city, and three others who died in infancy.

183. AMELIA   born 1809; m., 1830, Christopher Gwyer. Mrs. Gwyer died in 1839. No ch.

†184. HENRY,   born April 20, 1811, in Springfield, Mass.

†185. LINUS,   born Dec. 18, ——, in Boston, Mass.

†186. BENJ. FRANKLIN, born April 3, 1814, in Stoughton, Mass.

77.

HEMAN WORTHINGTON married, March 6, 1788, Martha Barber. Believed to have left one daughter.

87.

SAMUEL WORTHINGTON of Salem, N. Y. married three times; 1st, Olive Dewey, who died in 1772; 2nd, Esther Patch, who died Feb. 25, 1789; 3rd, Aug. 12, 1789, Mrs. Martha Savage Stocking, dau. of William Savage and Sarah Gibson.

Mrs. Martha Worthington died April 5, 1818.

Mr. Samuel Worthington died July 25, 1821.

CHILDREN BY 1ST WIFE.

†187. JOHN,   born Jan. 20, 1771.

CHILDREN BY 2ND WIFE.

188. OLIVE,   born April 2, 1779; married, 1st, David Rider of Springfield, Mass.; 2nd, Joseph Whittredge of Rochester, Mass., son of Joseph Whittredge and Abigail ——. He was a widower with three children—Mary, Abigail and Joseph. Mrs. Olive Whittredge d. Aug. —, 1846.

CHILDREN BY 1ST HUSBAND.

1. Mary Rider, m. Thomas Cushman of Springfield, O., and d. in 1837.

2. Olive Rider, m. Henry Chapin and d. about 1845 in White Pigeon, Mich.

CHILDREN BY 2ND HUSBAND.

1. Thomas Whittredge, b. and d. near Springfield, O.
2. William Whittredge.
3. Worthington Whittredge, b. May 22, 1820, in Springfield, O.; m., Oct. 16, 1867, Euphemia Foot (b. Dec. 22, 1837, in N. Y. city), dau. of Samuel A. Foot and Jane Campbell. Worthington Whittredge is an artist of N. Y. city.

Ch.

1. Jeannie Campbell Whittredge, b. Nov. 1, 1871; d. March 18, 1873.
2. Effie Whittredge, b. Jan. 27, 1874.
3. Olive Whittredge, b. June 24, 1875.
4. Mary Whittredge, b. Sept. 30, 1879.

189. HANNAH, born Sept. 12, 1781; married Andrew Watson of York, N. Y. She died May 1, 1864.

CHILDREN.

1. David R. Watson, b. Marel 5, 1806, in York, N. Y.; mar

ried, Oct. 29, 1873, Lois Ann Worthington (b. Jan. 22, 1842, in Great Valley, N. Y.), dau. of Squire Worthington and Annise Preston of Farmersville, N. Y. Mr. David Watson died Oct. 6, 1890.

Ch.

1. Walter D. Watson, b. Jan. 25, 1875, in York.

2. Sarah Watson, m., in 1835 Jno. McCleary, and died Nov. 1882. No ch.

3. Huldah Watson, died July 16, 1868; unm.

4. Maria Watson, b. 1807; m., 1st, John Root, who d. 1841 2; m., 2nd, Sept. 1843, David B. Prosser. Mrs. Maria Root Prosser d. Sept. 5, 1882. Had no ch.

5. William Henry Watson, b. Aug. 24, 1814; m., 1st, May 24, 1835, Catherine Barr of Barre, N. Y., who d. April 8, 1836. Mr. Watson m., 2nd Sept. 24, 1842, Mary L. Bottom. He d. Jan. 24, 1888.

Ch. by 1st Wife.

1. Catherine Maria Watson, b. Feb. 27, 1836; m., April 5, 1858, Wm. Whipple of Medina, N. Y. Had 3 ch.

Ch. by 2nd Wife.

2. Charles Jesse Watson, b. April 20, 1844; d. May 5, 1889.
3. Marietta Watson, b. May 6, 1848.
4. Henrietta Watson, b. May 6, 1848; d. Aug. 4, 1890.
5. Francis Huldah Watson, b. Dec. 8, 1851.

6. Samuel Watson, b——; d. in infancy?

190. MARY,   born Jan. 18, 1784; married Henry Doney.

CHILDREN.

1. Maria Doney.
2. Catherine Doney.
3. A son.

†191. TIMOTHY,   born June 30, 1786.

192. ESTHER,   born Feb. 10, 1789; married, Sept. 25, 1817, in Hebron, N. Y., Samuel Quaw (b. Sept. 14, 1790).

Mr. Samuel Quaw died Oct. 19, 1831.

Mrs. Esther Quaw died Dec. 25, 1861.

CHILDREN.

1. James Quaw, b. June 15, 1818; d. Sept. 6, 1819, in Hebron.
2. Martha Jane Quaw, b. Feb. 22, 1820, in Hebron; m.,

Dec. 4, 1845, William R. Cook, and d. July 10, 1860.

3. Nancy Quaw, b. Aug. 21, 1822, in Hebron; d. March 25, 1825, Hebron.

4. Hannah Maria Quaw, b. Aug. 2, 1824, in Hebron; m., Feb. 23, 1847, Moses Fisk. Had no ch.

5. Andrew William Quaw, b. Nov. 23, 1826; d. July 13, 1851.

6. Harriet Stocking Quaw, b. Dec. 27, 1828; m., June 30 1853, J. Fleming Craig. Had 6 ch.

CHILDREN BY 3RD WIFE.

193. SABRINA   born Aug. 25, 1790, in Salem N. Y.; m., Feb. 21, 1808, Solomon Fisk (b. Feb. 20, 1787, in Grand Isle, Vt.), son of Ichabod E. Fisk and Eleanor Roberts, who died April 23, 1809, and Mr. Fisk m., Sept 26, 1809, Catherine Worthington, sister to Sabrina.

Mr. Solomon Fisk died March 28, 1859, at Chazy, N. Y.

Mrs. Catherine Fisk died Sept. 21, 1861.

1. S. Newell Fisk, b. April 16, 1809, in Chazy, N. Y.; m.,

1st, Maria North of Chazy, who d. in 1849; m., 2nd., July 19, 1852, Mrs. Phebe Ann Raymond Fisk, widow of Almond Dunbar Fisk.

Mr. S. Newell Fisk d. June 11, 1856, at Chazy.

Mrs. Phebe Fisk d. May 29, 1880, at Brooklyn, N. Y.

Ch. bv 2nd Wife.

1. Harry Newell Fisk, b. Aug. 2, 1854, in Chazy.

194. CATHERINE,   born March 12, 1793, in Salem, N.Y.; married, Sept. 26, 1809, Solomon Fisk (b. Feb. 20, 1787, in Grand Isle, Vt.), son of Ichabod E. Fisk and Eleanor Roberts. She was his 2nd wife, his first being Sabrina, sister to Catherine.

Mr. Solomon Fisk died March 28, 1859, at Chazy, N. Y.

Mrs. Catherine Fisk died Sept. 21, 1861.

CHILDREN.

1. Joel Savage Fisk, b. Oct. 24, 1810; d. May, 1877, at Ft. Howard, Wis.
2. Sabrina Arazetta Fisk, b. Dec. 24, 1812; m., Dec. 24,

1833, Charles M. Scott of Chazy, N. Y.

Mrs. Scott d. 1879 at Waupaca, Wis.

Mr. Scott d. 1890 at Waupaca, Wis.

Ch.

1. John Ogden Scott, b. April 24, 1835.
2. Julia Ellen Scott, b. April 30, 1837; d. April 30, 1841.
3. Caroline Leslie Scott, b. Aug. 25. 1839.
4. Charles M. Scott, b. Jan. 24, 1842; d. Jan. 11, 1843.
5. Martha Ellen Scott, b. May 5, 1844.
6. Winfield Scott, b. March 30, 1847.
7. Cornelia Trimble Scott, b. ——; d. 1873.
8. Charles Scott.
9. Catherine Scott.

3. William C. Fisk, b. July 20, 1814; d. April 12, 1844, at Oxford, Miss.

4. Almond Dunbar Fisk, b. April 26, 1818; m., May 13, 1840, in N. Y. city, Phebe Ann Raymond.

Mr. Fisk d. Oct. 13, 1850, at Newtown, L. I., and Mrs. Phebe Fisk m., 2nd, July 19, 1852, Mr. S. Newell Fisk,

and d. May 29, 1880, at
Brooklyn, N. Y.

Ch.

1. Wm. M. L. Fisk, b. May
10, 1841, in N. Y. city.
2. Helen Martha Fisk, b. May
28, 1843, in N. Y. city; m.,
April 4, 1866, Austin
Adams.
3. Josephine I. Fisk, b. Jan.
12, 1847, in Newtown, L. I.
4. Phebe Ann Fisk, b. Aug. 24,
1848, in Newtown, L. I.;
m., Jan. 18, 1887, John H.
Wagner. Had 2 ch.
5. Almond Dunbar Fisk, b.
March 7, 1850, in Newtown,
L. I.; m., June 26, 1878, in
Brooklyn, N. Y., Anna L.
Rorback, who d. Oct. 17,
1888, in Brooklyn. Had 4
ch.

5. Martha Ellen Fisk, b. March
15, 1821, in Chazy, N. Y ;
m., May 9, 1843, at Chazy,
Rev. Newton B. Wood.

Ch.

1. Ellen Amelia Wood, b. Aug.
25, 1844; d. May, 1846.
2. Martha A. Wood, b. April
6, 1847, in Champlain, N.
Y.; m., May 7, 1873, Dr.
W. H. McLenathan of
Brooklyn, N. Y.

3. Charles Newton Wood, b. April 26, 1849, in Alburgh, N. Y., m., Oct. 21, 1874, Olive A. Clark of Millsborough, N. Y.

4. Francis F. Wood, b. Mav 8, 1852, in Grand Isle, Vt.; m., April 9, 1883, in Corning, Iowa, Chas. W. Hager.

5. Juliette Wood, b. Oct. 10, 1854, in Beekmantown, N. Y,; m., Jan. 19, 1882, in Brooklyn, Harry B. Gibbird.

6. Wilbur Fisk Wood, b. July 4, 1858, in Ausable Forks, N. Y.; m., Jan. 13, 1889, in Kansas City, Mo., Katharine Wittler.

7. Julian Worthington Wood, b. Aug. 7, 1861, in Mooers, N. Y.

6. Wilbur W. Fisk, b. Sept. 19, 1833; d. June 5, 1855, at Chazy, N. Y.

†195. WILLIAM SAVAGE, born July 4, 1800, in Salem, N. Y.

FIFTH GENERATION.

95.

ELIAS WORTHINGTON of Colchester, Ct., married, Oct. 24 1771, Anna Morgan (b April 10, 1752).

Mr. Elias Worthington died about 1804.

CHILDREN.

†196. CHARLES MORGAN, born Aug. 15, 1772, at Colchester.
197. RHODA,   born Aug 21, 1775; m., William
                          Marvin, and died, 1862, at
                          Minneapolis, Mich.

CHILDREN.

1. Harriet Marvin.
2. Elizabeth Marvin.
3. Jeannette Marvin.
4. William Marvin.

198. ALCOTT,   born March 28, 1780; died July 20,
                         1834, at Colchester, Ct.; un-
                         married.

†199. JEFFREY.

97.

JOEL WORTHINGTON of Colchester, Conn., married, Jan. 23,
1777, Eunice Newton.
    Mr. Joel Worthington died Jan. 29, 1817.
    Mrs. Eunice Worthington died Aug. 16, 1846.

CHILDREN.

200. CLARISSA,   born Jan. 30, 1778; married Nov.
                         24, 1800, Artemas Worthing-
                         ton (b. Dec. 11, 1777), son of
                         Elijah Worthington and Anna
                         Lovet. Mrs. Clarissa Worth-
                         ington died Aug. 27, 1847. Mr.
                         Artemas Worthington died ,
                         1858, at Colchester.

CHILDREN.

1. Nicholas Worthington, b. Aug. 16, 1802, in Colchester; m., 1st, Harriet Stark; 2nd, Sarah Sears of Hillsdale, Mich. He lived at Hillsdale and died Feb. 13 1861.

   Ch. by 1st Wife.

   1. Harriet Virginia Worthington, b. March 25, 1831, in Virginia; m., Sept. 13, 1851, Charles Ferdinand Dimmers of Hillsdale (b. Sept. 25, 1820, in Coblenz, Prussia). He d. Sept. 19, 1883. Had 4 ch.

   Ch. by 2nd Wife.

   2. Leslie Worthington, b.—, in Salem, Conn.
   2. Anna Worthington, b.—, in Salem, Conn.
   3. Marv Worthington, b—, in Adams, Mich.

2. Caroline Worthington, b. Nov. 6, 1804, in Colchester; m., Sept. 28, 1824, Seth E. Lathrop of Colchester (b. Jan. 6, 1797), son of Seth Lathrop and Maria Harris.
   Mrs. Caroline Lathrop d. May 5, 1860.

Mr. Lathrop d. Nov. 1, 1877.

Ch.

1. Caroline Maria Lathrop, b. July 30, 1846, in Salem, Ct.; m., April 30, 1862, David M. Jones of Turnerville, Ct. Had 3 ch.

3. Clarissa Ann Worthington, b. Dec. 29, 1806, in Colchester; m., June 10, 1828, James Fitch Stark of Trinidad, Colo. (b. Feb. 25, 1806).

Mrs. Clarissa Stark died July 16, 1890, at Cincinnati, Iowa.

Ch.

1. Caroline Lathrop Stark, b. July 24, 1829.
2. Ruth Allen Stark, b. March 6, 1831.
3. James Worthington Stark, b. March 4, 1833.
4. Harriet Louise Stark, b. June 22, 1835.
5. John Henry Stark, b. Sept. 26, 1837.
6. Lewis Cass Stark, b. May 22, 1844.
7. Clarissa Amelia Stark, b. Jan. 24, 1847.

4. Louisa Worthington, b. Apr. 27, 1808, in Colchester, Ct.;

m. John Griffin of Platte,
Mich. (b. June 1, 1798, in
Lyme, Ct.), son of Nathan
Griffin. Mrs. Louisa Griffin
d. Jan. 3, 1881. Mr. Griffin
d. Nov. 27, 1882. No ch.

5. Artemas Ward Worthington, b. July 21, 1813, in Colchester; m. Phœbe Sammis.

Ch.

1. Isabel Worthington.
2. Robert Worthington.
3. A son.
4. A son.

6. Eunice Elizabeth Worthington, b. Oct. 13, 1815, in Colchester; m., April ——, 1843, Cyrus Mann of Hebron, Ct., son of Reuben Mann. Mrs. Eunice Mann died Nov. 7, 1890.

They had a dau. who m. Charles Phelps of Hebron, Ct.

7 Albert Brummell Worthington, b. May 23, 1819, in Colchester; m., July 23, 1848, Mary E. Selden (b. May 25, 1822), dau. of Huntington Selden and Laura Hurd of Middle Haddam,

Conn. They lived at Middle Haddam, Conn.

Ch.

1. Albert Selden Worthington, b. Oct. 9, 1849, in Middle Haddam; m., April 20, 1887, Katie Goin, (b. Dec. 19, 1860, in Seneca, Can.), dau. of Eber Goin and Abigail Drake. Had no ch.
2. Arthur Huntington Worthington, b. Jan. 14, 1851.
3. Clara Louisa Worthington, b——.

8. Arthur Worthington, b. —, 1821; was killed in the Civil War; unmarried.

†201. Henry,   born Sept. 3, 1780.
202. Israel N.   born May 22, 1782; was married, and died Dec. 19, 1819, but no further record can be found.
203. Lois,   born Oct. 1, 1785; m., Feb. 15, 1811, Elijah Foot (b. Sept. 14, 1784) son of Israel Foot. They removed to Delaware Co., O. She died Dec. 26, 1818.
†204. Elias,   born June 24, 1788.

98.

Asa Worthington of Colchester, Conn., married Lucretia Kellogg (b. March 10, 1760). Mr. Asa Worthington died Nov. 13, 1822.

CHILDREN.

205. LAURA,

born Jan. 1, 1786; married, March 29, 1804, Ralph Isham of Col chester (b. June 25, 1776). Mrs. Laura Isham died Sept. 29, 1845. Mr. Isham died June 7 1847.

CHILDREN.

1. Laura Esther Isham, b Jan. 29, 1805.
2. Lucretia Isham, b. Feb. 3, 1807
3. Ralph Henry Isham, b. Feb. 17, 1809; m. Ann Heyward.

Ch.

1. Catherine Worthington Isham, b. Nov. —, 1839; d. March 4, 1858.
2. Ralph Isham, b. July —, 1843; d. Mav 16, 1874.

4. Joseph Giles Isham, b. Jan. 13, 1811.
ɔ. Ann Isham, b. June 13, 1813.
6. Asa Worthington Isham, b. May 1, 1815; d. Oct. 11 1824.
7. Frances Fedora Isham, b. March 11, 1817.
8. Catherine Isham, b. Jan. 14, 1819; d. Dec. 31, 1830.

206.	ANTHONY,	born 1785; d. 1875; unmarried.
†207.	ASA,	born 1789, in Colchester.

101.

DANIEL WORTHINGTON of Albany, N. Y., where he settled in 1810, removing from Colchester, Conn. He married, Feb. 9, 1766, Elizabeth Hazard of Westerly, R. I., a relative of Oliver Hazard Perry, who was often at their house, as also was Chancellor Kent and Thomas Addis Emmet (son of the Irish Patriot). Daniel Worthington was a lawyer, and died in Al bany, N. Y., Sept. 25, 1825.

CHILDREN.

208.	DANIEL,	born 1794, in Colchester.
209.	JOEL,	born 1796, in Colchester.
210.	SAMUEL,	born 1798, in Colchester; was vale-dictorian of his class at Yale College, and died soon after graduating.
211.	ELIZA,	born 1800, in Colchester; was the only daughter married; she left one son, Robert Crawford.
†212.	ROBERT HAZARD,	born Aug. 17, 1802.
213.	GILES	born 1804.
†214.	DENISON,	born March 4, 1806, in Colchester.
215.	OPHELIA,	born 1808, in Colchester, and three others who were born in Albany and died in infancy.

104.

DAVID WORTHINGTON of Peru, Mass., married Affa Gilbert of Sherburne, Mass., and settled in Belchertown, Mass. They returned to Sherburne in 1787, and again went to Belchertown in 1794; finally settled in Peru, where both died.

Mr. David Worthington died April 20, 1818.

Mrs. Affa Worthington died April 18, 1834.

CHILDREN.

†216. ERASTUS,   born Oct. 8, 1779, in Belchertown.

217. LUCINDA,   born Feb. 2, 1781, in Belchertown;
m., Nov. 26, 1806, Isaac King
of Chesterfield, Mass. (b. Feb.
11, 1778, in Chesterfield), son
of Eleazer King and Elizabeth
Day

Mr. King died July 17, 1838.

Mrs. King died Aug. 7, 1864.

CHILDREN.

1. Lucinda King, b. Sept. 25
1807; d. Dec. 26, 1807.

2. Franklin King, b. Dec. 8,
1808; m., Sept. 25, 1841,
Sarah C. Gelston, who d.
May 2, 1883.

Ch.

1. Sophia King, b. July 19,
1844; d. June 8, 1886.

2. Ann Gelston King, b. Sept.
5, 1845; m., Nov. 29, 1870,
Frank E. Brigham.

3. Sarah Frances King, b.
Oct. 26, 1849.

4. Bertha King, b. March 5
1852; d. June 21, 1878.

5. Abby C. Lawrence King, b.
March 4, 1855.

6. Samuel Gelston King, b.
Feb. 8, 1857; m., Oct. 30
1882, Alice T. Clark.

7. William Bates King, b.
Dec. 12, 1859; d. Aug. 17,
1863.

8. Theodore Winthrop King,
b. Feb. 2, 1862.

3. Sophia King, b. Jan. 21,
1811; m., May 28, 1868,
Mr. Phineas Nash, who d.
Jan. 23, 1880.
Mrs. Nash d. June 11,1890.

4. Edward King, b. March 31,
1813; m., Sept. 22, 1836,
Susan Cornelia Jours, who
d. Sept. 8, 1857. Mr. King
d. Jan. 17, 1867.

Ch.

1. Lucretia Ann King, b. July
2, 1837; m., Nov. 3, 1858,
Francis B. Snow.

2. Cornelia King, b. Aug. 19,
1839.

3. Helen King, b. June 21,
1841; d. Sept. 9, 1858.

4. Emma King, b. Sept 8,
1843; m., May 17, 1871,
Edward O. Blanchard.

5. Ella Susan King, b. July 1,
1846; m., Oct. 21, 1874,
Wm..Butlers.

6. Georgiana King, b. March
10, 1849; d. Sept. 28, 1849.

7. George Edward King, b.
Aug. 13, 1850; m., Oct. 30,

1872, Lilla T. Folsom,who
d. Sept. 25, 1877, and Mr.
King m., 2nd., June 20,
1883, Mrs. Florence Whit-
nev.

8. Isaac Worthington King,
b. Nov. 20, 1851; d. Sept.
19, 1853.

9. Frederick King, b. April 3,
1853; d. Nov. 9, 1861.

5. Lucinda King, b. Nov. 29,
1815; m., Oct. 10, 1838,
Thomas Nash.

Ch.

1. Franklin K. Nash, b Julv
2, 1842; d. Nov. 2, 1848.

2. Edward W. Nash, b. Aug.
24, 1844; m. Feb. 1, 1871,
Martha W. Child.

3. Harriet L. Nash, b. July 19,
1847.

4. Franklin K. Nash, b. May
11, 1850.

5. Helen M. Nash, b. Jan. 13,
1853; m., June 13, 1883.
Arthur Hinds.

6. Mary S. Nash, b. July 24,
1854; d. Nov. 27, 1869.

7. Susan L. Nash, b. April 30,
1857; d. Dec. 24, 1875.

8. Thomas Nash, b. July 29,
1859; d. July 24, 1863.

6. Lucretia King, b. Nov. 5,
1817; d. April 7, 1837.

7. Merrilla King, b. Nov. 8,

1819; m., 1st, Feb. 9, 1857, Henry White, who d. March 15, 1872, and his widow m., 2nd, June, 1875, Elbridge B. Kingsley. He d. June 9, 1889.

8. George Worthington King, b. July 30, 1822; m., 1st, July 1, 1850, Harriet Emily Mason, who d. Sept. 25, 1855, and Mr. King m., 2nd, Feb. 9, 1857, Harriet Warner. He d. April 29, 1866.

Ch. by 2nd Wife.

1. Isaac Worthington King, b. Jan. 17, 1859.
2. Emily Harriet King, b. Aug. 26, 1860.
3. Franklin King, b. May 11, 1863.
4. Ann Lucinda King, b. May 26, 1866; d. Aug. 1, 1878.

218. TEMPERANCE,   born Feb. 12, 1783, in Belchertown, Mass.; m., about 1806, Harvey Spalding of Royalton, N. Y. (b. Aug. 24, 1780).

Mrs. Temperance Spalding died ——, 1821, at Elbe, N. Y.

Mr. Spalding died, Jan. 21, 1837, at Vicksburg, Miss.

CHILDREN.

1. Eliza Sheperd Spalding, b. Nov. 24, 1808; m., Jan. 1, 1835, at Royalton, Jonathan Ingalls.

   Mr. Ingalls died —, 1875.?

   Mrs. Eliza Ingalls died May, 1877, at Green Bay, Wis.

   Ch.

   1. Charles Edward Ingalls, b. Jan. 6, 1836.
   2. George H. Ingalls, b. Oct. 23, 1841.
   3. Mary Eliza Ingalls, b. Oct. 27, 1845.

2. Charles Spalding.

3. Emily Temperance Spalding, b. Nov. 30, 1815, in Berkshire, Mass.; m., March 27, 1842, David Samuel Worthington of Sandusky, Ohio (b. March 26, 1818), son of Samuel Worthington and Nancy Miller.

   Mrs. Emily Worthington d. March 1, 1887.

   Ch.

   1. Elizabeth Worthington, b. Nov. 30, 1842; d. March 24, 1862.

2. Martha Worthington, b. Aug. 9, 1845; d. March 30, 1865.

3. Nettie Worthington, b. Aug. 10, 1857; m., Oct. 8, 1879, Charles Henry Wilson of Sandusky, O. Had 2 ch.

4. Laura Wilder Spalding, b. May 9, 1818; m., 1st, Nov. 19, 1840, David R. Dunn of Lockport, N. Y., who d. Feb. 24, 1850, and his widow m., 2nd, Aug. 12, 1851, M. M. Southworth of Lockport, N. Y. Mrs. Laura Southworth died May 31, 1883, at Lockport, N. Y.

Mr. Southworth died Sept. 24, 1889.

Ch. bv 1st Husband.

1. Frances E. Dunn, b. July 8, 1843; m., May 30, 1877, Charles E. Grisson. No ch.
Ch. by 2nd Husband.

1. Charles M. Southworth, b. March 6, 1853.

5. David Worthington Spalding, b. June 2, 1820; m., 1st, Lovita Ross of Peru, Mass.; had 4 ch.; 2nd, Elizabeth Hinkley; had 3 ch.; 3rd.——.

219. ELIZABETH,   born   , 1784, at Belchertown, Mass.; m. April —, 1808, William Dick

inson of South Williamstown,
Vt., and Hadlev, Mass. (b.   ,
1785, in Hadley, Mass.), son
of John Dickinson and Abigail
Alexander.

Mrs. Elizabeth Dickinson died
Dec.   , 1856.

Mr. William Dickinson died
Nov. —, 1868.

CHILDREN.

1. Mary Worthington Dickinson, b. March 16, 1809; m.
   —— Johnson, and d. May —,
   1872.
2. Edward Dickinson, b. June
   15, 1810; d. Feb. 24, 1812.
3. Elizabeth Wells Dickinson,
   b. Aug. 13, 1811
4. Edward Alexander Dickin
   son, b. Jan. 3, 1813; m. Ma
   ria Fletcher, and d. Feb. 24,
   1880.
5. Julia Franklin Dickinson, b.
   Aug. 3, 1814; d. June, 1872.
6. William Dickinson, b. April
   11, 1816.
7. Amelia Newton Dickinson,
   b. July 24, 1820; m. ——
   Eddy, and d. Feb. 17, 1884.
8. John Woodbridge Dickinson,
   b. Oct. 12, 1825, in Boston,
   Mass.

9. Emily Sophia Dickinson, b. Oct. 20, 1827; m. —— Stow of Jamestown, N. Y.

?20. AFFA, born —, 1785; married, Oct. 18, 1818. Nathan Miner of Peru, Mass. (b. March 28, 1770, in Conn.), son of Christopher and Lucy Miner

Mrs. Affa Miner died Jan. 25, 1850, at Ware, Mass.

Mr. Nathan Miner died July 4, 1855, at Winchester, N. H. Both were buried in Peru, Mass.

CHILDREN.

1. Dr. David Worthington Miner (b. Oct. 6, 1820, in Peru; m., Sept. 24, 1845, Mary H. Warner (b. Nov. 24, 1821, in Northampton Mass.), dau. of Joseph Warner and Nancy ——. They lived at Ware, Mass.

Ch.

1. Worthington Warner Miner, b. Nov. 5, 1847.
2. Mary Affa Miner, b. July 9, 1851; d. Jan. 9, 1857.
3. Eliza Nancy Miner, b. Oct. 20, 1853; m., Aug. 24, 1882, Charles E. Garman of Amherst, Mass.
4. Affa Sophia Miner, b. March 28, 1859.

5. Mary Warner Miner, b. Jan. 23, 1863; d. July 21, 1863.

2. Dr. Julius Fráncis Miner, b. Feb. 16, 1823, in Peru; m., Sept. 8, 1847, Mary Cordelia Cogswell, (b. Feb. 25, 1824, in Pittsfield, Mass.), dau. of Richard Cogswell. Dr. Miner died Nov. 5, 1887.

Ch.

1. Julius Cogswell Miner, b. Sept. 14, 1850; d.—, 1859.
2. Mary Estella Miner, b. May 22, 1858; m. Nathaniel Willis Norton, and d. June 26, 1889.
3. Worthington Cogswell Miner, b. May 31, 1861.

221. MARY, born March 5, 1788, in Sherburne, Mass.; m., Dec. 12, 1812, at Peru, Mass., Ezra Harwood of Lockport, N. Y., (b. July 28 1788, in Berkshire Co., Mass.), son of Marville H. Harwood (who was son of Dr. John Harwood) and Mary Southworth.

Mr. Ezra Harwood d. May 5 1859.

Mrs. Mary Harwood d. Feb. 11, 1873.

CHILDREN.

1. Emerson Harwood, b. Dec. 15, 1813, in Worthington,

Mass.; m., May 17, 1837, Mary Trowbridge, dau. of Cyrus Trowbridge and Nancy Whipple.

Ch.

1. Ann Elizabeth Harwood, b. Feb. 28, 1838; d. Aug. 11, 1856.
2. Martha Whipple Harwood, b. Nov. 28, 1839; m., Sept. 17, 1861, Thomas Cabot Boynton, and d. Oct. 27, 1872.
3. Frances Ransom Harwood, b. Sept. 16, 1841; m., Jan. 30, 1867, Eli S. Nichols.
4. John Emerson Harwood, b. June 4, 1845; m., 1st, Aug. 2, 1870, Georgie Belle Gardner, who d. Nov. 21, 1883; m., 2nd, Aug. 25, 1885, Adelaide V. Cropsey.
5. Jennie Colton Harwood, b. March 12, 1850; unm.
6. Mary Trowbridge Harwood, b. Aug. 5, 1853.

2. Mary Harwood, b. May 8, 1817, in Royalton, N. Y.; m., Jan. 5, 1837, Charles L. Safford, son of Elias.

    Mr. Charles Safford d. Dec. 13, 1864, in Detroit, Mich.

Ch.

1. Charles H Safford, b
2. Lucretia Safford.

3. Mary Safford, m. Dr. Wm. H. Lathrop.
4. Arthur R. Safford, m. Maria —— of Otsego, N. Y

3. Lucretia Agnes Harwood, b. May 21, 1819, in Royal ton, N. Y.; m., Nov. 24, 1840, Edwin L. Boardman, of Lockport, N. Y., son of William Boardman and Abi gail North of Sheffield, Mass.
   Mrs. Lucretia Boardman d. March 17, 1854.

Ch.

1. Minerva North Boardman, b. April 16, 1842, in Lockport; m., Jan. 29, 1868, Marcus Edmund Tobey of Gt. Barrington, Mass. Had 3 sons.
2. Cornelia Lucretia Boardman, b. July 6, 1845; m. Wm. H. Pulsifer of St.Louis, Mo., now residing in Newton, Mass.

4. Jane Elizabeth Harwood, b. Feb. 4, 1826, in Lockport; m., Sept. 13, 1849, Rev. Therin Gaylord Colton of Rootstown, O. (b. July 24, 1820, in Otsego, N. Y.), son of Rev. George Colton and Lucy Cowles.

Ch.

1. Mary Worthington Colton, b. Sept. 23, 1850; m., Aug. 22, 1875, Hon. J. K. Boies of Hudson, Mich., and d. Sept. 10, 1888, at Hudson, leaving a dau., Bessie.

2. George H. Colton, b. Feb. 22, 1854; d. Feb. 5, 1858.

3. Abbie Amelia Colton, b. Sept. 2, 1857; m., Aug 26, 1883, Frank M. Childs of Hudson.

4. Rev. Alfred Ely Colton, b. Nov. 9, 1859; m. Clara Porter Smith, dau. of Henry M. Smith of Cummington, Mass. They reside in Gatesbury, Ill.

5. Hubert Gaylord Colton, b. June 15, 1863; resides in Portland, Ore.

6. Walter Safford Colton, b. Oct. 26, 1867.

5. Worthington B. Harwood, b. May 19, 1822; was a soldier in a California regiment and died July—, 1865; unm.

6. Emily Harwood, b. June 27, 1829, in Royalton, N. Y., m., 1st, Oct. 3, 1849, John H. Lull (b. in Otsego, N. Y.; d. Jan. 3, 1855); m., 2nd, Nov. 1, 1868, Erastus Bowen (b. in Homer, N. Y).

Ch. by 1st Husband.

1. Fred Lull, b. July 28, 1852.
2. Julia H. Lull, b. March ,
   1855.

7. Julia Harwood, b. May 27,
   1831, in Rovalton; m., Jan.
   22, 1863, Sidnev Strong of
   Northampton. Mass. (b.
   Aug. 2, 1816, in Westhamp-
   ton, Mass.), son of Paul
   Strong and Sarah Chapman.
   Mr. Sidney Strong d. Aug.
   5, 1888.

Ch.

1. Gilman Harwood Strong,
   b. March 31, 1865.
2. Cornelia Boardman Strong,
   b. Oct. 17, 1868.
3. Julia Worthington Strong,
   b. March 20, 1871.

†222. SAMUEL,   born Jan. 8, 1792, in Sherburne, Mass.
†223. DAVID,   born Oct. 12, 1794, in Peru, Mass.
 224. SOPHIA,   born May 16, 1790, in Brookfield,
                  Mass.(?); married Samuel E.
                  Hitchcock of Sandusky, Ohio
                  (b. June, 1798, in New York
                  state).
                      Mrs. Sophia Hitchcock died
                  Feb., 1857.
                      Mr. Hitchcock died Feb. 9,
                  1881.

CHILDREN.

1. Cordelia Antoinette Hitch
   cock, b. Aug. 15, 1831; m.
   June 5, 1851, Walter F.
   Stone of Sandusky, O. (b
   Nov. 18, 1822).
       Mr. Stone died Dec. 24,
   1874·
       Mrs. Cordelia Stone died
   Jan. 9, 1887.   .

Ch.

1. Mary S. Stone, b. Feb. 13,
   1854; m., Oct. 27, 1875,
   John L. Moore of Sandusky,
   Ohio, son of Philander and
   Iulia Moore.
2. Pralla Cordelia Stone, b
   July 20, 1858; m., April 21
   1886, Frank Graham Sco
   field, son of Sidney and
   Eliza Scofield.
3. Walter H. Stone, b. June
   24, 1866. Unm.

107.

AMASA WORTHINGTON of Williamstown, Vt., married Nov
12, 1801, Asenath Stebins, dau. of Moses Stebins of Wilboro
ham, Mass.

Mr. Amasa Worthington died Jan. 30, 1859, in Williamstown, Vt.   .

Mrs. Asenatl Worthington died after 1855.

CHILDREN.

225. MARGARET,   born April 7, 1803, died April 12, 1803.

226. ELIAS,   born March 15, 1805; died Feb. 10 1817.

227. CLARISSA,   born April 13, 1807; married, Oct. 13, 1825, Jonathan C. Farnham. She died October 7, 1877. Had 3 ch.

228. ASENATH,   born April 16, 1809, in Williamstown, Vt.; married, July 8, 1862, Robert Seaver. Had no ch.

†229. JOHN JEWETT,   born Feb. 18, 1812, in Williamstown, Vt.

230. AMASA,   born Aug. 6, 1814; died Oct. 13, 1821.

108.

DANIEL WORTHINGTON of Williamstown, Vt., married, Feb. 27, 1800, Mary Fiske (b. May 12, 1780), dau. of Judge Jonathan Fiske of Williamstown. They removed in 1838 to Wisconsin; settled first at Milwaukee, and then at Round Point, and finally at Oconomowac.

Mr. Daniel Worthington died July 4, 1866, in Oconomowac. Mrs. Mary Worthington died in Oconomowac.

CHILDREN.

231. HULDAH   born July 31, 1801, in Williamstown; married, 1st, Dec. 19, 1821 John Richardson (b. 1791, in Northfield, Vt.), son of Stanton Richardson and Anna Double-

day, who died in 1834; m., 2nd,
May, 1838, Hosea Clark, son of
Stephen Clark and Dinah Pres-
ton.

Mrs. Huldah Richardson
Clark died Sept. 14, 1847.

CHILDREN BY 1ST HUSBAND.

1. Sarah Richardson, b.   ,
   1823; d.   , 1826.
2. George M. Richardson, b.
   , 1824; d.   , 1827.
3. John Harris Richardson,
   b.   , 1826; d   1876.
4. Marshall H. Richardson,
   b.   , 1827; d.   , 1859.
5. George S. Richardson, b.   ,
   1829; d.   , 1850.
6. Mary Richardson, b.   ,
   1831; d.   , 1832.
7. Daniel W. Richardson, b.   ,
   1833; m., Marcia Helen Lane
   (b. March 5, 1836, in Northfield, Vt.), dau. of Josiah
   Lane and Alpha Chamberlain.

CHILDREN.

1. Ella Maria Richardson, b.
   Jan. 22, 1856; d. Jan. 28,
   1856.
2. Mary Lane Richardson, b.
   Aug. 3, 1862.

    3. Helen Worthington Rich-
ardson, b. Oct. , 1864; d.
April 5, 1865.

    4. Ernest Ensign Richardson,
b. Jan. , 1866.

    5. Grace Helen Richardson, b.
July —, 1870.

    6. Robert Worthington Rich
ardson, b. Aug. 4, 1879.

CHILDREN BY 2ND HUSBAND.

    1. Lucia Ann Clark, b. March
27, 1839; m., Aug. 7, 1867
Samuel F. Paine.

Ch.

    1. Charles Clark Paine, b. Dec.
13, 1869.

    2. Stephen Alonzo Clark, b.
Jan. 6, 1842, in Northfield;
m., April 24, 1869, Frankie
Fanning (b. June 10, 1849),
dau. of —— Fanning and
Jane A. Breckenridge. Had
no ch.

†232. ELIJAH,   born July 31, 1803, in Williamstown
Vt.

233. SOPHIA,   born April 9, 1805; married, May
5, 1833, Nathan Strong
Green of Clinton, Mich. (b.
March 31, 1805, in Conn).
Mr. Green died Feb. 27,
1883, in Clinton.

Mrs. Sophia Green died July 11, 1887.

CHILDREN.

1. Mary Sophia Green, b. May 29, 1836, in Northfield, Vt.; m., April 10, 1856, George Minot Pomeroy (b. Dec. 3, 1828), son of Quartus Wells Pomeroy and · Minerva Champney.

   #### Ch.

   1. Lebbeus Dan Pomeroy, b. June 2, 1859; m., March 19, 1884, Leona E. Lamb. Had 2 ch.
   2. Carrie Strong Pomeroy, b. Feb. 7, 1851; d. Aug. 20, 1864.
   3. Charles Lyman Pomeroy, b. Feb. 11, 1863; d. Aug. 22, 1864.
   4. Julia Edith Pomeroy, b. Feb. 6, 1867; m., Oct. 16, 1889, Charles J. Becker.

2. George Worthington Green, b. March 14, 1838; m., Oct. 25, 1860, Mary E. Townson (b. Dec. 10, 1837), dau. of Joseph Townson and Mary White.

   They reside in Brooklyn, Mich., where Mr. Green is a hardware merchant.

Ch.

1. George E. Green, b. June 15, 1862.
2. Charles T. Green, b. Oct. 1, 1867.
3. Leon W. Green, b. Oct. 29 1874.
4. Clark S. Green, b. July 16, 1879.

3. Charles Milford Green, b. March 14, 1840; m., 1st. Dec. 25, 1871, Florence Amanda Clough; m., 2nd, Dec. 31, 1878, Hattie Brad ner.

Ch. by 1st Wife.

1. Frances Aroxy Green, b. June 13, 1874; d. in infancy.
2. Florence Amanda Green, b. June 13, 1874.

†234. LYMAN, born Feb. 16, 1807.

235. MARY, born Sept. 26, 1808, in Williamstown, Vt.; married, May 2, 1833, Moses Lane.

Mr. Lane died Dec. 18, 1889. Mrs. Mary Lane living (1890) at Northfield, Vt. Had no ch.

236. RHODA born June 18, 1811, in Williamstown, Vt.; m., Sept. 1, 1834, at Woodstock, Vt., Gilman Comings (b. July 31, 1805, in Cornish, N.H.), son of Warren Comings. Mr. Gilman Comings died Dec. 16

1876, at Metuchen, N. J. Mrs.
Rhoda Comings died March 14
1883.

CHILDREN.

1. George Taylor Comings, b.
   Dec. 17, 1836, in Wood
   stock, Vt.; d. Jan. 11, 1839,
   in Snufftown, N. J.
2. Elvira Amy Comings, b. Oct.
   31, 1839, in Snufftown, N.
   J.; m., Jan. 18, 1864, Henry
   LaFarge of Metuchen, N. J.

Ch.

   1. Nettie O. LaFarge, b. June
      23, 1866, in Metuchen; m.,
      Dec. 31, 1884, Andrew J.
      Tappan.
   2. Daniel D. LaFarge, b. Aug.
      11, 1868, in Metuchen.
   3. Annie A. LaFarge, b. Jan.
      6, 1870, in Metuchen.
   4. Rhoda C. LaFarge, b. April
      8, 1872, in Metuchen.
   5. Charles C. LaFarge, b. Feb.
      16, 1881, in Metuchen.

3. George Taylor Comings, b.
   May 23, 1841, in Petersburg, N. J.; m. May 23, 1867,
   at Sparta, N. J., Sarah L.
   Corv.

Ch.

   1. Virgil Comings, b. June 18,
      1868, in Metuchen; d. June
      17, 1869, in Metuchen.

2. Ella C. Comings, b. July 4, 1870, in Metuchen.

3. Worthington G. Comings, b. Nov. —, 1871, in Kansas.

4. Robert M. Comings, b. —, in Kansas.

5. Frank Comings, b. —, in Metuchen.

6. Raymond G. Comings, b. —, in Perth Amboy, N. J.

7. Harry Comings, b. —, in Perth Amboy, N. J.

8. Walter Comings, b. —, in Perth Amboy, N. J.

4. Jenette Comings, b. July 16, 1844, in Milton, N. J.; d. Nov. 9, 1852, in Sparta, N.J.

5. Martin Luther Comings, b. Aug. 10, 1846, in Sparta, N. J.; d. Oct. 19, 1852, in Sparta, N. J.

6. Daniel Gilman Comings, b. May 17, 1850, in Sparta, N. J.; m., July, 1884, at Newark, N. J., Louisa C. Smith.

Ch.

1. Viola May Comings, b. July —, 1885, in Middletown, N. Y.

2. Bertha L. Comings, b. June 27, 1887, in Middletown, N. Y.

3. Florence A. Comings, b. Nov. —, 1889, in Middletown, N. Y.

†237.	DANIEL,	born Feb. 3, 1813, in Northfield, Vt.
†238.	DAVID,	born Feb. 13, 1815, in Williamstown, Vt.
†239.	THEODORE,	born May 17, 181?, in Northfield, Vt.
240.	ELIAS,	born July 16, 1819; died Jan. 12, 1824.
241.	FRANCIS,	born Feb. 3, 1822; died Sept. 12, 1823.

121

WILLIAM WORTHINGTON of Dorchester, Mass. married, May 25, 1814, Rachel Glover Howe (b. June 4, 1749), daughter of John and Martha Howe of Dorchester.

Mr. William Worthington died March 6, 1857, in Dorchester.

Mrs. Rachel Worthington died Oct. 26, 1857, in Dorchester.

On the day of Mr. Worthington's funeral the flags on the shipping in Boston harbor were at half mast, the first time in the history of the city, for a private citizen.

[From a Boston daily paper.]

"DEATH OF A GOOD MERCHANT.—We regret to report the sudden death of William Worthington, Esq., one of the oldest and most respected merchants of Boston. The event took place yesterday at his residence in Dorchester. His disease was hemorrhage of the lungs. It is the lot of but few men engaged in active business to reach the age of more than three-score and ten years, with so pure a reputation, so upright and honorable a character, as will be universally awarded to the deceased. Such men serve to redeem the mercantile profession from the stain it oftentimes receives by the action of selfish, mean or unprincipled merchants. Mr. Worthington was a native of Colchester, Conn. He came to Boston when a lad and has been known in business circles for more than half a century. His age was 73 years. We believe he has occupied a store on Central Wharf for a longer period than any merchant thereon. He has been a director of the New England Bank for some thirty-three years, and during the last quarter of a century he has been an active member and wise counsellor of most of the well-established benevolent organizations

WILLIAM WORTHINGTON.

of this city. He was a life member of the American Unitarian Association, and for more than thirty years has served as deacon of the New South Church. In all the relations of life the deceased was known as a man of sterling integrity, whose actions were based upon the deepest Christian principles. The funeral services will take place at his late residence in Dorchester on Monday afternoon next, at three and a half o'clock. As we contemplate the useful life and noble example of the deceased, the following lines from an anonymous poet seem to have almost been written for the comfort of his relatives and friends:

> " ' I looked upon the righteous man
> And heard the holy prayer,
> Which rose above the breathless form
> To soothe the mourner's care,
> And felt how precious was the gift
> He to his loved ones gave—
> The stainless memory of the just,
> The wealth beyond the grave.' "

CHILDREN.

242. MARTHA HOWE, born April 6, 1815; d. April 23, 1824.

243. SARAH WELLES, born April 1, 1817; married, June 28, 1836, W. H. Richardson.

Mrs. Sarah Richardson died Oct. 30, 1884.

CHILDREN.

1. Anna Caroline Richardson; m. Dr. R. T. Edes of Washington, D. C.

2. Stanley Worthington Richardson. Unm.

3. Martha Linette Richardson.

4. Rachel Howe Richardson; m. George F. Roberts, now deceased.

244. WILLIAM FRANCIS, born June 18, 1819; died Jan. 17, 1873. Unmarried.
245. JOHN HOWE,   born July 24, 1821; died Aug. 24, 1884. Unmarried.
246. MARTHA HOWE, born Feb. 21, 1824; married, May 25, 1847, Olcott Banv. Had no ch.

122.

FRANCIS WORTHINGTON married Caroline Lovering, dau. of Joseph Lovering of Boston, Mass.

Mr. Worthington died about 1846.

CHILDREN.

247. FRANCIS,   born —; died —; unmarried.
248. JOSEPH,   born —; died —; unmarried.

126.

ERASTUS WORTHINGTON of Colchester, Conn., and Brooklyn, N. Y., married Ann Taintor (b. July —, 1767), eldest daughter of Captain Charles Taintor and Mary Skinner, dau. of Rev. Thomas Skinner of Westchester. Capt. Charles Taintor (b. Feb. 8, 1723), was son of Michaiel (b. Sept., 1680, in Windsor, Conn.), and Eunice Foote of Wethersfield, who were married Dec. 3, 1712.

Michaiel Taintor was son of Michaiel (b. Oct., 1652) and Mary Loomis.

Michaiel was son of Charles, who was in New England in 1643.

Erastus and Ann Worthington died about 1836 in Brook lyn, N. Y.

CHILDREN.

†249. ERASTUS,   born ——.
†250. ALFRED   born ——.
†251. WILLIAM,   born March 13, 1798, in Colchester.

127.

ELIJAH WORTHINGTON married, Sept. 8, 1791, Sarah P Lewis.

CHILDREN.

252. SAMUEL,   born ——
253. ELIJAH,   born ——.
254. HARRIET,   born July 25, 1793.
255. INFANT SON,   born July 25, 1793; died 2 days later.

128.

JOSEPH WORTHINGTON of Harvey's Lake, Pa., married, 1st, Sept. 10, 1791, Mary Adams Bulkeley (b June 25, 1770), daughter of Eliphalet Bulkeley and Mary Adams; married, 2nd, in the fall of 1820, Sarah Perry, daughter of Daniel.

Mrs. Mary Bulkeley Worthington died July —, 1814.

Mr. Joseph Worthington died Jan. 21, 1853, at Harvey's Lake.

CHILDREN BY 1ST WIFE.

256. NANCY,   born July 1, 1792, in Colchester, Ct.; married, 1st, Feb. 8, 1808, Isaac Fuller, son of Bermajah Fuller and Katharine ——; married, 2nd, in 1830, Isaac Cook.

CHILDREN BY 1ST HUSBAND.

1. Charles Fuller.
2. Harrison Fuller.
3. Eliphalet Fuller.
4. Elijah Fuller.
5. Frances Fuller.
6. Ellen Fuller.
7. Justin Fuller.
8. Isaac Fuller.

CHILDREN BY 2ND HUSBAND.

1. Maria Cook.

†257. JOSEPH LOVETT, born Sept. 6, 1795, in Colchester, Ct.
†258. ELIPHALET B., born Sept. 1, 1795, in Colchester, Ct.
259. MARIA born Feb. 28, 1800, in Colchester, Ct.; married Thomas Stewart.

CHILDREN.

1. Joseph W. Stewart, deceased.
2. Emma Stewart, deceased.
3. Delphine Stewart, deceased.

†260. ELIJAH, born in Colchester.
261. ELIZA, born 1805, in Colchester; married, in 1824, Asaph W. Pratt, son of Calvin Pratt.

CHILDREN.

1. Edmund Pratt.
2. Henrietta Pratt, m. ——— Foster.
3. Asaph Pratt.
4. Julia Pratt.

5. Frank Pratt.
6. Mary Pratt.

†262. JONATHAN BULKELEY, born Jan. 16, 1807 in Harvey's
Lake.
†263. THOMAS BARTLETT, born April 6, 1810, in Harvey's
Lake.

CHILDREN BY 2ND WIFE.

†264. HENRY, born July 9, 1821.

129.

JUSTIN WORTHINGTON of Ogden, N. Y., married, Nov. 27,
1794, Sallie Sparrow (b. Sept. 27, 1771, in East Haddam)
daughter of James Sparrow and Sally Holmes.
Mr. Justin Worthington died Aug. 14, 1848.
Mrs. Sally Worthington died June 9, 1851.

CHILDREN.

265. SALLY HOLMES, born Jan. 11, 1796; married, July 5,.
1819, Arnold Eddy of Ogden, N.
Y. (b. March 31, 1795), son of
John Eddy and Sally Smith.
Mr. Arnold Eddy died Feb.
22, 1827.
Mrs. Sally Eddy died May 2,.
1885.

CHILDREN.

1. Leroy Eddy, b. Oct. 5, 1820 ·
d. Nov. 15, 1852.
2. Almont Eddy, b. Dec. 16,
1821, d. Nov. 4, 1829.

3. Sally Sparrow Eddy, b. June
5, 1823, in Ogden; m., Sept.
13, 1849, Samuel Emery Ellinwood (b. Jan. 20, 1820, in
Clinton, N. Y.), son of Eli
Ellinwood and Sophia Ma-
ria Gridley.

Ch.

1. Charlotte Mariah Ellinwood, b. June 24, 1855.
2. Eli Groves Ellinwood, b.
Feb. 14, 1859.
3. Allie Holmes Ellinwood, b.
Feb. 14, 1859.

4. Sarepta Reid Eddy, b. Sept.
9, 1824; d. July 17, 1825.
5. Delos Eddy, b. April 25,
1826, in Ogden, N. Y.; m.,
April 12, 1870, Helen M.
Marsh of Darien Centre, N.
Y. Had no ch.
6. Ellen Geraldine Eddy, b. Oct.
2, 1827, in Ogden; m., Sept.
25, 1890, Adin Gage of Spencer Port, N. Y. (b. March,
1820, in Henrietta, N. Y.)

†266. JUSTIN LOVETT, born Aug. 19, 1797.

267. ELIZABETH S., born Aug. 19, 1797; died Jan. 16,
1872.

268. CAROLINE MUNFORD, born March 7, 1799; married,
Sept. , 1843, Stephen Gates.
Mr. Gates died in 1867, at
Parma, N. Y.

Mrs. Caroline Gates died May
19, 1890. Had no ch.

†269. JAMES SPARROW, born Dec. 15, 1802.

†270. HENRY SPENCER, born May 31, 1812, in Ogden, N. Y.

131.

ARTEMAS WORTHINGTON of Colchester, Conn., married, Nov.
24, 1800, Clarissa Worthington (b. Jan. 30, 1778), daughter
of Joel Worthington and Eunice Newton of same town).

Mr. Artemas Worthington died April 16, 1853, in Colchester.
Mrs. Clarissa Worthington died Aug. 27, 1849.

CHILDREN.

†271. NICHOLAS, born Aug. 16, 1802, in Colchester.

272. CAROLINE, born Nov. 6, 1804, in Colchester;
married, Sept. 28, 1824, Seth E.
Lathrop of Colchester, (b. Jan.
6, 1797), son of Seth Lathrop
and Maria Harris.

Mrs. Caroline Lathrop died
May 5, 1860.

Mr. Lathrop died Nov. 1, 1877.

CHILDREN.

1. Caroline Maria Lathrop, b.
July 30, 1846, in Salem, Conn;
m., April 30, 1862, David
M. Jones of Turnerville, Conn.
(b. July 6, 1838, in Hebron,
Conn.), son of William G.
Jones and Mary E. Northam.

Ch.

1. Mabel Caroline Jones, b. March 3, 1876.
2. Myron William Jones, b. July 16, 1879.
3. Herman David Jones, b. March 4, 1883.

273. CLARISSA ANN, born Dec. 29, 1806, in Colchester; married, June 10, 1828, James Fitch Stark of Trinidad, Colo. and Cincinnati, Iowa (b. Feb. 25, 1806, in Colchester), son of James Stark.

Mrs. Clarissa Stark died July 16, 1890, in Cincinnati, Iowa.

CHILDREN.

1. Caroline Lathrop Stark, b. July 24, 1829, in Colchester; m., March 13, 1851, Beni Bishop of Huron, Dakota. She d. Feb. 16, 1889.

Ch.

1. George Stevens Bishop.
2. James Stark Bishop.
3. William Arthur Bishop.
4. John Henry Bishop.
5. Clara Bell Bishop, deceased.
6. Frank Ward Bishop
7. Chas. Worthington Bishop.
8. Harriet Louisa Bishop.

2. Ruth Allen Stark, b. March 6, 1831, in Colchester; m., in 1854, Walter Buel.

Mr. Buel died many years
ago.

Mrs. Ruth Buel died in
1856, in Coldwater, Mich.

Ch.

1. Julia Ellen Buel, b. ——; m.
—— Clark.

3. James Worthington Stark
b. March 4, 1833, in Col
chester; m., Sept. 5, 1861,
Cynthia Buck (b. March 4,
1836, in Hanover, N. Y.),
dau. of Rev. Elijah Buck and
Mary Ann Butler

Mrs. Cynthia Stark died
Aug. 1, 1891. Had no ch.

4. Harriet Louisa Stark, b. June
22, 1835; d. Sept. 18, 1836.

5. John Henry Stark, b, Sept.
26, 1837; d. April 7, 1862;
unm.

6. Lewis Cass Stark, b. May
22, 1844; d. Nov. 25, 1863

7. Clarissa Amelia Stark, b.
Jan. 24, 1847, in Jonesville,
Mich.; m., March 4, 1866,
Wilson L. Woodburn of Cin
cinnati, Iowa (b. March 29,
1836, in Wyrox, Pa.), son
of Moses Woodburn and Es-
ther Whitney.

Ch.

1. Harry Woodburn, b. July 6, 1868; d. July 31, 1870.
2. James Fitch Woodburn, b. Oct. 16, 1870.
3. John Lewis Woodburn, b. Jan. 13, 1873.
4. Lucy Esther Woodburn, b. March 19, 1875.
5. Mary Clara Woodburn, b. Feb. 14, 1878.
6. Charles Wilson Woodburn, b. Nov. 26, 1881.
7. Ernest Clarence Woodburn, b. July 19, 1885.

274. LOUISA,   born April 27, 1808, in Colchester; married John Griffin of Platte, Mich. (b. June 1, 1798, in Lyme, Conn.), son of Nathan Griffin.

Mrs. Louisa Griffin died Jan. 3, 1881.

Mr. John Griffin died Nov. 27, 1882. Had no ch.

†275. ARTEMAS WARD, born July 21, 1813, in Colchester.

276. EUNICE ELIZABETH, born Oct. 13, 1815, in Colchester ; married, April   1843, Cyrus Mann of Hebron, Conn., son of Reuben (?).

Mrs. Eunice Mann died Nov. 7, 1890.

Had a dau. who m. Charles Phelps, of Hebron, Conn.

†277. ALBERT BROWNELL, born May 23, 1819, in Colchester.

278. ARTHUR YOUNG, born 1821, in Colchester; went west

about 1850, and joined the
Union army at the Rebellion,
and died in the hospital; was
unmarried.

Four other children who died in infancy.

132.

DUDLEY WORTHINGTON of Colchester, Conn., married, 1st
Oct. 5, 1792, Nancy Swan (b. 1775; d. Jan. 27 1814); 2nd
Oct. 12, 1814, Sarah Reid (b. 1790).

Mr. Dudley Worthington died April 1, 1838, in Colchester.

Mrs. Sarah Worthington died Dec. 28, 1865.

CHILDREN BY 1ST WIFE.

†279. DUDLEY WRIGHT, born Aug. 19, 1795, in Colchester.

280. GERSHOM BUCKLEY, born Mav 19, 1798, in Colchester ·
died May 17, 1801.

281. NANCY SWAN, born Dec. 30, 1800, in Colchester ;
married April 13, 1823. Reuben
Bradley of West Mystic, Conn.
(b. Feb. 28, 1799), son of Abraham and Elizabeth Bradley of
Russell, Mass.

Mrs. Nancv Bradley died April
7, 1885.

Mr. Reuben Bradley living
(1890) at West Mystic, Conn.
Had no children.

282. SOPHIA EMILY, born July 15, 1803; married in Wall-
ingford, Conn., Oct. 20, 1858,

John C. Dudley (b. 1779). Had
no ch.

†283. GERSHOM BUCKLEY, 2ND, born Aug. 1, 1805, in Colchester.

284. CLARISSA ABIGAIL, born April 1, 1808; died about 1850;
unmarried.

CHILDREN BY 2ND WIFE.

285. SARAH REID   born June 25' 1816; married, Sept.
22, 1833, Simon Huntington of
Croton, Conn. (b. July 24,
1810), son of Daniel Huntington
and Elizabeth Lord.

Mrs. Sarah Huntington died
Nov. 4, 1889. Had no ch.

133.

JOHN WORTHINGTON of Colchester, Conn., married Lydia
Bulkeley (b. April 25, 1781), daughter of John Bulkeley and
Judith Worthington of Colchester.

Mr. John Worthington died June 5, 1806, and his widow
married Dr. William Mason.

134.

ιRALPH WORTHINGTON of Cooperstown, N. Y., having removed about 1802 from Colchester, Conn.; he married, Sept.
6, 1803, at Hartnick, near Cooperstown, N. Y., Clarissa Clark
(b. May 27, 1784), eldest daughter of Jerome Clark and Anna
Pinneo. Of the other children of Jerome and Anna Clark:
Jerome Clark, bap. Jan. 28, 1780, at Lebanon, Conn.; Tenas P.
Clark, bap. Jan. 5, 1800, at Lebanon, Conn.; Mary Clark, mar-

RALPH WORTHINGTON.

ried, May 15, 1815, Melanthon Barnett (b. Oct. 2, 1792, in New Lebanon, Conn.), and was mother of Gen. James Barnett of Cleveland, Ohio, and Augustus Barnett of San Diego, Cal.

Mr. Ralph Worthington died Sept. 9, 1828, in Cooperstown, N. Y. Mrs. Clarissa Worthington died Dec. 20, 1871, in Elmira, N. Y.

CHILDREN.

†286. JOHN RICHARD, born Dec. 13, 1804 in Cooperstown, N. Y.

†287. ALBERT, born Sept. 30 1806, in Cooperstown, N. Y.

†288. RALPH HENRY, born June 15, 1809, in Cooperstown, N. Y.

289. MARY SOPHIA, born Aug. 26, 1811, in Cooperstown, N. Y.; married, April 2, 1833, Dr. Tracy Beadle of Elmira, N. Y. (b. Nov. 21, 1808, in Otsego, N. Y.), son of Henry Beadle and Susan Squires.

Dr. Tracy Beadle died March 22, 1877, in Elmira, N. Y

Mrs. Mary Beadle died Oct. 4, 1889, in Elmira, N. Y.

CHILDREN.

1. Ralph Worthington Beadle, b. Jan. 9, 1834, in Cooperstown.

2. Henry Watson Beadle, b. October 11, 1837, in Elmira; m., Oct. 23, 1861, at Poughkeepsie, N. Y., Henrietta De

Graff. He died Dec. 24, 1881, in Elmira.

Mrs. Henrietta Beadle d. June 20, 1871, in Elmira.

Ch.

1. Mary Beadle, b. Sept. 14, 1862, in Elmira; d. July 26, 1864, in Elmira.
2. Harriet Beadle, b. July 16, 1865, in Elmira; d. May 14, 1882, in Elmira.
3. Nenrietta Beadle, b. June 25, 1867, in Elmira; d. Feb. 17, 1884, in Elmira.

3. Chauncev Moore Beadle, b. April 5, 1842, in Elmira.
4. George Tracy Beadle, b. Aug. 23, 1848, in Elmira; d. Aug. 2, 1849, in Elmira.

†290. GEORGE,   born Sept. 26, 1813, in Cooperstown.

291. CLARISSA,   born Jan. 1, 1817, in Cooperstown; married, Aug. 1, 1836, Chauncev Watson Moore of Brooklyn, N. Y. (b. Sept. 24, 1804), son of Uriah Moore and Catharine Terry.

Mr. Chauncey Moore died April 30, 1873.

CHILDREN.

1. Rev. Nathaniel Schuyler Moore, b. Feb. 16, 1839;

m., 1st., June 22, 1864, Marv M. Young. M., 2nd, June 16, 1880, Bolinda Pier son (b. in Sweden). They reside at Winsted, Conn.

Ch. by 1st Wife.

1. Fred Dwight Moore, b. June 20, 1865.
2. Harriet Moore, b. July 10, 1867.
3. Frank Cook Moore, b. Nov. 10, 1870.

Ch. bv 2nd Wife.

4. George Pierson Moore, b. Sept. 12, 1883.

2. George Worthington Moore, b. Feb. 28, 1841; d. Feb. 7, 1887. Unm.
3. Chauncey Watson Moore, b. Feb. 26, 1845; d. Nov. 2, 1865.
4. Clarissa Worthington Moore, b. Oct. 17, 1850; d. Feb. 23, 1851.

292. ABIGAIL, born Sept. 24, 1819, in Cooperstown; married, May 14, 1845, Noah H. Robinson of Elmira, N. Y. (b. Jan. 26, 1816, in Granville, Mass.), son of Hezekiah Robinson and Rebecca Cooley.

Mr. Noah Robinson died May 7, 1863, in Elmira.

Mrs. Abigail Robinson died
Oct. 11, 1890, in Elmira.

CHILDREN.

1. Richard Worthington Rob-
    inson, b. April 17, 1846, in
    Elmira; m., Oct. 3, 1866,
    Harriet Louise Carrier.

    Mr. Richard Robinson
    died Aug. 17, 1871, and his
    widow m., Nov. 9, 1873,
    John C. Seelev of Elmira.

Ch.

1. Richard Worthington Rob-
    inson, b. April 4, 1869; m.,
    Dec. 15, 1890, Ada Jones of
    Knoxville, Tenn.
2. John Bliss Robinson, b. June
    4, 1850, in Elmira.
3. George Tracy Robinson, b.
    Feb. 1, 1852, in Elmira; m.,
    Nov. 23, 1889, in N. Y. city,
    Alma Beatrice Tanner.

135.

GEORGE WORTHINGTON of Irasburgh, Vt., married, Oct. 1,
1806, Clarissa Davis, daughter of Col. Jacob Davis and (his
cousin) Rebecca Davis of Montpelier, Vt.

Mr. George Worthington died June 15, 1862.

CHILDREN.

†293. JOHN,   born March 22, 1807, in Irasburgh.
 294. GEORGE,   born Oct. 8, 1808, in Irasburgh.

136.

ELIJAH WORTHINGTON of Rome, N. Y., where he settled in early life, removing from Colchester, Conn., in 1808. Married Eunice Bartlett (b. ——, 1787, in Danbury, Conn.).

Mrs. Eunice Worthington died ——, 1855.

Mr. Elijah Worthington died ——, 1860.

CHILDREN.

295. ABIGAIL, born ——, 1814, in Rome, N. Y., married, ——, 1841, William Lovett Howland (b. ——, 1809, in Mass.).

Mr. Howland died ——, 1872.

Mrs. Abigail Howland died Aug., 1885. Had no ch.

296. SARA, born ——, 1816, at Rome; m., in 1840, Winfield Scott Sherwood (b. ——, 1812, in Kings Co., N. Y.), son of Thomas Adiel Sherwood and Sarah Whiting.

Mr. Winfield Sherwood d. Jan. 10, 1869, in California.

Mrs. Sara Sherwood d. Jan. 10, 1891, in New York city, and is buried in Philadelphia, Pa.

CHILDREN.

1. Elizabeth Percy Sherwood, b. ——, 1844; m., in 1883, William Gardner MacDowell of Philadelphia (b. —, 1846 in Phila.).

Ch.

1. Eloise MacDowell, b. ——,
   1884; d. in infancy.
2. William Harrison Mac
   Dowell, b. ——, 1884; d. in
   infancy

2. Worthington Sherwood, b.
   1846.

297. ELIZABETH,   born ——, 1809; married Ralph Shirl,
                    and died in 1828.

CHILDREN.

1. Charles Worthington Shirl,
   b. ——, 1828; d. ——, 1858.

141.

CAPTAIN DAN WORTHINGTON married, Feb. 6, 1800, Sally
Geer.

Capt. Worthington sailed from Baltimore for St. Domingo
in Nov., 1807, and was never heard of afterwards. His ship
was never reported. He was engaged in the China trade and
sailed his own ship.

Mrs. Sally Worthington died Jan. 31, 1830.

CHILDREN.

298. SALLY GEER,   born Jan. 28, 1802; married Judge
                    John Hollister, who died in
                    Buffalo, N. Y.

                    Mrs. Sally Hollister died in
                    1888, in Buffalo. Had no ch.

143.

DR. CHARLES WORTHINGTON, a physician of Lenox, Mass. and identified with the medical school at Pittsfield, Mass.; married, Aug. 5, 1802, Sarah Walker (b. Aug. 1, 1783), daughter of Judge William Walker of Lenox and Lucy Adams, who was formerly of Canaan, Ct.

Dr. Worthington died May 23, 1840, at Lenox.

Mrs. Sarah Worthington died Oct. 18, 1846.

CHILDREN.

299. MARY WALKER, born Feb. 10, 1804; d. May 5, 1863; unm.

300. SARAH, born March 3, 1806; married April 19, 1831, John Zacchrus Goodrich of Stockbridge, Mass. (b. Sept. 27, 1804, in Sheffield, Mass.), son of Zacchrus Goodrich and Amanda Landon.

Mrs. Sarah Goodrich died Dec. 22, 1856.

Mr. John Goodrich died April 19, 1885, at Stockbridge.

CHILDREN.

1. Mary Goodrich, b. —, 1833; d. June 25, 1851.
2. Sarah Worthington Goodrich, b. 1835; m., Sept. 17, 1861, Joseph R. French of Stockbridge, and d. March 21, 1869.

Ch.

1. Mary Goodrich French, b·
    Sept. 4, 1862.
2. Isabella French, b. Jan. 18,
    1865.

3. Infant, b. ——, 1837; d.
    Sept. 6, 1837.
4. Landon Goodrich, b. Nov.,
    1839; d. Sept. 17, 1840.
5. Isabella Goodrich, b. April
    13, 1845; m., June 1, 1864,
    John M. Fiske of Cambridge,
    Mass.

Ch.

1. Sally Goodrich Fiske.
2. John Landon Fiske.

301. ELIZABETH   born June 16, 1808; married, June
22, 1837, John Hooker Strong
of Stockbridge, Mass. (b. May
31, 1810, in Middle Haddam,
Conn.), son of Asabel Hooker
Strong (son of Rev. Cyprian
Strong and Sarah Bull), and
Nancy Ames of Middle Haddam,
Conn.

Mrs. Elizabeth Strong died
April 28, 1852, at Lenox, Mass.,
and Mr. Strong married, 2nd,
Harriet A. Farnham of Hard
wick, Vt.

Mr. John Strong died Jan. 25,
1882, at Stockbridge, Mass.

CH. OF JOHN AND ELIZABETH STRONG.

1. Charles Worthington
Strong, b. May 9, 1840, in
Lenox, Mass.; m., Aug. 10,
1864, Sarah Elizabeth Burg-
hardt of Stockbridge.

Ch.

1. Mary Elizabeth Strong, b.
May 18, 1867, in Stock-
bridge.
2. Margaret Dewey Strong,
b. June 11, 1870, in St.
Joseph, Mo.
3. John Frederick Strong, b.
Feb. 22, 1873, in St. Joseph,
Mo.
4. Henry Walbridge Taft
Strong, b. Dec. 21, 1879, in
Pittsfield, Mass.
5. Isabella Worthington
Strong, b. Nov. 15, 1882,
in Pittsfield, Mass.

2. Charlotte Elizabeth Strong,
b. Sept. 10, 1846, in Stockbridge; m., Oct. 10, 1874,
Charles Dunning, at Lenox,
Mass.

Ch.

1. Lucy Dunning, b. in Eddy,
Texas.
2. Mary Raymond Dunning,
b. July 14, 1877, in Eddy,
Texas.

3. Harry Walbridge Taft Dunning, b. July 14, 1880, in
Eddy, Texas.

CH. OF JOHN AND HARRIET STRONG.

1. Laurel Terrill Strong, b.
Sept. 25, 1856.
2. John Frederick Strong, b.
April 27, 1859; d. Jan. 31,
1860.

302. HARRIET,   born July 27, 1813; married, Oct. 12
1842, Henry W. Taft, and died
October 17, 1860, at Lenox.
Had no ch.

303. CHARLES,   born Feb. 23, 1822; died May 28,
1847, at Lenox. Unmarried.

147.

GAD WORTHINGTON, a merchant of Lenox, Mass., and
Batavia, N. Y.; married Aug. 27, 1812, at Lenox, Fannie
Belden (b. Feb. 26, 1793, in Lenox), daughter of Oliver Bel
den, Jr., and Anna Steel of Lenox.

Mr. Gad Worthington died March 10. 1861, at Batavia.

Mrs. Fannie Worthington died June 9, 1885.

CHILDREN.

†304. DAN LEANDER,   born August 14, 1813, in Lenox.
†305. GAD BELDEN,   born Oct. 2, 1815, in Lenox.
306. FANNIE,   born July 17, 1817, in Lenox; married, Nov. 20, 1845, Oscar Pack
ard of Buffalo, N. Y., son of
Joseph. Mr. Oscar Packard died

July 18, 1891, at Loudonville, N. Y., aged 82 years.

Mrs. Packard is living (1891) at Loudonville.

Mr. Oscar Packard was well known among the business men of Albany, N. Y. He was born there and his family is a very old one. In early life he engaged in the produce commission business in Buffalo, N. Y., and there laid the foundation of his latter successes as a business man. After spending several years in Buffalo, he returned to Albany and continued in the commission business for about three years, when he went to St. Louis, Mo., as organizer and general manager of the American Express Company's first agency there. He returned to Albany in a few years, and in 1867, during the term of Wheeler H. Bristol, as state treasurer, he filled the office of deputy state treasurer.

CHILDREN.

1. Catharine Margaret Packard, b. Sept. 3, 1846; m., Sept. 1, 1870, at Albany,

N. Y., James Cassety of Buffalo, N. Y.

Ch.

1. Edward Cassety, b. May 16, 1871, in Fredonia, N.Y.
2. Louisa Cassety, b. Jan. 3. 1873, in Fredonia, N. Y.
3. John Cassety, b. Aug. 12, 1873, in Fredonia, N. Y.; d. Aug. 15. 1874, in Fredonia, N. A.

2. Marv Worthington Packard, b. Sept. 17, 1848 ; m., June 14, 1871, at New York, Edwin Ellis of Albany, N. Y.

Ch.

1. Delancv Montrose Ellis. b. Dec. 8. 1873, at Owego, N. Y.

3. Edward Winslow Packard, b. July 1, 1852.

†307. SAMUEL K., born July 16, 1822. in Richford, N.Y.
†308. JOHN, born Jan. 29, 1824, in Lenox, Mass.
309. MARY ANN, born June 15, 1827, in Batavia, N. Y.; married, Oct. 5, 1848, Wheeler, Hutchinson Bristol (b. Jan. 18, 1818, in Canaan, N. Y.), son of George Bristol and Sally Hutchinson.

CHILDREN.

1. GeorgeWorthington Bristol, b. Oct. 12, 1849, in Batavia.

2. Fanny Louise Bristol, b. Feb. 10, 1856, in Batavia; m., Dec. 19, 1877, William Alexander Smyth.

Ch.

1. Stuart Worthington Smyth, b. May 22, 1879.

3. May Bristol, b. May 3, 1861, in Owego, N. Y.; d. Sept. —, 1861

†310. ROBERT, born Jan. 25, 1829, in Richford, N. Y.

148.

GUY WORTHINGTON, a merchant of Lenox, Mass., married, May 27, 1824, Lydia Ophelia Dewey of Becket, Berkshire Co., Mass., daughter of Abel Dewey and Lydia Burchard.

Mr. Guy Worthington died Feb. 11, 1847, at Owego, N. Y.

Mrs. Lydia Worthington died Jan. 4, 1870, at Owego, N. Y.

CHILDREN.

311. JOHN CHAMBERLAIN, born Dec. 12, 1825, in Lenox, Mass.
312. LYDIA LOUISE, born Nov. 23, 1828, in Lenox, Mass.; died Sept. 12, 1889.
†313. GEORGE, born Oct. 14, 1838, in Lenox, Mass.

149.

DR. ROBERT WORTHINGTON, a physician, of Lenox, Mass., and Richford, N. Y.; married, 1st, May 22, 1815, Laura Sherrill (b. April 4, 1791, in Richmond, Mass.), daughter of Henry

Sherrill and Lois Chidsey. She died April 30, 1822, and Dr. Worthington married, 2nd, June 3, 1823, Sarah W. Shepard (b. Feb. 1, 1797), daughter of Rev. Samuel Shepard and Lucy Ames.

Mrs. Sarah Worthington died Aug. 28, 1849.

Dr. Worthington died Aug. 5, 1856.

CHILDREN BY 1ST WIFE.

314. JANE ANN, born March 26, 1816, in Lenox; married Oct. 4, 1837, William Hull Hill (b. July 4, 1812, in Delphi, N. Y.), son of Ensign Hill and Marv Hastings Kellogg.

      Mr. William Hill died May 31, 1878, at Lenox.

CHILDREN.

1. Laura Sherrill Hill, b. July 27, 1838; d. April 11, 1842.
2. Marv Jane Hill, b. Aug. 20, 1845; d. Oct. 7, 1845.
3. Robert Ensign Hill, b. March 11, 1843; m., July 2, 1874, in Cortland, N. Y., Louise M. Pomeroy. Had no ch.
4. Marv Jane Hill, b. May 5, 1849.

315. HENRY SHERRILL, born Aug. 7, 1817; died Feb. 6, 1820.

†316. HENRY SHERRILL, born Nov. 10, 1820, in Lenox.

317. LAURA, born April 27, 1822, in Lenox; died April 28, 1822.

318. CATHARINE MARIA, born Feb. 26, 1828; died Aug. 25 1843.

153.

AMOS WORTHINGTON of Cincinnati, Ohio, married, June 22, 1798, Dezier Gallup (b. Nov. 20, 1773, in Groton, Conn.), daughter of Benadam Gallup and Bridget Palmer of Groton, Conn., and was descended from Capt. John Gallup of Boston, Mass.

Mr. Worthington established himself in early life at Agawam, Mass., as a merchant, and about 1811 became interested in the "Agawam Cotton Factory Company," a newly organized stock company for the manufacture of yarns, coarse sheetings, etc., in which venture he lost heavily. For several years afterwards he was the principal proprietor of a distillery, but this also proved unprofitable. In 1819 or 20 he sold his stock of merchandise to Norman Warriner for lands in Champagne Co., Ohio. In 1820 Amos and his son Amos made the journey in their own wagon to visit the land with a view of removing there; but, his family objecting, Mr. Worthington again entered into business in Agawam, and continued there until 1847, when he removed, with his wife and grandson, Henry Julius Appleton, to Cincinnati, Ohio.

Mr. Amos Worthington died Jan. 31, 1852, at Cincinnati.

Mrs. Dezier Worthington died ——, 1862.

CHILDREN.

319. HIRAM,   born Sept. 17, 1799; died Feb. 23, 1801.

†320. Amos,   born April 22, 1801 in Agawam, Mass.

321.	JOB,	born Nov. 22, 1802; died April 14, 1804.
322.	LUCY,	born July 26, 1804, in Agawam; died June 25, 1846, in Agawam; unmarried.
323.	TIMOTHY,	born April 12, 1806. Removed from Cincinnati in April, 1849, to California, where he died April 5, 1862; unmarried.
†324.	LEWIS,	born Feb. 24, 1808, in Agawam.
325.	MARIA,	born Feb. 10, 1810, in Agawam, married, about 1835, Nathaniel Buckland Moseley of Bryn Mawr, Pa. (b. Sept. 3, 1801), son of Nathaniel Moseley and Electa Buckland.

Mrs. Maria Moseley died May 1, 1851, in Philadelphia.

CHILDREN.

1. Elizabeth Worthington Moseley, b. Feb. 15, 1837, in Philadelphia.
2. Edward Buckland Moseley, b. Jan. 16, 1846. Was surgeon in the U. S. army. Married, Dec. 9, 1875, Florence E. David (b. Oct. 9, 1853, in Mobile, Ala.), dau. of Francis David and Mary El LeBaron.

Ch.

1. Eleanor Moseley, b. Nov. 23, 1876.
2. Lillian Moseley, b. May 2, 1880.
3. Lewis Worthington Moseley, b. Dec. 27, 1881

3. Lucv Haley Moseley, b. Jan. 29, 1849; died Nov. 1, 1850.

†326. EDWARD,   born March 17, 1812, in Agawam.
327. BENJAMIN,   born Dec. 16, 1813, in Agawam. Removed to Cincinnati, O.; and, after engaging in a trading expedition to the rivers for two years, he commenced the studv of law in the office of Gen. Carv and William Groesbeck in Cincinnati, and was admitted to practice in the courts of the State of Ohio. He died a few years later, on May 1, 1851; unmarried.

328. LOUISA BASSETT, born Dec. 6, 1815; married, May 5, 1836, Henrv Appleton of Springfield, Mass. (b. —, 1812), son of Julius Appleton and Elizabeth Adams.

Mr. Henrv Appleton died Mav 4, 1842, at Springfield.

Mrs. Louisa Appleton died Sept. 9, 1844, at Philadelphia, Pa.

CHILDREN.

1. Edward Worthington Appleton, b. April 4, 1838, in Springfield; m., Jan. 28, 1879, Katharine Elizabeth Bodker.

Ch.

1. Vivian Appleton, b. Feb. 2, 1881.
2. Adrian Appleton, b. May 17, 1883.
3. Edith Louise Appleton, b. May 3, 1887.
4. Ralph Henry Appleton, b. May 10, 1889; d. July 5, 1889.
5. Julian Felix Appleton, b. Sept. 7, 1890; d. Feb. ——, 1891.

2. Henry Julius Appleton, b. Oct. 22, 1839; m., April 14, 1864, Rebecca Bodley; resides in Cincinnati, O.

Ch.

1. Henry Appleton, b. Dec. 21, 1864.

329. SIMEON GALLUP born Sept. 18, 1818; removed to California and died there; unmarried.

154.

AMBROSE WORTHINGTON, a farmer, of Bloomfield, N. Y., married, May 6, 1801, Ruth Chapin (b. Nov., 1778), and settled at Agawam, Mass, where they lived for thirty years, then removing to Bloomfield, N. Y.

Mrs. Ruth Worthington died Aug. 22, 1831, at West Bloomfield.

Mr. Worthington died Dec. 15, 1854, at West Bloomfield.

CHILDREN.

†330. AMBROSE,   born Sept. 21, 1802, in Agawam.

†331. JAMES,   born Aug. 3, 1804, in Agawam.

332. JULIA,   born Sept. 12, 1806, in Agawam; married, May 14, 1829, Amasa Ainsworth, Jr., of Agawam; they removed in 1836 to Michigan City, Ind., where Mr. Ainsworth died.

CHILDREN.

1. Julia E. Answorth, b.   , 1830; m. her first cousin, Luther H. Ainsworth, son of Luther Ainsworth, and lived in Monmouth, Ill. Had no ch.

333. LUCIA,   born Oct. 27, 1808, in Agawam; married Josiah G. Perry of.Worcester, Mass.

Mrs. Lucia Perry died March 28, 1880. Mr. Perry died May —, 1880. Had no children.

334.	LAVINIA,	born June 8, 1814, in Agawam; died Nov. 5, 1842, in Bloomfield; unmarried.
†335.	ROBERT,	born April 6, 1811, in Agawam.
336.	MARY,	born Jan. 18, 1816, in Agawam; married, May 8, 1834, William Chapman Clark of Worcester, Mass. (b. Nov. 13, 1809, in Hubbardston, Mass.), son of Moses Clark and Arethusa Parkhurst.

Mrs. Mary Clark died July 9, 1842, in Worcester, and Mr. Clark married, 2nd, Dec. 27, 1843, Cynthia Ball (b. Feb. 23, 1817), dau. of Norman Ball and Betsey Warriner, who was grand-dau. of Lucy Worthington and Eli Ball.

CHILDREN.

1. William Watson Clark, b. Feb. 14, 1836; d. March , 1836.
2. James W. Clark, b. Feb. 6, 1839; unmarried.

337.	JONATHAN,	born, April , 1818, in Agawam; died Nov. 29, 1820, in Agawam.

155.

JONATHAN WORTHINGTON, 4th, of Agawam, Mass., married, 1st, Dec. 26, 1803, Phebe Smith (b. Jan. 6, 1781), daughter of Capt. Samuel Smith and Abigail Woodmansee. Mrs. Phebe

Worthington died May 17, 1809, at Agawam, and Mr. Worthington married, 2nd, June 2, 1811, Fanny Smith (b. April 29, 1784, in Groton, Conn.), sister to Phebe.

Mrs. Fanny Worthington died May 7, 1855.

Mr. Worthington died Feb. 26, 1870, at E. Groveland, N. Y., and was buried at Agawam.

CHILDREN BY 1ST WIFE.

338. SAMUEL SMITH, born Nov. 10, 1805; died in infancy.

†339. HENRY, born Aug. 3, 1807, in Agawam.

CHILDREN BY 2ND WIFE.

†340. MINER born Sept. 17, 1812.

†341. JOB, born June 24, 1815, in Groton, Conn.

†342. ROLAND, born Sept. 19, 1817, in Agawam.

†343. SOLOMON, born April 3, 1820, in Agawam.

344. PHEBE S., born June 4, 1822, in Agawam; married, Oct. 24, 1867, Gilbert L. Deane of E. Groveland, N. Y. (b. Dec. 23, 1840, in Allen, N. Y.), son of Apollos Deane and Wealthy Lincoln.

CHILDREN.

1. Mable Deane, b. May 3, 1869, in Middletown, Vt.; an adopted daughter.

345. JONATHAN HIRAM, born Feb. 2, 1825, in Agawam; unmarried; was a member of the firm of book publishers—Jewett, Proctor and Worthington of Cleveland, Ohio; died at Cleveland, O., Sept. 11, 1854.

346. FANNY SMITH,   born Nov. 9, 1829, in Agawam; married, July 26, 1854, Amos Beach of Circleville, O. (b. 1828, in Aurora, N. Y.), son of Jabez Beach and Abigail Gates.

CHILDREN.

1. Fanny Worthington Beach, b. Jan. 25, 1856; m., Aug. 28, 1878, A. C. Wilkes.

160.

DAVID WORTHINGTON of Agawam, Mass.; married, 1st, May 21, 1794, Mary Rogers (often called Polly, b. 1777), daughter of David Rogers and —— Flower, and grand-daughter of Ozias Flower. She died Dec. 6, 1808, and Mr. Worthington married, 2nd, in 1809, Sally Ball Remington (b. 1769, in W. Springfield, Mass.), daughter of Seth Remington and Elizabeth Ball.

Mr. David Worthington died Nov. 20, 1843, at Agawam.

Mrs. Sally Worthington died April 7, 1857, at Agawam.

CHILDREN BY 1ST WIFE.

†347. RANSFORD,   born Jan. 2, 1795, in Agawam.
†348. DAVID 2nd,   born July 5, 1797, in W. Springfield.
†349. ALBERT,   born 1801, in W. Springfield.

CHILDREN BY 2ND WIFE.

350. MARY or POLLY, born 1810, in W. Springfield; died Nov. 13, 1831; unmarried.
351. SARAH or SALLY
    BALL,   born Feb. 19, 1812, in Agawam;

married, April 19, 1832, Oliver
Sykes Larned (b. Oct. 1, 1810,
in Suffield, Conn.), son of John
Larned and Chloe Sykes.

Mrs. Sarah Larned died 1843.
Mr. Oliver Larned died ——.

CHILDREN.

1. Sarah Remington Larned, b.
   Oct. 28, 1836, in Agawam :
   m., June 28, 1856, Lucius
   Stock of Toledo, O. (b. Dec.
   6, 1825, in W. Springfield,
   Mass.), son of John Stock
   and Martha Whiting.

   #### Ch.

   1. Lucia Worthington Stock,
      b. Feb. 6, 1855, in Canan-
      daigne, N. Y.; d. Sept. 29,
      1859.
   2. Mary Lavinia Stock, b. Jan.
      30, 1862, in Memphis, Tenn;
      d. March 1, 1862, in Mem-
      phis, Tenn.
   3. Theodore Williams Stock,
      b. June 10, 1864, in Canton,
      Miss.; d. June 30, 1864, in
      Canton, Miss.
   4. Clara Morey Stock, b. Oct.
      24, 1865, in Canton, Miss.
   5. Albert Cage Stock, b. Jan
      23, 1868, in Canton, Miss.
   6. Antoinette Worthington
      Stock, b. Aug. 25, 1879, in
      Toledo, O.

2. Mary Worthington Larned,
    b. Oct. 20, 1838, in Canan-
    daigne, N. Y.; m., July 4,
    1855, Amos L. Symonds of
    Allen's Hill, N. Y. (b. April
    29, 1833), son of Chancey
    Symonds and Lida Nelson.
      Mrs. Mary Symonds died
    Jan. 31, 1890, at Allen's
    Hill.
3. David Worthington Larned,
    b. June 18, 1840; d. Nov.
    20, 1843.
4. Catherine Larned, b July 19,
    1842; d. Dec. 4, 1842.

161.

JOHN WORTHINGTON of Grafton and Petersburg, N. Y., married, Dec. 11, 1797, Lovisa Robinson (b. Dec. 20, 1775),
daughter of —— Robinson and —— Persons or Parsons.
  Mrs. Lovisa Worthington died May 23, 1839.
  Mr. John Worthington died June 19, 1850, at Petersburg.

CHILDREN.

352. EUNICE,   born July 6, 1797; married, April 17,
                        1816, Henry A. Clum (b. July
                        1, 1795, in Brunswick, N. Y.),
                        son of Adam Clum and Magde-
                        lene Havner. Mrs. Eunice Clum
                        died Sept. 24, 1865. Mr. Henry
                        Clum died June 12, 1879.

CHILDREN.

1. Adam H. Clum, b. Sept. 30,
1818; m., Jan. 1, 1844,
Mary Smith, and d. June
10, 1848.

Ch.

1. Sherman Clum b. Jan. 2,
1845; d. Nov. , 1856.
2. Amelia Frances Clum, b.
Feb. , 1847.

2. John W. Clum, b. Oct. 10,
1819; m., Nov., 1849, Caroline Lohnes, and d. Nov. 12,
1884.

Ch.

1. Frank M. Clum, b. 1851.
2. Richard H. Clum, b. 1853.

3. Sally E. Clum, b. July 9,
1821; m., Oct. 26, 1841
Joseph B. Betts.

Ch.

1. Thomas H. Betts, b. Oct.
17' 1842.
2. Maria A. Betts, b. Jan. 1,
1844.
3. Clarence E. Betts, b. Sept.
13, 1846.
4. Caroline A. Betts, b. Feb.
29, 1848.
5. Frances O. Betts, b. April
30, 1855.

4. Caroline Clum, b. Aug. 12, 1823; unm.

5. Lovisa Clum, b. Jan. 19, 1825; d. Oct. 16, 1826.

6. William B. Clum, b. Aug 16, 1827, m., Aug., 1851, Oliver Higgins.

Ch.

1. Etta F. Clum, b. Aug. —, 1853.
2. Allen Clum, b. Jan. —, 1857 dec.
3. Melvin Clum, b. Jan.   , 1857; dec.
4. Hattie, dec.
5. Frank, dec.
6. Maud.
7. Eugene.
8. William.
9. Millie.

7. Mary Clum, b. Sept., 1828; d. Aug., 1829.

8. Henry R. Clum, b. March 27, 1830; m., Dec., 1849, Sarah Lohnes.

Ch.

1. William Clum, b. —, 1850; d. —, 1853.
2. A. H. Waldo Clum, b. Aug., 1853.

9. Julia Frances Clum, b. April 14, 1835; m., Nov., 1859, Andrew Haynes, and d. Feb. 18, 1863.

Ch.

1. Arthur D. Haynes, b. March 9, 1861.

353. JOHN, born March 31, 1799; d. , 1808.

354. SALLY, born Sept. 2, 1801, in Grafton, N. Y.; married, April 15, 1825, Martin Clum (b. April 6, 1800, in Brunswick, Y. Y.), son of Adam Clum and Magdelene Hayner. Mrs. Sally Clum died Oct. 1, 1858.

Mr. Martin Clum died Dec. 30, 1870.

CHILDREN.

1. Henrv M. Clum, b. Feb. 2, 1826, in Brunswick, N. Y.; m., Jan. 9, 1858, Matilda Allen (b. Oct. 13, 1838).

Ch.

1. Harvey A. Clum, b. March 15, 1859; d. July 25, 1868.
2. Henry M. Clum, b. Aug. 27, 1860; d. Nov. 22, 1862.
3. Albert Clum, b. Dec. 12, 1861.
4. Eva G. Clum, b. Sept. 14, 1864.
5. Alfred W. Clum, b. Aug. 12, 1867; d. Sept. 4, 1868.
6. Henry M. Clum, b. March 6, 1870; d. Sept. 4, 1878.
7. Matilda A. Clum, b. Sept. 10, 1871.

8. Robbie A. Clum, b. April 4,
    1873; d. May 25, 1874.
9. Isabella A. Clum, b. Sept.
    21, 1876.

2. Aaron Worthington Clum,
    b. Jan. 25, 1827, in Bruns
    wick; m., Dec. 25, 1847,
    Helen C. Lewis (b. Sept. 27,
    1827).

Ch.

1. Charles Henry Clum, b.
    May 7, 1849; m., Nov. 14,
    1874, Lydia Rysdorph (b.
    Oct. 3, 1856). Had 4 ch.
2. Ida Imogene Clum, b. Dec.
    31, 1851; d. June 29, 1854.
3. Mary Ann Clum, b. Sept.
    24, 1853; d. Jan. 20, 1854.
4. Adna Clum, b. Oct. 16,
    1854; d. Feb. 19, 1858.
5. Elizabeth Clum, b. Nov. 3,
    1856.
6. Nellie Clum, b. June 28,
    1858; d. March 29, 1860.
7. Adaline Clum, b. Nov. 20,
    1860; m., May 7, 1890,
    Adam Ross(b. May 8,1864).
8. Clarence Clum, b. March
    20, 1864; d. July 3, 1864.
9. A. Russell Clum, b. Dec. 4,
    1868.
10. Fred Clum, b.Dec. 18,1870.

3. Lovisa Clum, b. June 8,
    1828; m., Sept. 17, 1851,
    Robert E. Myers (b. Dec. 9,
    1825, and died Feb. 4,1871.

Ch.

1. Edna A. Myers, b. July 10, 1852; d. Sept. 1, 1852.
2. Ida Augusta Myers, b. May 2, 1854.
3. Jessie Adelaide Myers, b. Dec. 13, 1855.
4. Herbert Augustus Myers, b. Aug. 1, 1857.
5. Cornelia Myers, b. Jan. 8, 1859; d. April 12, 1864.
6. Mary Blanch Myers, b. Jan. 14, 1860; d. Aug. 7, 1863.
7. Robert Henry Myers, b. Sept. 24, 1862; d. Aug. 22, 1872.
8. Winifred Ada Myers, b. Oct. 24, 1866.
9. Edward Beekman Myers, b. March 24, 1864; d. March 7, 1866.
10. Martin Clum Myers, b. Nov. 24, 1869; d. March 1, 1887.

4. Ananias Clum, b. April 18, 1829; d. Oct. 6, 1850.

5. Christina Clum, b. Jan. 1, 1831.

6. Martin J. Clum, b. Oct. 8, 1832; m., June 16, 1858, Susan Spoar (b. Dec. 9, 1832).

Ch.

1. Victoria Maria Clum, b. Nov. 11, 1860, in St. Paul, Minn.; m., Nov. 14, 1888 Anson P. Batcham, (b. June 22, 1855). Had 1 ch.

2. Maud Kate Clum, b. Aug. 8, 1863, in St. Paul.
3. Kitt May Clum, b. Nov. 7, 1865, in St. Paul.
4. Edna Julia Clum, b. Jan. 8, 1868, in St. Paul.
5. Orville Jay Clum, b. Dec. 15, 1871, in St. Paul.

7. Marv Clum, b. March 14, 1834; m., Feb. 12, 1862, Martin Coon Tifft (b. April 2, 1830).

Ch.

1. Blanch Clum Tifft, b. July 12, 1864, in Greenwich, N. Y.; d. March 14, 1883.
2. Oscar Worthington Tifft, b. Sept. 1, 1865, in Greenwich, N. Y.
3. Nellie Frances Tifft, b. Aug. 26, 1869, in Greenwich, N.Y.
4. Susan Jane Tifft, b. Feb. 10, 1872, in Greenwich, N. Y.; d. Sept. 8, 1878.
5. Grant Joseph Tifft, b. Oct. 4, 1874, in Greenwich, N. Y.

8. Harvey G. Clum, b. July 5, 1836; d. June 2, 1864.
9. Charles Edgar Clum, b. Jan. 22, 1842; m., Jan. 18, 1867, Lydia Augusta Tifft (b. Jan. 18, 1841, in Greenwich, N.Y.)

Ch.

1. Grace Castella Tifft, b. Feb. 4, 1868, in Troy, N. Y.

2. Frank Harvey Tifft, b. May
    16, 1872, in Troy, N. Y.

355. MARY,   born Nov. 7 1803, in Grafton, N. Y ·
                   married, July 5, 1827, Ebenezer
                   Stevens of Grafton (b. June 10,
                   1802, in Sandlake, N. Y.), son of
                   John Stevens and Elizabeth Gil-
                   lett. Mr. Ebenezer Stevens died
                   Dec. 22, 1883, at Petersburgh,
                   N. Y. Mrs. Mary Stevens died
                   May 26, 1888, at New York.

CHILDREN.

1. John Worthington Stevens
    b. Aug 4, 1828, in Grafton ·
    m·, June 25, 1850, Maria
    Saturna Waite, dau. of Ru-
    fus S. Waite.

Ch.

1. John Elmer Stevens, b. Dec.
    4, 1860; married.
2. Minnie Stevens, b. Sept. 30,
    1861; married.
3. Flora Estella Stevens, b.
    Dec. 16, 1862; married.

2. Calvin Stevens, b. Jan. 12,
    1830, in Grafton; m., Oct.
    28, 1850, Mary Francis
    Clark of Grafton.

Ch.

1. Florence Adelah Stevens.

3   Henry Ebenezer Stevens, b.
July 15, 1834, in Grafton,
m. Mary Jane Davison, dau.
of Paul R. Davison.

Ch.

1. Antoinette Stevens.
2. Henry.
   Several other ch., deceased.

4. Mary Antoinette Stevens, b.
April 14, 1836, in Grafton;
d. March 21, 1852.
5. Plowdon Stevens, b. May.
2, 1840, in Grafton; m.
Laura McEwen.

Ch.

1. Plowdon Stevens.
2. Alfred L. Stevens.
3. Ralph Stevens.
4. Rosco C. Stevens.
5. Eugene Stevens.

6. Helen Elizabeth Stevens, b.
May 22, 1844, in Grafton,
m., Oct. 3,1867, Isaac Bevier.

Ch.

1. John L. Bevier.

356. LOVISA,   born Sept. 9, 1805, in Grafton, N. Y.;
married, Aug. 29, 1832, James
Butler of Lima, N. Y. (b. June
22, 1795, in Hardwick, Mass.),
son of John Butler and ——
Black.

Mr. James Butler died Nov. 13, 1863.

Mrs. Lovisa Butler died Sept. 26, 1891, at Troy, N. Y.

CHILDREN.

1. James Henry Butler, b June 13, 1833, in Lima, N. Y.; d. Nov. 18, 1843.
2. John Worthington Butler, b. April 11, 1836, in Grafton, N. Y.
3. Leydou Erving Butler, b. June 23, 1839, in Livonia, N. Y.; m., Sept. 20, 1864, Susannah Berwick Cursons of Buffalo, N. Y., dau. of Josiah Cursons and Sarah Berwick.

Ch.   •

1. Charles Leydou Butler, b. Oct. 9, 1865.

4. Lovisa Worthington Butler, b. April 13, 1842, in Alden, N. Y.; d. April 1, 1875; unm.
5. Emma Lovisa Butler, b. June 11, 1845, in Alden, N.Y.

357. AARON FERRE,   born Sept. 5, 1807; d. – , 1814.

†358. LYNUS PERSONS, born Oct. 5, 1809, in Grafton, N. Y.

359. JULIA,   born Oct. 7, 1812, in Grafton, N. Y.; married, Aug. 11, 1836, Obediah McChesney of Troy, N. Y. (b.

Sept. 19, 1809, in Brunswick,
N. Y.), son of Walter McChesney
and Chloe Wellman.

Mrs. Julia McChesney died
July 16, 1854.

Mr. Obediah McChesney died
Dec. 15, 1884.

CHILDREN.

1. Elmina McChesney, b. Aug.
   9, 1838, in Brunswick, N.Y.;
   m., Dec. 6, 1865, Jacob H.
   Pratt of Troy, N. Y.

   Ch.

   1. Kittie Worthington Pratt,
      b. Dec. 10, 1866, in Troy;
      m., Sept. 29, 1886, Wm. G.
      White of Greenwich, N. Y.;
      have 1 dau.

2. Lovisa McChesney, b. Oct.
   26, 1839; d. Dec. 25, 1854.
3. Mary McChesney, b. June
   30, 1841, in Brunswick, N.
   Y.; m., Dec. 14, 1870, Jacob
   Schermerhorn of Brunswick.

   Ch.

   1. Rachael Schermerhorn, b.,
      Aug. 13, 1877, in Bruns-
      wick.
   2. Harvey Obed Schermerhorn,
      b. Dec. 14, 1879, in Bruns-
      wick.

3. Henrietta Schermerhorn, b.
July 15, 1882, in Brunswick.

4. Harvey Worthington Mc-
Chesney, b. Sept. 17, 1844
in Brunswick; m., Aug. 27,
1885, Carrie Ellen Collins
of Troy, N. Y.

Ch.

1. Harvey Bosworth McChesney, b. June 26, 1886.
2. Anna Julia McChesney, b.
Dec. 1, 1887.

5. Julia Frances McChesney, b.
Nov. 12, 1847; d. Nov. 22,
1849.
6. Albert McChesney, b. Sept.
14, 1850; d. Dec. 31, 1851.
7. Julia Augusta McChesnev,
b. July 12, 1852, in Brunswick.

360. ELIZA, born April 13, 1815; died the same
year.

†361. DAVID FERRY, born July 8, 1816, in Grafton, N. Y.

163.

AARON WORTHINGTON of Petersburgh, N. Y., married, March
17, 1798, Abigail Ross (b. Aug. 14, 1781, in Petersburgh, N.
Y.), daughter of William Ross and Sarah Coon of Petersburgh.
Mr. Aaron Worthington died Oct. 28, 1842, at Petersburgh.
Mrs. Abigail Worthington died Sept. 20, 1860.

CHILDREN.

362. SARDINIA,   born Oct. 1, 1799, in Petersburgh;
married, 1st, Oct. 19, 1820,
Wanton Sweet of Canaan, N. Y.
(b. Oct. 6, 1789, in N. Kingston,
R. I.), son of Sylvester Sweet
and Hannah Tanner.   Mr. Wanton Sweet died April 8, 1830,
at Petersburgh, N. Y.,and his
widow married, 2nd, Sept. 20,
1833, Warren T. Ford of Canaan, N. Y. (b. June 25, 1793,
in Red Rock, N. Y.), son of Jesse
Ford and Azubah Lee.

Mr. Warren Ford married, for
his 1st wife, Abigail Pixley of
Gt. Barrington, Mass., and had
ch.

    1. Lucinda Ford, b. July 22,
       1822; d April 1, 1886.
    2. Wm. Alexander Ford, b.
       Oct. 2, 1824.
    3. Edward Warren Ford, b.
       April 22, 1826.
    4. Mary Ann Ford, b. April
       13, 1828.

Mr. Ford died Dec. 14, 1861,
at Canaan.

Mrs. Sardinia Ford died April
14, 1863, at Canaan.

CHILDREN BY 1ST HUSBAND.

1. Aaron Sweet, b. July 31, 1821, in Petersburgh, N. Y.; d. July 3, 1825, in Ellisburg, N. Y.
2. William Sweet, b. June 1, 1824, in Ellisburg, N. Y.; m., July 1, 1847, Cornelia C. Atwood (b. June 2, 1830, in Austerlitz, N. Y.), dau. of MillsAtwood and Sophronia Stickles, and he died Aug. 17, 1884, at Austerlitz.

Ch.

1. Sarah Melissa Sweet, b. Nov. 28, 1849, in Austerlitz; d. Dec. 3, 1850.
2. William Wanton Sweet, b. June 8, 1852, in Canaan; m., Sept. 9, 1874, Minnie Pettit of Brooklyn, N. Y. (b. March 17, 1853). They reside at Gilman, Ill. Have 4 ch.
3. Paulina Elizabeth Sweet, b. Nov. 14, 1859, in Austerlitz.

3. Paulina Abalina Sweet, b. Sept. 26, 1826, in Ellisburgh; m., Dec. 14, 1843, Matthew A. Bemis of Spencertown, N. Y. (b. May 25, 1814), son of Ephraim Bemis and Chloe Spencer.

Ch.

1. Charles Wanton Bemis. b.
    Jan. 1, 1846; d. March 28,
    1866, in Spencertown, N. Y.
2. Sarah Sophia Bemis, b.
    Feb. 26, 1848; m., Feb. 10,
    1866, David E. Budlong of
    New Lebanon, N. Y.; had
    11 ch.
3. Ida Elizabeth Bemis, b. Oct.
    21, 1851; m., April 18,
    1883, DeRett O. Sawyer of
    Spencertown, N. Y.

CHILDREN BY 2ND HUSBAND.

1. Abigail Ross Ford, b. Aug.
    26, 1834, in Canaan, N. Y.·
    m., March 18, 1856, William
    Henry Hastings of Suffield,
    Conn. (b. May 10, 1830, in
    Suffield), son of William
    Hastings and Lydia Rem-
    ington.
2. Roland Thomas Ford, b.
    April 22, 1838, in Canaan.

363. SALLY,   born Jan. 31, 1802, in Petersburgh;
                      married, 1st, 1818, John W.
                      Reynolds of Petersburgh, son of
                      John Reynolds and Waity ——.
                      Mr. Reynolds died April 8, 1826
                      aged 32 years, and his widow
                      married, 2nd, in 1838, Nathan-
                      iel Worden of Troy, N. Y., son
                      of Arnold Worden,

Mr. Worden died —, 1857.

Mrs. Sally Worden died April 7, 1875, in Chatham, N. Y.

CH. BY 1ST HUSBAND.

1. Emily Melissa Reynolds b. November 14, 1819; m., April 1, 1836, Sidney L. Reynolds of Petersburgh, N. Y.; she died in 1871.

    He died in 1873. Had no ch.

2. John W. Reynolds, b. June 18, 1822, in Petersburgh; m. Caroline Bremmer and d. in 1853.

    Ch.

    1. Emily Reynolds, m. Franklin Wells of Chatham, N.Y.

3. Waity Elizabeth Reynolds, b. April 1, 1825; m., Nov. ?8, 1843, Sandford K. Sterns of Chatham Corners, N. Y. Mr. Sterns died in 1862.

    Ch.

    1. Elizabeth Sterns, m. John B. Haskins of Chatham. 1 ch.
    2. Thomas E. Sterns, m. Maggie Shufelt.
    3. Nellie M. Sterns.

CH. BY 2ND HUSBAND.

1. Hiram Moses Worden, b.
April, 1839, in Chatham
Corners, N. Y.; m. Kate
Graves and d., in 1868, at
Chatham Corners. Had
several ch. All deceased.

364. PAULINA,   born Feb. 11, 1805, in Petersburgh·
died Nov. 2, 1813, in Peters-
burgh.

365. JOHN,   born Sept. 16, 1806, in Petersburgh;
died July 6, 1808, in Peters
burgh.

366. ABALINE A.   born May 6, 1808, in Petersburgh;
married Dr. Hiram Moses of
Petersburgh, who died June 4,
1885, aged 85 years.

Mrs. Abaline Moses died July
6, 1877, at Petersburgh.

CHILDREN.

1. Hiram Moses, b. Feb. 14,
1829; m. Philena M. Col-
lard and resided in Petersburgh.

Ch.

1. Carrie Moses.

2. Aaron Thomas Moses, b.
July 14, 1831, in Peters
burgh; m., Oct. 18, 1850,
Deborah Elizabeth Harts
horn (b. Feb. 20, 1833, in

Berlin, N. Y.), dau. of Sanford Hartshorn and Susan
Matteson.

Ch.

1. Harriet Elizabeth Moses,
   b. August 23, 1851, in
   Petersburgh; m., Sept. 30,
   1879, George Henry White
   (b. Sept. 6, 1846, in W.
   Wardsboro, Vt.), son of
   James Lawrence White and
   Luthera Jackson. Had 1
   dau.
2. Ruth Estella Moses, b.
   Oct. 4, 1854, in Peters-
   burgh; m., March 14, 1882,
   James Nichols Barber (b.
   Feb. 4, 1857, in Petersburgh), son of Darius W.
   Barber and Harriet M.
   Dill. Had 3 eh.
3. Charles Augustus Moses, b.
   April 25, 1856, in Petersburgh; m., Sept. 3, 1874,
   Edy Frances Odell (b. Sept.
   13, 1853, in Petersburgh),
   dau. of John Odell and
   Fannie Hakes. No ch.
4. Sandford Hiram Moses, b.
   Dec. 8, 1858, in Petersburgh; m., Elizabeth M.
   Kennedy (b. May 22, 1861,
   in Troy, N. Y.), dau. of
   Peter Kennedy and Elizabeth Van Valkenburgh.
   Had 1 dau.
5. William Hartshorn Moses,
   b. Feb. 21, 1862, in Peters-

burgh; m., March 14, 1883, Alice May Hakes (b. May 26, 1863, in Petersburgh), who d. Aug. 1, 1887, in New York. Had 2 ch.

6. Fred Moses, b. Jan. 10, 1873, in Petersburgh.

3. Charles Jefferson Moses, b. June 28, 1834; m. Margaret Hewitt.

Ch.

1. Jennie Moses.
2. Solon Moses.
3. Frank Moses.

4. Adelbert Archelaus Moses, b. March 24, 1837, in Petersburgh; m., Jan. 27, 1856, Harriet A. Lewis.

Ch.

1. Julia C. Moses, b. July 26, 1857; d. Dec. 23, 1858.
2. Lewis A. Moses, b. Sept. 5, 1859; d. Jan. 19, 1861.
3. Mary A. Moses, b. July 20, 1862; m., Feb. 1, 1885, Harry A. Lewis. Have 1 dau.
4. H. Jesse Moses, b. Sept. 16, 1864; m., Sept. 3, 1887, L. M. Gorham. Had 2 dau.
5. Berthia Moses, b. Oct. 30, 1867.

5. Solon Worthington Moses, b. March 5, 1842; m., Jan.

1, 1862, Mary E.. Hovey, dau. of Smith Hovev and Cornelia ———. Had 2 ch.

Ch.

1. Cornelia Moses, b. April 7, 1864.
2. Marth Moses, b. May 20, 1866.

†367.   AARON FERRE,   born Dec. 5, 1812, in Petersburgh.
†368.   DAVID ROSS,   born May 6, 1817, in Petersburgh.
†369.   WILLIAM CHAPIN, born March 14, 1819, in Petersburgh.
370.   AMBROSE,   born March 18, 1822, in Petersburgh; died July 8, 1843.
†371.   WINFIELD SCOTT, born Jan. 20, 1826, in Petersburgh.

166.

SETH WORTHINGTON of Petersburgh, N. Y., married 1st., October 24, 1819, Sophia Main (b. Nov. 8, 1799, in Ellisburgh, N. Y.), daughter of Rhuben Peckham Main and Sally Burdick, who died October 28, 1834, and Mr. Worthington married, 2nd, June 14, 1835, Nancy M. Clark, daughter of James Clark and Rhoda Brumley.

Mr. Seth Worthington died Sept. 3, 1847.

CHILDREN BY 1ST WIFE.

†372.   JOHN MAIN,   born Nov. 6, 1820, in Petersburgh.
373.   THOS. FRANKLIN, born Dec. 25, 1823, in Petersburgh; died Nov. 8, 1854; unmarried.
†374.   HARVEY REYNOLDS, born June 14, 1827, in Ellisburgh, N. Y.

375. MARYLINE JENETTE, born Dec. 24, 1828, in Ellisburgh,
             N. Y.; married, Sept. 9, 1847,
             Dyer Fillmore of Rural Hill,
             N. Y. (b. June 7, 1827, in Ellis-
             burgh), son of Amaziah Fill-
             more and Sally Richerson. Mrs.
             Maryline Fillmore died Oct. 3,
             1875, and Mr. Fillmore married
             for 2nd wife, Oct. 19, 1876,
             Sophia Wood (b. Sept. 1, 1834;
             died May 30, 1890).

CHILDREN OF DYER AND MARYLINE FILLMORE.

             1. Fanny Sophia Fillmore, b.
             July 19, 1859.
376. AARON SETH,   born April 2, 1831, in Petersburgh;
             died Oct. 13, 1833.
†377. DAVID MORTMER, born Sept. 9, 1834, in Petersburgh.

CHILDREN BY 2ND WIFE.

378. LAMIRA SOPHIA, born March 14, 1836, in Petersburgh;
             married John H. Hewitt, son of
             John B. Hewitt.
379. HANNAH CELESTIA, born Sept. 27, 1837; married
             Thomas Crandall, son of Phillip
             of Petersburgh; had no ch
380. ROWLAND NATHAN, born March 7, 1838, in Peters-
             burgh.

168.

THOMAS WORTHINGTON married, ——, 1832, Mrs. Nancy Hoyt Stiles, daughter of Amos Hoyt and widow of Garwood Stiles.

Mr. Thomas Worthington died Sept. 12, 1845.

Mrs. Nancy Worthington died Jan. 1, 1874, in Westville Conn., aged 74 years.

CHILDREN.

†381.	HARVEY,	born Oct. 21, 1833.
†382.	THOMAS E.,	born Aug. 25, 1835, in Oxford,Conn.
†383.	GEORGE,	born Jan. 4, 1838, in Oxford, Conn.
384.	ALBERT D.,	born Sept. 16, 1841, in Oxford,Conn.; died Oct. 18, 1883; unmarried.

170.

HARVEY WORTHINGTON of Talbot County, Ga , married, in Redbone,Ga., in 1835, Zilpha Amelia Adkins (b. Nov. 10, 1818, in Ware, Mass.), daughter of Henry Adkins and Lucinda Clark of Whately, Mass.

Mr. Harvey Worthington died Oct. 10, 1861, in Macon, Ga.

Mrs. Zilpha Worthington died Nov. 1, 1867, in Millen, Ga.

CHILDREN.

385. JULIA AMELIA, born April 28, 1836, in Redbone, Ga., married, Nov. 24, 1858, in Greenville, S. C., Abiel Abbot Foster of Greenville, S. C. (b. Sept. 30, 1836, in Columbus, O.), son of Abiel Foster (b. in Canterbury, N. H.) and Pamelia Judd (b. in Northampton, Mass.).

Mrs. Julia Foster died March 1, 1873, in Greenville, S. C., and Mr. Foster married, 2nd, May, 1876, Mrs. E. E. McCann.

CH. OF ABIEL AND JULIA FOSTER.

1. Kate Worthington Foster, b. Oct. 18, 1869, in Greenville.
2. Lewis Foster, b. Feb. 22, 1873, in Greenville.
3. Julia Amelia Foster, b. Feb. 22, 1873, in Greenville.

386. LUCINDA CLARK, born Sept. 3, 1838, at Redbone; married, Aug. 30, 1860, at Macon, Ga., Leander Stewart of Eastman, Ga. (b. in Baltimore, Md.), son of —— Stewart and Rebecca Griffith.

CHILDREN.

1. Coralie Stewart, b. July 24, 1861, in Macon, Ga.; d. Oct. 8, 1868, in Millen, Ga.
2. Julia Worthington Stewart, b. Nov. 13, 1867, in Millen, Ga.; m., March 23, 1886, in Eastman, Ga., Charles T. Thompson (b. June 10, 1863, in S. Starksboro, Vt.).
3. Harry Colcord Stewart, b. June 10, 1869, in Millen, Ga.

387. ELLEN SOPHIA, born Feb. 1, 1841, at Redbone; married, May 4, 1859, in Savannah, Ga., John Milton Fiske of Holliston, Mass. (b. Feb. 20, 1836), son of Abner Fiske (b. in Hollister, Mass.), and Lorinda Bellows (b. in Shrewsbury, Mass.).

Mr. John Fiske died Oct. 27, 1889.

CHILDREN.

1. Alice Imogene Fiske, b. Feb 29, 1860; m., March 30, 1879, at Woonsocket, R. I., I. Edward Loring of Yarmouth, Mass.

Ch.

1. Harvey Wells Loring, b. Nov. 28, 1879, in Hollister, Mass.

2. William Harvey Fiske, b. Nov. 18, 1861, in Hollister, Mass.

3. Henry Fiske, b. April 27, 1864, in Natick, Mass.; m., Feb. 14, 1885, Ada Gifford of West Brookfield, Mass.

Ch.

1. Lewis Worthington Fiske, b. April 6, 1887, in Hollister.
2. Alice Marion Fiske, b. Oct. 20, 1888, in Hollister.

388. MARY JANE,   born Sept. 3, 1844, in Macon, Ga.;
                      died in infancy.
389. INFANT SON,   born Sept. 20, 1845, in Macon, Ga,;
                      died in infancy.
390. INFANT SON,   born July 30, 1846, in Macon, Ga.;
                      died in infancy.
391. MARY ELIZABETH, born Sept. 23, 1847, in Macon, Ga.;
                      married, Aug. 12, 1866, in Mil-
                      len, Ga., to Jacob Tyng Colcord,
                      of Eastman, Ga. (b. Oct. 27
                      1839), son of Frederick Colcord
                      and Elizabeth Mary Jenness).
                      Mr. Jacob Colcord was a native
                      of Exter, N. H., and a half
                      brother of Frank J. Dudley, who
                      was husband of Henrietta Ad-
                      kins Worthington.

CHILDREN.

1. Frederick Worthington Colcord, b. Dec. 25, 1867, in
   Blackshear, Ga.; d. Jan. 25,
   1868.
2. A. Reppard Colcord, b. Oct.
   22, 1869, in Blackshear, Ga.
3. Lula Pearl Colcord, b. April
   23, 1873, at Blackshear, Ga.
392. HENRIETTA ADKINS, born April 1, 1854, in Brooklyn,
                      N. Y.; married, Oct. 9, 1879, in
                      Exter, N. H., Frank Jenness Dud-
                      ley (b. Aug. 7, 1851, in Brent-
                      wood, N. H.) son of Jeremiah

Dudley and Mrs. Elizabeth Mary Jenness Colcord.

CHILDREN.

1. Marion Dudley, b. March 12, 1882, in Eastman, Ga.; d. March 12, 1886, in Eastman, Ga.
2. Walter Dudley, b. Feb. 6, 1885, in Eastman, Ga.
3. Malcolm Dudley, b. April 10, 1887.
4. Henry D. Dudley, b. June 28, 1889.

172.

DEACON ALFRED WORTHINGTON of Agawam, Mass., married, July 19, 1831, at Agawam, Cynthiaetta Chapin (b. Dec. 12, 1809, in Suffield, Conn.), daughter of Obadiah Chapin and Lois Rose of Suffield.

Deacon Worthington died April 14, 1878, at Agawam.

CHILDREN.

†393. WATSON ALFRED, born Sept. 17, 1833, in Agawam.
†394. LEWIS NELSON, born Sept. 1, 1836, in Agawam.
395. MARTHA CYNTHIAETTA, born Nov. 27, 1840, in Agawam; died, May 31, 1891, at Northampton, Mass., and buried at Agawam; was unmarried.
396. MARY LOIS, born Aug. 19, 1846, at Agawam; married, April 2, 1874, Abel Jackson (b. in Baldwinville,

Mass.), son of Abel Jackson and
Betsey Foster. Mr. Jackson had
one son by a former marriage,
Elbridge R. Jackson, b. Sept.
12, 1844.

CHILDREN.

1. Harry Everett Jackson b.
    May 22, 1878, in So. Gard
    ner, Ms.; died the same day.

173.

LEWIS WORTHINGTON of Greenville, S. C., married Nov. 21,
1844, Maria King (b. Aug. 24, 1814).

Mr. Lewis Worthington died April 7, 1869, at Greenville, S.
C., and his widow removed to Endfield, Conn., and died July 28,
1883, at Thompsonville, Conn.; was buried at Greenville, S. C.

CHILDREN.

397. HARRIET EMMA, born Sept. 25, 1846; died July 13,
      1847.
398. ELLEN MARIA, born Aug. 25, 1848; died Sept. 14,
      1850.

174.

DEACON SYLVESTER WORTHINGTON of Springfield, Mass.,
married, in 1864, Eunice Hannam.

CHILDREN.

399. EDWIN B., born May 1 1808; died Jan. 13,1809.
400. ADOPTED DAU., who married a Mr. Smith.

176.

THEODORE WORTHINGTON of Flowerfield, Mich., married Eliza Irwin, daughter of James Irwin.

Mrs. Eliza Worthington died May 17, 1851, at Flowerfield.

Mr. Worthington died Dec. 24, 1856, at Flowerfield.

CHILDREN.

†401. WILLIAM LESTER, born Nov. 24, 1823, in Chenango Co., N. Y. ·

†402. WARREN SYLVESTER, born Nov. 24, 1823, in Chenango Co., N. Y.

403. WASHINGTON IRVING, born Nov. 15, 1829.

404. EMMER R., born Sept. 23, 1832; died Oct. 24, 1837.

†405. THEODORE, born May 4, 1838

406. EMILY ADELIA, born July 7, 1841, in Flowerfield; died Jan. 2, 1856.

407. EMMER ELIZA, born July 7, 1841, in Flowerfield; married, 1st, Dec. 25, 1874, Samuel Albaugh (born in Carroll Co., Ohio, and died Feb. 2, 1876); had no ch.; married, 2nd, Oct. 6, 1881, Daniel W. Hull, of Fort Dodge, Iowa (b. April 16, 1833, in Delaware Co., O.), son of James Hull and Mary Brundage.

CH. BY 2ND HUSBAND.

1. William Lester Hull.
2 Warren Sylvester Hull.
3. Washington Irving Hull.

177.

JOEL WORTHINGTON of Enfield, Ct., married Rachel Warriner (b. Sept. 20, 1793, in W. Springfield, Mass.), daughter of Gad Warriner and Eunice Worthington. They removed to Ohio, where Mr. Worthington died and his widow married Joshua Howse.

CHILDREN.

†408.	WILLIAM,	born July 5, 1813, in Enfield, Ct.
†409.	HENRY,	born 1815, in Springfield, Mass.

184.

HENRY WORTHINGTON of Manorville, L. I., married in 1834, Hannah Raynor (b. April 15, 1813), daughter of Jonathan Raynor (d. at 80 years of age) and Bethia Edwards (d. at 82 years of age) of Calverton, L. I.

Mr. Worthington died Aug. 17, 1865, in Manorville.

Mrs. Hannah Worthington died Sept. 5, 1865, in Manorville.

CHILDREN.

†410. GEORGE WASHINGTON, born July 20, 1836, in Manorville, L. I.

411. HENRY VANBUREN, born Sept. 10, 1838, in Manorville, L. I. He enlisted in the war in 1862, was taken sick and returned home, where he died of Typhus fever two weeks later, in July 31, 1865. His father and mother took the fever from him and both died within five weeks. He was unmarried.

412. BEULAH, born Aug. 6, 1840, in Manorville, L. I., married, Nov. 1, 1863, Warren Sherry (b. July 11, 1837, in Middle Island, L. I.), son of Enos Sherry and Mary Howe of Patchogue, L. I.

CHILDREN.

1. Ella F. Sherry, b. Oct. 13, 1864; d. Oct. 15, 1866.
2. Cortland Sherry, b. July 16, 1867.
3. Margiana Sherry, b. Aug. 28, 1871.
4. DeForrest Sherry, b. June 28, 1877.

†413. JOHN TYLER, born June 27, 1842, in Manorville, L. I.

414. SARAH JANE, born April 7, 1844, in Manorville; married, April 3, 1864, Elbert S. Ruland of Middle Island, L. I. (b. April 25, 1843, in Middle Island), son of Lertes Ruland and Hannah Howell.

CHILDREN.

1. Willard Worthington Ruland, b. June 18, 1865.
2. Wallace Wellington Ruland, b. June 18, 1865.
3. Howard Ruland, b. Nov. 9, 1867.

4. Eugene Ruland, b. May 4
1870.

5 Effie R. Ruland, b. March
11, 1874.

6. Bertha L. Ruland, b. March
11, 1874.

ι. Irving Baker Ruland, b.
Nov. 8, 1879.

415. MARY AMELIA, born Oct. 13, 1846, in Manorville
L. I.; married, Nov. 10, 1870,
John Bradley of East Haven,
Ct. (b. Nov. 7, 1844), son of
Jared and Marv Bradlev.

CHILDREN.

1. John Wesley Bradlev, b.
Aug. 16, 1871.

2. Ambrose Clayton Bradley,
b. April 1, 1874.

3. Archer Clifton Bradley, b.
April 1, 1874.

4. Claud Linwood Bradley, b.
October 1, 1875.

5. Beatrice Worthington ,Brad-
ley, b. Jan. 18, 1882.

6. Grover Cleveland Bradley,
b. Oct. 18, 1886.

416. HENRIETTA, born Oct. 9, 1848, in Manorville,
L. I.; married. Dec. 11, 1869,
William Riley Benjamin of
Greenport, L. I. (b. April 17,
1841, in Goodground, L. I.)

son of John C. Benjamin and Hetty Carter of Aquebque, L. I.

CHILDREN.

1. Herbert Eugene Benjamin, b. Sept. 18, 1870.
2. Inez Benjamin, b. March 23, 1873; d. June 23, 1876.
3. Charles Edwin Benjamin, b. Oct. 21, 1881.

†417. JONATHAN BRADFORD, born March 8, 1851, in Manorville, L. I.

418. IDA MAY, born July 20, 1854, in Manorville, L. I.; married, Dec. 20, 1875, Isaac Swezev of Middle Island, L. I. (b. Dec. 17, 1854, in Middle Island), son of Azel Swezev and Rhoda Gerard.

CHILDREN.

1. Eva Swezev, b. Feb. 16, 1880.

419. JAMES PARKER, born Sept. 11, 1856, in Manorville L. I.; died May 9, 1876.

185.

LINUS WORTHINGTON of Mattituck, L. I.; married, in 1836, Electa Raynor (b. April 3, ——, in Manorville, L. I.), daughter of Jonathan Raynor and Bethia Edwards of Calverton, L. I.
Mr. Worthington died March 11, 1884.
Mrs. Electa Worthington died Sept. 15, 1867.

CHILDREN.

420. CHARLES HENRY, born March 26, ——, in Manorville,
L. I.; died Sept. 15, 1866, un-
married.

421. EMMA JANE,   born Dec. 26, 1839, in Manorville,
L. I.; married, Dec. 11, 1859
George Robinson of Mattituck
L. I. (b. Oct. 21, 1833, in Man
orville, L. I.), son of Stephen
Robinson and Caroline E. Over-
ton.

CHILDREN.

1. Laura Elmore Robinson b.
May 13, 1862.
2. Alonzo Francis Robinson, b.
Nov. 21, 1873.
3. Lila May Robinson, b. Aug.
12, 1884.

422. WILLIAM ALBERT, born Jan. 5, 1842, in Manorville,
L. I. Is unmarried.

423. MARY CATHERINE, born June 5, 1845, in Manorville,
L. I.; died June 15, 1863.

424. HARRIET LOUISA, born 1847, in Manorville, L. I.

425. SEREPTA AUGUSTA, born May 6, 1849, in Manorville,
L. I.; died in 1872.

426. MARIA ANN,   born Nov. 27, 1851, in Manorville,
L. I.; died Nov. 25, 1876.

427. AGNES M.,   born Sept. 13, 1855, in Manorville,
L. I

428. EDGAR F.,   born Dec. 28, 1858.

186.

BENJAMIN FRANKLIN WORTHINGTON of East Hampton, L. I. married, Sept. 10, 1837, Hannah Cook (b. April 11, 1824), daughter of Calvin Cook (son of Calvin, son of Calvin, son of Calvin), and Hannah Youngs of Baiting Hollow, L. I.

CHILDREN.

429. EDWIN FOREST, born Sept. 30, 1838, died in the war.

430. AMELIA ANN, born Feb. 13, 1840, at Riverhead, L. I.; married, Nov. 2, 1861, Alfred Willard Beers of East Hampton (b. at Sag Harbor, L. I.), son of Orlando Beers and Mary Lydia Whipple. No children. Mr. Beers died July 14, 1883.

431. LUCETTA PRISCILLA, born Oct. 30, 1841, in Riverhead, L. I.; married, Aug. 28, 1864, Henry Glover of Sag Harbor, L. I. (b. Feb., 1840, at Sag Harbor, L. I.), son of Benjamin Glover and Rebecca Case.

CHILDREN.

1. Frank Benjamin Glover, b. Sept. 18, 1866.
2. Frederick Worthington Glover, b. Sept. 22, 1870.

†432. JAMES BURKE, born Nov. 22, 1843, in Wading River, L. I.

433. SUSAN MARIA, born May 11, 1845, in River Head L. I.; married, April 9, 1865,

Sylvester Miller (b. in Amagan-
sett, L. I.), son of Sylvia Miller
and — Osborne.

Mrs. Susan Miller died April,
1867.

Mr. Sylvester Miller died July
4, 1871. No children.

434.   ALICE JOSEPHINE, born July 18, 1847, in Bridge Hamp
ton, L. I.; married, March 2
1865, Edward Baker, son of
David Baker and Rebecca
Osborne.

Mr. Edward Baker died Sept.
16, 1882, aged 47 years.

CHILDREN.

1.   Rosa De Bevoise Baker, b.
Dec. 20, 1866.
2.   Charles David Baker.
3.   Edward Charles Baker; d.
March 25, 1885, aged 13
years and 4 months.

†435.   JOHN ALONZO,   born April 18, 1849, in Bridge Hampton, L. I.

436.   EUGENE COOK,   born July 20, 1851, in Bridge Hampton, L. I.

437.   FRANK ROBERT,   born Dec. 26, 1852.

†438.   WILLIS COLEMAN, born Sept. 17, 1854.

439.   IDA FRANCIS,   born Jan. 19, 1857, in Bridge Hampton, L. I.; married, May 12,
1879, Henry C. Merrick of
Rochester, N. Y.

CHILDREN.

1. Florence Louise Merrick, b. Feb. 23, 1880.
2. Arthur Burchel Merrick, b. July, 1886.

440. ADELBERT, born April 7, 1859.
441. FLORENCE NIGHTINGALE, born Jan. 12, 1861, in Bridge Hampton, L. I.; married, Jan. 15, 1885, Joseph Osborne of East Hampton, L. I. (b. Feb. 11, 1852, in East Hampton, L. I.), son of Charles Osborne and Harrietta Eliza Cook.

CHILDREN.

1. Charles Joseph Osborne b. Aug. 13, 1886.
2. Nelson Cook Osborne, b. March 4, 1888.
3. Mary Gelston Osborne, b. Oct. 17, 1889.

442. BENJAMIN, born May 19, 1863.
443. AMOURETTE LEE, born Feb. 1, 1865.
444. LILLIAN MILLER, born April 7, 1868.

187.

JOHN WORTHINGTON of Freedom, N. Y., married, in 1800, Prucilla Smith (b. Aug. 4, 1776).

Mrs. Prucilla Worthington died March 2, 1849.

Mr. Worthington died April 18, 1885.

CHILDREN.

†445. THADDEUS,   born Feb. 24, 1803, in Galen, Seneca
                      Co., N. Y.

446. OLIVE,   born April 10, 1804, in Galen, Seneca
                      Co., N. Y.; married, Oct. 9,
                      1829, Henry Hills, who was
                      born Aug. 9, 1809, and died
                      October 20, 1876.
                          His widow died Dec. 17, 1885.
                          Had one child, who died in
                      infancy.

†447. SAMUEL,   born Sept. 30, 1805, in Galen, Seneca
                      Co., N. Y.

†448. JOHN, 2ND,   born Jan. 17, 1807, in Galen, Seneca
                      Co., N. Y.

449. REBECCA,   born Dec. 14, 1808, in Galen, Seneca
                      Co., N. Y.; married, October 14,
                      1835, Edmond Stone of Lyndon,
                      N. Y. Was his 2nd wife, he
                      having married, 1st, Sally Bierce
                      by whom he had six children.
                          Mr. Edmond Stone died Sept.
                      12, 1889.
                          Mrs. Rebecca Stone died July
                      25, 1884.

CHILDREN.

1. Priscilla Stone, b. March 19,
    1837, in Farmersville, N. Y.;
    m., Feb. 4, 1860, Nelson
    Warner (b. May 25, 1836,

in New Berlin), son of
Alpheus Warner and Dia-
damy Campbell. 2 ch.

2. James M. Stone, b. Sept. 2
1838: m., Jan. 1, 1861,
Caroline M. Grinnell (b. Jan.
25, 1839, in Victor, N. Y.),
daughter of Joseph Grinnell
and Sylvia Skinner. 5 ch.

3. Edmund Stone, b. Oct. 2ı,
1841; killed in the battle of
Gettysburgh, July 2, 1862.

4. Lucy Stone, b. Sept. 8, 1843,
in Lyndon, N. Y.; m., March
31, 1867, Albert L. Warren
(b. April 11, 1843, in Rus
ford, N. Y.), son of Michael
Warren and Elmira Wood.
4 ch.

5. Mary Stone, b. Feb. 12,
1845, in Lyndon, N. Y.; m.,
Oct. 21, 1865, John E. Grin-
nell (b. Jan. 13, 1835, in
Victor, N. Y.), son of Joseph
Grinnell and Sylvia Skinner·
Mr. John Grinnell died
July 10, 1876. 3 ch.

†450. SQUIRE, born Nov. 18, 1810, in Galen, Seneca
Co., N. Y.

451. CHARLES, born June 7, 1812, in Galen, Seneca
Co., N. Y.; died in infancy.

452. LYDIA, born April 2, 1816, in Galen, Seneca
Co., N. Y.; married, Jan. 14,

1845, Nathaniel Greenwood of Sandusky, N. Y. (b. Aug. 27, 1818), son of Thomas Greenwood and Catherine Camp.

Mrs. Lydia Greenwood died Feb. 1, 1881. No ch.

453. SARAH,   born April 14, 1820, in Galen, Seneca Co., N. Y.; married, April 15, 1850, Abel Ames (b. July 26, 1808, in Shaftsbury, Vt.), son of Jacob Ames.

Mrs. Sarah Ames died Jan. "2, 1888.

Mr. Abel Ames died April 28, 1876.

CHILDREN.

1. Mary O. Ames, b. Feb. 11, 1851, in Rushford, N. Y.; married William Miner of Portville, N. Y.
2. Alice A. Ames, b. Feb. 27, 1853.
3. Helen A. Ames, b. Aug. 27, 1855; d Jan. 18, 1863.
4. F. Adelaide Ames, b. Sept. 7, 1859; d. Sept. 22, 1891.

191.

TIMOTHY WORTHINGTON of Hillsdale, Mich., married Maria Merrills.

Mr. Worthington died Dec. 30, 1878.

CHILDREN.

454. SAMUEL MERRILLS, born——
455. MARY   unmarried.
456. JULIA,   married John Sixby and lived near Hillsdale Mich.
457. HARRIET,   born ——; unmarried.

195.

WILLIAM SAVAGE WORTHINGTON of Winfield Junction, L. I. married, April 2, 1834, Sarah Alvia Jenkins (b April, 1816, in Albany, N. Y.), daughter of Herman Jenkins and Elizabeth Fryer.

Mrs. Sarah Worthington died April 14, 1884.

Mr. W. S. Worthington died June 22, 1890, in Winfield Junction.

CHILDREN.

458. ELIZABETH,   born Jan. 1, 1835, in Navarino, N. Y.; married, Dec. 22, 1857, Norman Judson (b. Jan. 18, 1833, in Conquest, N. Y.), son of Joshua Dakin Judson and Deborah Haywood.

CHILDREN.

1. Herbert Judson, b. Nov. 8, 1858; m., Feb. 7 1883, Martha Van Deusen. Reside at Emerson, N. Y.
2. William Judson, b. May 6, 1862.

    3. Sarah Eliza Judson, b. April
      12, 1864; m., Dec. 22, 1886,
      Eugene Van Deusen of Butler
      Centre, N. Y.
    4. Homer Judson, b. March 30,
      1868; m., March 5, 1890,
      Lovina Jane Merritt. Reside
      at Conquest, N. Y.

CHILDREN.

†459. HERMAN,   born June 26, 1836, at Clyde, N. Y.
†460. SOLOMON FISK, born June 17, 1838.
  461. JOHN ROOT,   born April 26, 1840; died Sept. 14,
                      1841
  462. EDGAR,   born Aug. 4, 1843; died Aug. 5, 1843.
  463. SARAH M.,   born Sept. 20, 1845; died Dec. 20,
                      1847.
  464. WILLIAM,   born Oct. 19, 1848; died July 25, 1859.
  465. WALTER,   born Dec. 2, 1860; died Aug. 2, 1861.

SIXTH GENERATION.

196.

CHARLES MORGAN WORTHINGTON of Colchester, Conn., married, 1st, April 23, 1797, Margaret Bridges, who died May 2, 1832, in Colchester, and Mr. Worthington married 2nd, March 9, 1834, Mrs. Diadema Comstock.

Mr. Worthington died June 18, 1839.

CHILDREN BY 1ST WIFE.

†466. ELIAS MORGAN, born June 11, 1799, in Colchester.

467.	MARY ANN,	born June 14, 1802; died June 7, 1842. unmarried.
468.	HARRIET,	born March 29, 1805; died Sept. 22, 1806.
469.	HARRIET,	born Dec. 9, 1806; married, May 25, 1831, Alfred B. Pierce of Lebanon, Conn., son of Azel Pierce. Mrs. Harriet Pierce died Aug. 26, 1883. Had no ch.
†470.	OLCOTT,	born Aug. 21, 1809.

199.

JEFFREY WORTHINGTON married Mary Marshall.
Mr. Worthington died Sept. 5, 1828.

CHILDREN.

471. CHARLES,
472. JOHN,
473. JOEL,
474. WILLIAM,

Nothing can be learned of this family.

201.

DEACON HENRY WORTHINGTON of Colchester, Conn., married, Jan. 6, 1806, Sophia Ransom (b. —, 1782).

Deacon Worthington died Sept. 15, 1849, in Colchester.
Mrs. Sophia Worthington died Oct. 23, 1865.

CHILDREN.

475.	SOPHIA JANE,	born Feb. 26, 1807; married, Sept. 17, 1832, Alfred Otis of Colches

ter, son of David Otis (b. Aug.
20, 1773) and Fanny Fowler.
Mrs. Sophia Otis died Oct. 7,
1849.

CHILDREN.

1. Frances Sophia Otis, b. Sept.
    21, 1833.
2. Laura Emmeline Otis, b. Oct.
    , 1836; d. Sept. 1, 1842.

476. AUGUSTUS HENRY, born April 11, 1808; died April 30,
      1832; unmarried.
477. LAURA EMMELINE born Dec. 19, 1809; died Jan. 25
      1812.
478. MELANCTHON,   born Jan. 16, 1812; died March 1,
      1826.

204.

ELIAS WORTHINGTON married Althea Howe.
Mr. Worthington died Oct. 1, 1849.

CHILDREN.

479. JOEL,   born 1812.
480. ISRAEL.
481. JOHN.

207.

ASA WORTHINGTON of Colchester, Conn., married Frances
Meadowcroft, daughter of Cecil Edgar Meadowcroft of England.

Mr. Asa Worthington died Nov. 25, 1875, at Irvington on
Hudson, N. Y.

CHILDREN.

†482. HENRY ROSSITER, born Dec. 17, 1817, in New York.

483. KATHERINE J.,   married John W. Carrington.

CHILDREN.

1. John Carrington.
2. Raymond Carrington.

484. FRANCES L.,   born —; married William S. Ledyard.

CHILDREN.

1. Laura Ledvard.
2. Ella Ledyard.

485. GRACE ROMAINE, born —; married A. K. Thompson.

CHILDREN.

1. Ledyard Thompson.
2. Grace Thompson.
3. Emma Thompson.

486. MARIA FRAZER.

212.

ROBERT HAZARD WORTHINGTON, M.D., of Norfolk, Va., was surgeon U. S. N.; married, Jan. 29, 1839, Elizabeth James Herbert of Herbertsville, Va. (b. May 4, 1818).

Mr. Robert Worthington died Sept. 27, 1872.

Mrs. Elizabeth Worthington died June 4, 1882.

CHILDREN.

†487. ROBERT HERBERT, born Oct. 27, 1835, in Norfolk Co., Va.

†488. GEORGE WASHINGTON, born Feb. 22, 1839, in Norfolk Co., Va.

489, ELIZABETH JAMES, born May 14, 1841, in Norfolk Co.,
      Va.; died early.
†490. DENISON,   born Oct. 18, 1842, in Norfolk Co., Va.
†491. HERBERT LIVINGSTON, born March 14, 1844, in Nor-
      folk Co., Va.
492. JAMES BOUGHAM, born Dec. 2, 1846; was killed in the
      Battle of Sandy Point, May 6,
      1864; unmarried.
493. HATTIE ANN,   born Aug. 18, 1848; died Oct. 8
      1888; unmarried.
494. JULIA ALICE BOUGHAM, born Oct. 27, 1850, in Murfrees-
      boro, N. C.; married, April 21,
      1870, William Weston of Nor-
      fork, Va., son of Samuel Weston.
      Mrs. Julia Weston died Aug. 2,
      1872.
†495. DANIEL CHARLES, born June 12, 1853, in Murfreesboro,
      N. C.
496. ARTHUR SMITH,   born May 25, 1857, in Murfreesboro,
      N. C.
497. LILLIE,   born—; died in infancy.

214.

HON. DENISON WORTHINGTON, LL.D., of Albany, N. Y., afterwards removing to Wisconsin. "Born in Colchester, Conn.,
March 4, 1806. His father removed with his family to Albany, N. Y., in 1810. Denison served as clerk in several ca-
pacities, afterwards engaging in the retail grocery business,
and about 1835 entered with Mr. Gilbert in the wholesale
grocery business, which Worthington & Davis continued until
1847, when Mr. Worthington removed to Waukesha Co.,
Wisconsin, and engaged in farming. While in Albany served

HON. DENISON WORTHINGTON, LL.D.

in several positions of trust; was the second president of the Young Men's Association and a member of the city council.

In 1852 and 1854 he represented his assembly district in the Wisconsin legislature, and was state senator from 1855 to 1861; was also one of the regents of the Wisconsin State University; removed to Madison, Wisconsin, in 1858, and from 1861 to 1874 was secretary of Madison Mutual Insurance Co.; resigned on account of ill health; went to Denver, Colorado, and died there April 23, 1880.

His life was a useful one, his character pure; he was a loyal Churchman, a kind father and an honored citizen. Hon. Denison Worthington married, 1st, December 24, 1829, at Albany, Martha Searing (b. March 10, 1808, in Stillwater, N. Y.), daughter of Nathaniel Searing and Ursula Wright. She died March 23, 1839, and Mr. Worthington married, 2nd, June 3, 1840, Mary Ann La Grange (b. March 17, 1817, in Albany, N. Y.), daughter of Colonel Gerrit La Grange and Mary ——. Mrs. Mary Worthington died June 15, 1856, at Summit, Wis., and Mr. Worthington married for 3rd wife, about 1860, Julia McNaughton.

Mrs. Julia Worthington died in 1865.

Hon. Denison Worthington died April 23, 1880, at Denver, Colorado.

CHILDREN BY 1ST WIFE.

†498· ROBERT SEARING, born Oct. 4, 1830, in Albany, N. Y.
499. HARRIET, born July 20, 1833; died June 5, 1838.
500. WILLIAM HENRY, born May 23, 1836; died Sept. 19, 1837.

CHILDREN BY 2ND WIFE.

†501. DENISON LAGRANGE, born Sept. 19, 1841, in Albany, N.Y.
†502. WILLIAM HENRY, born Aug. 23, 1843, in Albany, N. Y.
503. MARY FRANCES, born May 21, 1845, in Albany, N. Y.;

married, April 15, 1869, Richard
Howard Hennegan (b. Dec. 25,
1838, in Rochester, N. Y.), son
of James Bradford Hennegan
and Margaret Howard. No
children. Reside at Oak Park,
Chicago.

504. MARTHA,   born Dec. 24, 1846, at Albany; married, and resides at Oak Park,
Chicago..

†505. JAMES LA GRANGE, born June 16, 1849, in Summit, Wis.

†506. GERRIT HAZARD, born April 29, 1854, in Summit, Wis.

507. FRANK TOWS,   born May 3, 1856, in Summit, Wis ;
a merchant in Denver, Colorado.

216.

ERASTUS WORTHINGTON, a lawyer of Dedham, Mass.; married, May 2, 1815, Sally Ellis, daughter of Abner and Martha
Ellis of Providence, R. I.

Mr. Erastus Worthington died June 27, 1842, at Dedham.

Mrs. Sally Worthington died June 30, 1856, at Dedham.

In the " Proceedings of the Celebration of the Two Hun
dred and Fiftieth Anniversary of the Incorporation of the
Town of Dedham, Mass., Sept. 21, 1886," is the following
sketch of the life of Mr. Worthington ·

"Erastus Worthington, the first of that name in Dedham, was
born in Belchertown, Mass., Oct. 8, 1779. He was graduated from
Williams College in the class of 1804. Among his classmates were
Luther Bradish and Henry Dwight Sedgwick of New York, Judge
Samuel Howe of Northampton, and Nathan Hale of Boston. After
his graduation, Mr. Worthington was employed for a time in teach.
ing, and then began the study of law, which he completed. in the
office of John Heard, Esq., of Boston. He was first admitted as an

attorney in Boston, but came to Dedham to reside in 1809. Here he began the practice of his profession, and was admitted as a counsellor of the Supreme Judicial Court in 1813. He devoted himself exclusively to legal practice until 1825, when the Norfolk Mutual Fire Insurance Company was organized mainly by his efforts, and he became its first secretary. From this time he gradually withdrew from practice, although as justice of the peace he was the magistrate of the town afterward during his life. In the spring of 1840, by reason of ill health, he was compelled to resign his office as secretary, and in the autumn of the same year he removed with his family to Dayton, Ohio. In the following spring, however, he returned to Dedham, where he continued to reside until his death, which occurred from chronic bronchitis, June 27, 1842. He left a widow and three sons, of whom Erastus Worthington, now of Dedham, is the youngest. Mr. Worthington was actively interested in politics as a Republican during the War of 1812, and as a Democrat during the administrations of Jackson and Van Buren. He delivered an oration in Dedham, July 4, 1809, on ' The Recent Measures of the American Government,' which was printed. He was a member of the General Court from Dedham in 1814 and 1815. He was also interested in the temperance reform, and was identified with the anti-slavery movement in its beginning. In 1810, Mr. Worthington wrote and published, anonymously, an elaborate pamphlet, entitled, ' An Essay on the Establishment of a Chancery Jurisdiction in Massachusetts.' This was a brief legal treatise, comprehending a general view of the whole subject; and upon the excellent authority of the late Judge Metcalf, who was contemporary in Dedham with Mr. Worthington, it was the first essay published in the commonwealth in favor of the establishment of an equity jurisdiction, which for a long time was viewed with disfavor by the legal profession, and which was not fully adopted until 1860.

"In 1827, Mr. Worthington wrote and published ' The History of Dedham from the Beginning of its Settlement in 1635 to May, 1827.' This history was written at a period when but few town histories had been published, and besides some brief notes to historical sermons, which related to church matters, nothing had been published concerning the history of Dedham. Mr. Worthington was the first carefully and intelligently to study the records of the town and of the churches and parishes in search of materials for history,

and he gathered and preserved such traditions as were well authen-
ticated sixty years ago. Moreover, he endeavored to exhibit a faithful view of society in Dedham in a retrospect of one hundred and
ninety years. His History is not merely a chronicle of events, but
these are connected and treated in the spirit and method of a true
historian. The narrative is concise, comprehensive, and accurate,
though not so exhaustive and minute as in town histories written in
more recent times. Mr. Haven, in a note to his centennial address
of 1836, accords to Mr. Worthington the credit of first undertaking
to develop the history of the town."

CHILDREN.

†508. ELLIS,   born Feb. 11, 1816, in Dedham.
†509. ALBERT,   born July 5, 1820, in Dedham.
†510. ERASTUS,   born Nov. 25, 1828, in Dedham.

222.

SAMUEL WORTHINGTON of Royalton, N. Y., was a carpenter
and joiner; married, 1st, October 30, 1815, Nancy Miller (b.
May 28, 1792, in West Springfield, Mass.), daughter of Jacob
Miller and Lucretia Ely. She died Jan. 15, 1826. Mr. Worthington married, 2nd, Abigail Harwood, and died Sept. 17,
1828, in Royalton, N. Y. He was one of the first settlers in
Rochester, N. Y., and it is said that he built the first frame
house there.

CHILDREN BY 1ST WIFE.

†511. DAVID SAMUEL, born March 26, 1818, in Rochester.
                     N. Y.
512. SOPHIA,   born May 8, 1820, in Royalton, N.
                     Y.; married, May 26, 1838, in
                     Royalton, Noah L. Bronson of
                     Lockport, N. Y. (b. Feb. 5, 1814,
                     in Manlius, N. Y.), son of Lee
                     Bronson and Armanda Upson.

CHILDREN.

1. George Worthington Bronson, b. March 19, 1839, in Lockport.

'› Helen Amanda Bronson, b. July 9, 1843, in Rovalton; m., Sept. 11, 1862, Augustus Stewart Gooding (b. Jan. 3, 1842, in Lockport, N. Y.). 5 ch.

†513. LORENZO   born May 1, 1822, in Rovalton, N. Y.

514. ELIZA JANE,   born May 8, 1824, in Royalton; married, 1st, Dec. 20, 1846, in Castalia, Ohio, Alonzo Plumb (b. in Mass., died in Kansas in 1859 ?), son of Comfort Plumb and Betsey Black. Married, 2nd, December 4, 1862, David Fuller of Townsend, Ohio (b. July 8, 1821, in Milan, Ohio), son of William Fuller and Mehitable Botsford. Mr. Fuller died May 18, 1878, in Townsend, Ohio.

CH. BY 1ST HUSBAND.

1. Frank Alonzo Plumb, b. Sept. 24, 1848, in Townsend, O.

2. Frederick Worthington Plumb, b. Jan. 12, 1851, in Townsend, O.; m., March

5, 1884, Anna Maria Whit
man.   They reside at Tip-
top, Arizona.   2 ch.

3. Eva Lena Plumb, b. Sept.
25, 1853, in Riley, O.; m.,
Oct. 27, 1875, Frederick
Haff of Townsend, O.   4 ch.

4. William Walter Plumb, b.
July 30, 1858, in Blissfield,
Mich.; m. Elizabeth Jane
Crippen. Reside at La Salle
N. Y.   4 ch.

CH. BY 2ND HUSBAND.

1. George Worthington Fuller,
b. Jan. 15, 1864, in Townsend, O.; m., Dec. 25, 1887,
Mable Hawley.   2 ch.

2. Mattie Fuller, b. Dec. 6,
1871.

223.

DAVID WORTHINGTON of Peru, Mass., married, 1st, Oct. 7,
1821, Marv Cushman (b. Nov. 11, 1796, in Goshen, Mass.),
daughter of Caleb Cushman of Peru and Bathsheba Spalding. She died Dec. 6, 1842, in Peru, and Mr. Worthington
married, 2nd, Sept. 26, 1844, Almira Thompson, daughter of
Amherst Thompson and Sarah Clark.

Mr. David Worthington died Dec. 26, 1851.

CHILDREN.

515. INFANT SON,   born Dec. 25, 1822; died same dav.

516. CORNELIA SOPHIA, born Nov. 10, 1824, in Peru; married, Nov. 27, 1845, William Roderick Ford of Hinsdale, Mass. (b. Feb. 13, 1811, in Peru, Mass.), son of Charles Ford and Anna Harris.

CHILDREN.

1. Sophia Cornelia Ford, b. May 16, 1847; m., March 11, 1867, Thomas Willwood Holmes (b. Jan. 4, 1847), son of Gideon Skull Holmes and Elizabeth Barr. 1 ch.
2. William Roderic Ford, b. Nov. 25, 1848; d. Feb. 17, 1849.
3. Charles Lineus Ford, b. June 2, 1850; m., April 16, 1874, Emma Harriet Thayer (b. July 29, 1852), dau. of Dwight Thayer and Amanda Brown. 4 ch.
4. Mary Antoinette Ford, b. April 2, 1852; m., Oct. 6, 1872, Charles Newell Dyer (b. Jan, 7, 1850), son of Charles Newell Dyer and Mary Ann Whitmarsh. 3 ch.
5. Lora Genevieve Ford, b. Nov. 21, 1854; m., Dec. 10, 1879, Clark Smith Taylor (b. Jan. 22, 1837, in Seneca, N. Y.),

son of Reserve Taylor and
Catherine Robson. No ch.

6. John Cushman Ford, b. Dec.
2, 1856; m., March 27, 1888,
Florence Vincent. 1 ch.

7. David Worthington Ford, b.
Oct. 9, 1858; d. Aug. 21,
1866.

8. Joseph Brainard Ford, b.
April 7, 1860; m., July 2,
1884, Georgiana Cynthia
Place (b. May 21, 1865),
dau. of David D. Place and
Dorothy Louisa Davis. Had
1 son.

9. William Harris Ford, b. Oct.
7, 1862; m., May 14, 1885,
Mary Ellen Mascraft (b.
April 9, 1863), son of Charles
Mascraft and Jennette Clay-
horn. 3 ch.

†517. RALPH CUSHMAN, born July 9, 1827, in Peru.

518. DAVID,   born Nov. 15, 1830, in Peru; died
Jan. 22, 1831.

519. SAMUEL,   born Nov. 15, 1830 in Peru; died
Feb. 27, 1838.

520. DAVID,   born April 18, 1834, in Peru; died
Feb. 25, 1855.

†521. BRAINARD TAYLOR, born Jan. 23, 1838, in Peru.

522. MYRA MINERVA, born Oct. 4, 1840, in Peru; married,
Feb. 22, 1874, Clark Smith
Taylor of Port Edwards, Wis.
(b. Jan. 22, 1837, in Seneca, N.

Y.), son of Reserve Taylor and
Catherine Robson. Mrs. Myra
Taylor died Aug. 23, 1873, and
Mr. Taylor married, Dec. 10,
1879, Lora Genevieve Ford.
Mr. Taylor died Feb. 4, 1888.

CHILDREN.

1. Infant daughter, b. Aug. 10
1873; d. Aug. 13, 1873.

229.

JOHN JEWETT WORTHINGTON of ——, Vermont, and Pots-
dam, N. Y., married, April 13, 1836, Belinda Washburn (b.
Feb. 1, 1812, in Rundolph?, Vt.), daughter of Liba Washburn
and Predy Courier. Mr. and Mrs. Worthington removed to
Potsdam, N. Y., about 1837. Mr. John Worthington died
Nov. 20, 1855, in Black Hawk County, Iowa. Mrs. Belinda
Worthington died Sept. 13, 1886.

CHILDREN.

†523. GEORGE GARY, born May 15, 1837, in —, Vermont.
524. ASINATH, born July 20, 1838, in Potsdam, N.Y·
†525. AMASA, born March 14, 1841, in Potsdam, N. Y.
526. JOHN JEWETT, born Aug. 29, 1842; died Nov. 27, 1855.
527. EMMA JANE, born Sept. 8, 1851; m., 1st, March 27, 1875, Harry Paine (b. —, in Princeton, Ill.), son of Judiah Paine and Harriet Alma; married, 2nd, Aug. 23, 1883, George

M.Sanborne, of Little Rock, Ark.
(b. April 15, 1860), son of David
J. Sanborne and Mary Annette
Page.

CHILDREN BY 1ST HUSBAND.

1.   Hattie Alma Paine, b. Jan.
10, 1876.

232.

REV. ELIJAH WORTHINGTON, a Methodist Episcopal minister
of LaGrange, Wis.; removed from Vermont in 1838; married
May 5, 1833, Emily E. Rand (b. Sept. 16, 1805, in Strafford,
Vt.), daughter of Samuel Rand and Alice Edmunds.

Rev. Mr. Worthington died June 4, 1858, in La Grange,
Wisconsin.

Mrs. Emily Worthington died June 4, 1888, in Mt. Pleasant,
Wisconsin.

CHILDREN.

†528.   FRANCIS ELIJAH, born   Dec. 14, 1834, in Northfield,
Vermont.

234.

LYMAN WORTHINGTON of Scio, Mich.; married, Oct. 30, 1833,
Caroline Blood (b. Feb. 15, 1813, in Hanover, N. H.), daughter of Enock Blood and Susan Caffron.

Mr. Lyman Worthington died Aug. 6, 1847, and his widow
married, April 23, 1850, James Foster of Tecumseh, Michigan.
She died May 16, 1877.

CHILDREN.

529. SUSAN, born Feb. 13, 1835; married, Sept. 3 1861, Dennis Van Duyn of Man chester, Mich. (b. Sept. 21, 1819, in Romulus, N. Y.), son of John Van Duyn and Elizabeth Sutten.

CHILDREN.

1. Carrie Van Duyn, b. Nov. 20, 1863.

†530. GEORGE L., born Aug. 30, 1837, in Tecumseh, Michigan.

†531. CHARLES, born Nov. 20, 1842, in Scio, Mich.

237

DANIEL WORTHINGTON of Chicago, Ill., and Memphis, Tenn., married, May 10, 1835, Ann Paine (b. Oct. 2, 1815), daughter of Elijah Paine and Fannie Morse (b. in Norwich, Conn.) of Tunbridge, Vt.

CHILDREN.

532. FRANCES ANN, born in Milwaukee, Wis.; married, June 21, 1858, Clarence Linden Hall of Memphis, Tenn.

CHILDREN.

1. Mary Hall, b. Feb. 9, 1860.
2. Belle Hall, b. May 11, 1862, m., Sept. 28, 1882, J. W. Robinson.
3. Clara Hall, b. July 1 1863 m., Nov. 2, 1885, W. D. Morrison.

4. Lulu Hall, b. Feb. 2, 1867

238.

Rev. David Worthington of Mt. Pleasant, Iowa, removed from Vermont in 1838; married, 1st, at Rock Island, Ill., Aug. 8, 1844, Orinda Lee (b. March 8, 1817, in Stanstead, P. Q., Canada), daughter of Henrv Lee (b. 1780, in Stafford, Conn.) and Sarah Davis (b. in Barrington, N. H.) of Stanstead, Can. Mr. and Mrs. Lee removed to Stanstead, Can., in 1804, where he died in 1848 and she died in 1846. Mrs. Orinda Worthington died Dec. 15, 1861, in Mt. Pleasant, and Rev. Mr. Worthington married, 2nd, Aug. 13, 1863, Lucretia Corbin (b. Aug. 15, 1835, in Fredericktown, Ohio), daughter of Ar temus Corbin and Ruth Beers.

Rev. David Worthington died March 1, 1866, in Mt. Pleasant.

The following is an extract from an obituary of Rev. David Worthington, written by Rev. T. E. Corkhill of Mt. Pleasant, Iowa, and published in the *Northwestern Christian Advocate*, Chicago:

"Rev. David Worthington was born in Williamstown, Vt., Feb. 13, 1815. When fifteen he accompanied his parents to a camp-meeting, where he was converted to God. Uniting immediately with the M. E. Church, he commenced a career of Christian usefulness which he followed with undeviating purpose until the close of his life.

"In 1835 he emigrated to the west and settled in the wilds of Wisconsin. He now began to visit the settlers around Milwaukee, talking with them at their work or praying with them in their rude homes or whenever a sufficient number could be gathered together he would hold a prayer-meeting. His diligence and success soon attracted the attention of the Church and he was licensed to exhort by Rev. J. R. Goodrich, then of the Illinois Conference. At a quarterly meeting held in Chicago, December 2, 1839, he was licensed to preach, and by Rev. John Clark, P. E., was employed as an assistant on Troy circuit the following year. He was received on trial in the Rock River Conference, August 26, 1840, graduated to full membership and was ordained Deacon by Bishop Roberts at a session of the same Conference held in Chicago, August 3, 1842.

" By division of the Conference he was placed upon the western side of the Mississippi and was one of the little group who organized the Iowa Conference at Iowa City, August 18, 1844. At this session he was ordained Elder by Bishop Morris. His appointments, as shown by the general minutes, have been as follows, to-wit: Rock River Conference, 1840, Burlington and Rochester, Wisconsin; 1841, Burlington, Wis.; 1842, Davenport, Iowa, Iowa Conference; 1844, Iowa City; 1845, Bloomington (now Muscatine); 1846, Fairport; 1847, 1848, Marion Mission; 1849, Iowa City Mission; 1850-1, Iowa City District; 1852 to 1855, Burlington District; 1856, Agent of the Iowa Wesleyan University. In this year he represented his Conference in the General Conference held in Indianapolis. In 1857, his appointment was to Augusta; 1858-9, Muscatine; 1860, Ottumwa; 1861-2, Mt. Pleasant Circuit; 1863, Fairfield; 1864-5-6, Mt. Pleasant District.

" His active ministry of twenty-six years was occupied, for seventeen years as pastor, for eight years as Presiding Elder, and for one year as agent of the I. W. University. For more than ten years he acted as president of the board of trustees of the university, and in every relation which he sustained to society, he won and retained both the confidence and esteem of all connected with him. As a preacher, his great object was to instruct, not to dazzle, his hearers. Ostentation or display never entered his mind. As a pastor he was faithful and affectionate. As a presiding officer he had but few equals and no superior in the Conference. His great spirit, swayed only by the highest principles of justice and right, led him to the strictest impartiality in all his rulings as a presiding officer, and in the filling of the various charges within his district. But the sublimest trait in his character was his unswerving, Christian integrity. Nature had endowed him with a keen preception, a sound judgment and a strong will.

" Soon after his appointment to Mt. Pleasant District he was thrown from his carriage, which resulted in fracturing his leg just above the ankle. This was the ' beginning of the end ' with him. A violent attack of lung fever followed from which he never fully recovered. Although able, occasionally, to attend his quarterly meetings, yet it became more evident, day by day, that his labors were drawing to a close. On the morning of the first of March his spirit passed away. His last words, whispered back to those around his bedside, were ' Down in the Valley.' "

CHILDREN BY 1ST WIFE.

533. MARY ADELAIDE, born June 15, 1845, in Iowa City, Iowa; married, June 12, 1867, John W. McLean (b. Feb. 6, 1834, in Chillicothe, O.), son of Daniel McLean and Elizabeth Long. Mrs. Mary McLean died Dec. 7, 1880.

CHILDREN.

1. Elizabeth Adelaide McLean, b. Sept. 24, 1868.
2. Thomas Evans McLean, b. July 28, 1873.

534. ADDIE, born June 15,1845,in Iowa City,Iowa.

535. JASON, born July 25, 1847, in Mt. Pleasant Iowa; died Dec. 19, 1864.

536. SARAH ELLEN, born May 28, 1849, in Mt. Pleasant; died Sept. 19, 1850.

†537. DAVID HENRY, born March 11, 1851, in Iowa City.

538. BELLE SARA, born Aug. 11, 1854, in Mt. Pleasant; married, Oct. 28, 1875, at Fairfield, Iowa, Albert Gallatin Adams of National City, Cal.(b. Oct. 25, 1849, in New Cumberland, W. Va.), son of Josiah Allen Adams and Elizabeth Welch.

CHILDREN.

1. Romola Mav Adams, b. July 17, 1876, in Colorado Springs, Colorado.
2. Rolland Worthington Adams, b. May 18, 1882, in Colorado Springs, Colorado.

539. WILLIAM,   born Jan. 17, 1857, in Mt. Pleasant.

CHILDREN BY 2ND WIFE.

540. CHARLES O.,   born July 10, 1864, in Mt. Pleasant; died July 11, 1865.

†541. FRANK C.,   born July 11, 1866.

239.

THEODORE WORTHINGTON of Oconomowac, Wis., where he settled in 1844, coming to Wisconsin from Vermont in 1836; married, March 29, 1846, Orilla Williams (b. Feb. 20, 1818, in Attica, N. Y.), daughter of Zudok Williams and Polly Muzzy. Mr. Theodore Worthington died ——, at Oconomowac, Wisconsin.

CHILDREN.

542. JAMES,   born —; died in infancy.
543. GEORGE L.,   born Aug. 3, 1847; died March 12, 1869.
544. HENRY H.,   born Feb. 28, 1849; died Feb. 24, 1869.
†545. FRANK,   born Aug. 14, 1851.

249.

ERASTUS WORTHINGTON married, ——, 1826, Julia Duncan.

250.

ALFRED WORTHINGTON of Deep River, Conn., married, ——, Sally Southworth.

Mr. Alfred Worthington died before 1840 in Deep River.

CHILDREN.

†546. WILLIAM D.

Several daughters.

251.

WILLIAM WORTHINGTON of Richford, N. Y., married Oct. 4, 1825, Eliza Cadwell Phelps of same place (b.Dec. 17, 1802), daughter of Noah Phelps and Anna St. John of Simsbury, Conn. They removed to Brooklyn, N. Y., about 1827, returning to Richford about 1837.

Mrs. Eliza Worthington died Nov. 9, 1839, in Richford.

Mr. William Worthington died Jan. 13, 1842, in Richford.

CHILDREN.

547. ANN ELIZA,   born July 16 1826, at Richford; died Feb. 5, 1829, in Brooklyn, N. Y.

257.

JOSEPH LOVETT WORTHINGTON, married Hannah Fuller, daughter of Joshua and Sybil Fuller. They lived in Pennsylvania, but no trace of them or their family can be found.

CHILDREN.

548. MARY,   born ——.

549. REBECCA,   born ——; m. Mr. Barnes and had one dau., Annie Barnes, who m.

A. N. Kellogg and had dau.,
Josie Worthington Kellogg.

550. LYDIA,

551. ELIZA ANN,

552. WILLIAM, supposed to have gone to California.

553. ANDREW R., supposed to have lived in Pennsylvania.

554. AUGUSTA,

555. GERTRUDE,

556. JAMES, supposed to have gone to California.

258.

ELIPHALET B. WORTHINGTON married Sally McShane. Nothing more can be heard of him.

260.

ELIJAH WORTHINGTON married Caroline M. Pratt daughter of Calvin Pratt. It is believed he lived a short time in Danville, N. Y., and published a paper there. He afterwards married a second time, but no trace of any of the family can be found.

CHILDREN BY 1ST WIFE.

557. HELEN, deceased.

558. ELIJAH, deceased.

CHILDREN BY 2ND WIFE.

559. CHARLES M., supposed to have lived in Illinois, but no trace of him can be found.

262.

JONATHAN BULKELEY WORTHINGTON of Laporte, Ohio, married, Feb. 14, 1828, Elizabeth Orr (b. Oct. 23, 1813), daughter

of John Orr.   Mrs. Elizabeth Worthington died Oct. 25, 1869.
Mr. Worthington died Sept. 5, 1884.

CHILDREN.

560. MARIA   born March 31, 1830; married, Oct.
                       28, 1857, Alfred Ruggles of Nor-
                       walk, Ohio (b. Feb. 12, 1827, in
                       Pennsylvania), son of Daniel
                       Ruggles and Louisa Fuller.
                           Mr. Alfred Ruggles died Aug.
                       29, 1871.

CHILDREN.

              1 Emma Alice Ruggles, b. Feb.
                 12, 1859; d. May 30, 1879.
              2. Estella Augusta Ruggles, b.
                 Aug. 30, 1861.

†561. ELDEN,   born March 9, 1833, in Carlisle, O.

562. BENJAMIN FRANKLIN, born Oct. 18, 1835, in Carlisle,
                       O.; died May 20, 1880.

563. ELIZABETH,   born July 16, 1839, in Eaton, Ohio;
                       married, Oct. 8, 1856, Jewry
                       Humphrey of Laporte, Ohio (b.
                       May 30, 1832, in Eaton, Ohio),
                       son of Orson J. Humphrey and
                       Lucina Sutliff.

CHILDREN.

              1. Helen A. Humphrey, b. Jan.
                  21, 1860.
              2. Elmer C. Humphrey, b. Jan.
                  27, 1862.

3. Mary E. Humphrey, b. March
1, 1865.
4. Orson J. Humphrey, b. April
20, 1868.
5. Clarence A. Humphrey, b.
April 10, 1871.
6. Edward B. Humphrey, b.
March 1, 1874; d. April 4,
1875.
7. Grace N. Humphrey, b. April
2, 1876.
8. Edward I. Humphrey, b.
July 20, 1878.
9. Hubert B. Humphrey, b.
March 22, 1881.

†564. ELIJAH,   born June 11, 1841, in Lorain Co., O.
†565. HENRY C.,   born Feb. 7, 1844, in North Eaton, O.
566. JOSEPH ERWIN,   born July 12, 1846.
567. AUGUSTA,   born Feb. 3, 1849, in Luzerne Co.,
                         Pa.; married Charles Warner of
                         Fields P. O., Ohio (b. July 14,
                         1843, in Medina, Ohio), son of
                         Edwin H. Warner and Clara
                         Hitchcock. Had no ch.
568. MARY,   born March 4, 1852; died July 22,
                         1888.

263.

THOMAS BARTLETT WORTHINGTON of Des Moines, Iowa,
married, 1st, Dec. 26, 1832, Hannah R. Lewis (b. Aug. 2,
1815, in Plymouth, Pa.), daughter of Griffin Lewis and Hannah Rogers. Mrs. Hannah Worthington died Oct. 4, 1837,

and Mr. Worthington married, 2nd, July 31, 1838, Elsie H. Mack, daughter of George Mack and Margaret Boggs of Mauch Chunk, Pa.

CHILDREN BY 1ST WIFE.

569. ADELAIDE   born Sept. 2, 1833, in Plymouth, Pa:; married, Oct. 5, 1851, General John A. Kellogg, of Minneapolis, Minn. (b. March 16, 1828, in Bethany, Pa.), son of Nathan Kellogg and Sarah Quidore of New York.

"General John Azor Kellogg was a lawyer by profession and held the office of district attorney when the war broke out. Entered military service in April, 1861, as first lieutenant in Co. K, Sixth Wisconsin Vol. Infantry. Was promoted to captaincy of Co. I, same regiment, in Dec., 1861, and served with the regiment until January, 1863; was then on duty as adjutant-general of brigade up to Dec., 1863. Returned to duty with the regiment in Jan., 1864; was wounded and made prisoner of war on the fifth day of May, 1864, at the Battle of the Wilderness; was prisoner for six months, and one of the six hundred placed under the fire of the Union guns at Charleston, S. C. Finally made his escape by jumping from a train of cars near Brunsville, S. C., Oct. 5, 1864; traveled thence by night to Calhoun, Georgia, reaching Union lines Oct. 26, 1864. He was promoted to major, lieutenant-colonel and colonel, respectively. Took command of regiment in Nov., 1864; assigned to the Iron Brigade, Feb., 1865; commanded same during last campaign and until the muster out of troops, Aug. 5, 1865. Was made brigadier-general by brevet; was U. S. pension agent at La Crosse, Wis., from 1866 until 1875, and a member of the state senate, 1879-80."

CHILDREN.

1. Ida D. Kellogg, b. April 11, 1854; m., March 21, 1888,

Edward L. Fúnk of Fari-
bault, Minn. 1 ch.

2. Elsie Worthington Kellogg,
b. July 28, 1857; m.,' Jan.
2, 1879, Frederick A. Sheldon of Troy, N. Y. Mr. Sheldon died ——, 1886. Mrs.
Sheldon diel July 21, 1890.

3. Stella L. Kellogg, b. Dec. 9,
1859; m., March 14, 1883,
Alban Haines of San Fran-
cisco, Cal., now of Min-
neapolis, Minn.

570. DILLA,   born March 16, 1835; d. Sept. 1,
1836.

571. DELIA,   born April 26, 1837, in Hazleton, Pa.;
married, Nov. 17, 1857, Wil-
liam W. Runyan (b. Nov. 17,
1833), son of John Runyan and
Anna Butterfield.

Mrs. Delia Runyan died Feb.
8, 1875.

CHILDREN.

1. Lewis Worthington Run-
yan, b. Nov. 10, 1859.

2. William Runvan, b. May 6,
1867.

3. Mary Mildred Runyan, b.
May 4, 1873.

CHILDREN BY 2ND WIFE.

†572. BARTLETT MACK, born Oct. 4, 1839, in Mauch Chunk,
Pa.

573. WILLIAM ARCHER, born Sept. 24, 1841; d. Nov. 8,
       1843.

†574. CHESTER BUTLER, born Nov. 17, 1843.

575. LENAH ALICE,   born Jan. 25, 1846, in Huntington,
                        Pa.; married, Dec. 26, 1866,
                        Jerome Edward Párker of La
                        Crosse, Wis. (b. Sept. 22, 1841,
                        in Troy, N. Y.), son of Edward
                        Smith Parker and Sallie Maria
                        Miller.

CHILDREN.

1. Edward Worthington
    Parker, b. Oct. 24, 1867
2. Adelaide Francis Parker, b.
    March 19, 1872.

264.

HENRY WORTHINGTON of Harvey's Lake, Pa. He married
after 1856 and died at Harvey's Lake, leaving a family, but
nothing can be learned of them.

266.

JUSTIN LOVET WORTHINGTON of Albion, Mich., married Jan.
7, 1826, at Ogden, N. Y., Eliza Olcott (b. Feb. 24, 1803, in
East Haddam, Ct.), daughter of Oliver Olcott and Jerusha
—— (b. in Hebron, Ct.).

Mr. Justin Worthington died Oct. 25, 1829, in Ogden, N. Y.,
and Mrs. Worthington removed with her children to Southern
Illinois, and died, May 29, 1888, in Mooresville, Mo.

CHILDREN.

576. OLIVER OLCOTT, born Oct. 25, 1826, in Rochester. N. Y.; died June 15, 1837, in Upper Alton, Ill.
577. EMMA LANISSA, born Jan. 8, 1828, in Ogden, N. Y.; married, March 29, 1849, at Upper Alton, Ill., James Friar Matthew (b. Aug. 11, 1825, in Fayette, Mo.), son of John Matthew and Rachel McKinney.

CHILDREN.

1. John Justin Matthew, b. Jan. 1, 1850, in Upper Alton.
2. Julia Ella Matthew, b. Aug. 8, 1852, in Upper Alton.
3. Mary Eliza Matthew, b. June 6, 1856, in Upper Alton; d. Dec. 25, 1866, at Mooresville.
4. Olcott Worthington Matthew, b. Oct. 12, 1857, at Upper Alton.

269.

JAMES SPARROW WORTHINGTON of Ogden, N. Y., Pittsford, N. Y., and Homer, Mich.; married, 1st, Dec. 28, 1826, Marv Lacey (b. Dec. 24, 1804, in Bennington, Vt.), daughter of Samuel Lacey and Ruth Sigourney. Mrs. Mary Worthington died Oct. 10, 1844, and Mr. Worthington married, 2nd, Oct.

5, 1847, Mrs. Lavina Cole (b. Jan. 14, 1809, in Albany, N. Y.), daughter of Noah Cole and Marv D. Germo, and widow of Peter Hopkins.

Mrs. Lavina Worthington died Oct. 28, 1876.

Mr. James Worthington died May 12, 1888.

CHILDREN BY 1ST WIFE.

†578. JAMES LACEY,   born Sept. 18, 1827, in Ogden, N. Y.

579. LAVINA AMELIA, born March 11, 1830, in Ogden, N. Y.; married, May 9, 1850, James Bellows (b. Dec. 30, 1829, in Pittsford, N. Y.), son of Ira Bellows and Marv Buck.

Mrs. Lavina Bellows died March 16, 1867, in Rochester N. Y.

Mr. James Bellows died Jan. 7, 1890.

CHILDREN.

1. Minnie Amelia Bellows, b. Nov. 4, 1851, in Pittsford.
2. Ira Worthington Bellows, b. Jan. 11, 1857, in Pittsford.

580. ALBERT SIGOURNEY, born Sept. 3, 1832, in Ogden, N. Y.; died June 15, 1839, in Pittsford.

581. MARY SIGOURNEY, born Sept. 8, 1842, in Pittsford; died Aug. 31, 1844, in Homer, Mich.

CHILDREN BY 2ND WIFE.

†582. CHARLES CARTER, born April 13, 1850, in Homer, Mich.

270.

HENRY SPENCER WORTHINGTON of Hope, Mich., married, 1st, Aug 3, 1834, Fanny Loomis Woodward (b. Nov. 8, 1813, in Connecticut), daughter of Asabel Woodward and Harriet House. Mrs. Fanny Worthington died Sept. 27, 1884, and Mr. Worthington married, 2nd, July 3, 1888, Jane Westervelt (b. April 19, 1830, in Penfield, N. Y.), daughter of Jacob Westervelt and Roxana Wakefield.

CHILDREN BY 1ST WIFE.

†583. JUSTIN WILLIAM, born June 21, 1835, in Ogden, N. Y.

†584. JAMES AMOS,   born March 11, 1837, in Ogden, N. Y.

585. ALBERT HENRY, born June 11, 1839, in Ogden, N. Y.; died Aug. 9, 1862, in camp, near Corinth, Miss., a soldier in the Union army.

†586. CHARLES NICHOLAS born Oct. 11, 1841, in Ogden, N. Y.

587. SARAH AMELIA, born May 9, 1845, in Ogden, N. Y.; married, Sept. 21, 1870, Robert W. Caskey (b. July 10, 1844, in Iasco, Mich.), son of William Salmon Caskey and Clarissa Wasson.

CHILDREN.

1. Julia Estelle Caskey, b. Aug. 2, 1871.
2. Clarissa Fanny Caskey, b. April 4, 1874.
3. William Henry Caskey, b. Aug. 13, 1876.

4. Helen Delaphine Caskey, b. May 29, 1879.
5. Luella Caskey, b. Aug. 9, 1883.
6. James A. Caskey, b. Nov. 8, 1885.
7. Mabel Caskev, b. April 1, 1890.

†588. DELOS IOTE,   born Oct. 24, 1856, in Hartland, Mich.

271.

NICHOLAS WORTHINGTON of Hillsdale, Mich., married, 1st, about 1829, Harriet E. Stark (b. May 13, 1812, in Colchester, Ct.), daughter of James Stark and Ruth Yeoman. Mrs. Harriet Worthington died May 25, 1832, in Colchester, Ct., and Mr. Worthington married, 2nd, June 2, 1840, Sarah M. Sears of Hillsdale, Mich. (b. October 4, 1819), daughter of James Sears and —— Gregory.

Mr. Nicholas Worthington died Feb. 13, 1861.
Mrs. Sarah Worthington died Nov. 10, 1862.

CHILDREN BY 1ST WIFE.

589. HARRIET VIRGINIA, born March 25, 1831, in Virginia; married, Sept. 13, 1851, Charles Ferdinand Dimmers of Hillsdale, Mich. (b. Sept. 25, 1820, in Coblenz, Prussia). Mr. Dimmers died Sept. 19, 1883.

CHILDREN.

1. Arthur Dimmers, b. Jan. 25, 1854; m., June 20, 1879.

2. Charles Dimmers, b. Jan. 13, 1857; m., Dec. 25, 1878.
3. Ellen Dimmers, b. June 28 1859; m. Nov. 11, 1878.
4. Alfred Dimmers, b. Feb. 26, 1866.

CHILDREN BY 2ND WIFE.

†590. LESLIE,   born Sept. 5, 1841, in Salem, Ct.

591. ANNA,   born Sept. 5, 1842, in Salem, Ct.; married, Sept. 4, 1864, William Henry Lancaster (b. April 27, 1838, in New Sharon, Maine), son of Ezekiel Lancaster and Lydia Hopkinson. They are living in the State of Washington.

CHILDREN.

1. Scott Gregory Lancaster, b. Aug. 26, 1870.
2. Leslie Worthington Lancaster, b. Oct. 7, 1872.
3. Henry Lewis Lancaster, b. March 29, 1874.
4. Harvey Belden Lancaster, b. March 29, 1874.
5. Mary Lancaster, b. May 25, 1876.
6. Nicholas Lancaster, b. Dec. 31, 1880; d. Jan. 3, 1881.

592... MARY SATTELEE, born March 25, 1845, in Adams, Mich.; died Oct. 17, 1846.

593. MARY GREGORY, born March 17, 1847, in Adams, Mich:; married, March 2, 1867, George T. Belden (b. March 23, 1840, in Rome, O.), son of George Belden and Mary Putnam. They are now living in the State of Washington.

CHILDREN.

1. Worthington Belden, b June 1, 1868; m., Sept. 14, 1890, Pearl Hoxie (b. March 15 1873, in Tacoma, Washington),
2. Winford Wingate Belden, b. June 22, 1870.
3. Ellen Gertrude Belden, b. April 30, 1872.
4. George Belden, b. Jan. 31, 1874.
5. Theodore Belden, b. Dec. 23, 1875.
6. Russell Goodwin Belden, b. Sept. 12, 1877.
7. Anna Belden, b. Sept. 7, 1879.
8. Harry Belden, b. Jan. 30, 1885.

594. ALBERT,   born April 3, 1849, in Adams, Mich.· died July 28, 1849.

275.

ARTEMAS WARD WORTHINGTON, a farmer of Rock River Rapids, Illinois, married Phoebe Sammis.

He died about 1856 from the effects of a rattlesnake bite.

CHILDREN.

595.	ISABEL,	born
596.	ROBERT,	born
597.	A SON,	born
598.	A SON,	born

277.

DR. ALBERT BROWNELL WORTHINGTON, a physician of Middle Haddam, Ct., married, July 23, 1848, Mary E. Selden (b. May 25, 1822), daughter of Huntington Selden and Laura Hurd of Middle Haddam.

CHILDREN.

†599. ALBERT SELDEN, born Oct. 9, 1849, in Middle Haddam.

600. ARTHUR HUNTINGTON, born Jan. 14, 1851.

601. CLARA LOUISA, born July 22, 1853.

279.

DUDLEY WRIGHT WORTHINGTON of Batavia, N. Y. married, April 30, 1820, Ataristá L. Bulkeley (b. May 29, 1799, in Colchester, Ct.), daughter of Peter Bulkeley of Colchester and Sally Wright.

Mrs. Atarista Worthington died Dec. 24, 1872, in Batavia.

Mr. Dudley Worthington died May 24, 1874, in Batavia.

CHILDREN.

602. HARRIET BULKELEY, born April 19, 1821, in Colchester, Conn.; died Feb. 11, 1841.

603. EMELINE, born Jan. 4, 1826, in Colchester, Conn.; d. Oct. 27, 1889, at Batavia; unmarried.

604. ABIGAIL, born June 9, 1828, in Colchester.

605. JOHN, born Nov. 15, 1830, in Colchester; living at Batavia; unm.

606. ELIZABETH, born March 11, 1833, in Batavia; married, Jan. 24, 1852, Oliver W. Nay (b. —, 1826, in Darian, N. Y.), son of David Nay and Thetis North. Mrs. Elizabeth Nav died June 1, 1859, in Batavia. Mr. Oliver Nay died Oct. 22, 1875, in Saginaw, Mich. Had no ch.

607. MARY, born Dec. 3, 1839, in Batavia; married March 7, 1867, David Lapp of Batavia (b. May 8, 1821, in Bucks Co., Pa.), son of John Lapp and Hannah Bydeler.

CHILDREN.

1. George Worthington Lapp, b. June 21, 1868, in Alexandria, N. Y.
2. Bermice Lapp, b. Sept. 6, 1882, in Batavia; d. March 28, 1883, in Batavia.

283.

GERSHOM BULKELEY WORTHINGTON of Colchester, Conn.; married, Sept. 18, 1831, Lucy A. Rathbone (b. Oct. 31, 1807), daughter of Àsa Rathbone of Salem.

Mrs. Lucy Worthington died Aug. 7, 1886.

Mr. Gershom Worthington died Nov. 9, 1888.

CHILDREN.

608. MARY JANE, born Feb. 19 1833, in Colchester; married, Feb. 15, 1855, Rvan Brooks of Colchester, son of Joseph Brooks and Mercy Ryan.

Mrs. Mary Brooks died Nov. 17, 1860.

Mr. Ryan Brooks died Feb. , 1888.

CHILDREN.

1. Hattie Jane Brooks, b. Nov. 25, 1855; m., April 22, 1879, John Northam Strong.
2. John Rvan Brooks, b. May 6, 1858; m., June 11, 1889, Kate M. Foote.

†609. ENOCH BROWN, born Dec. 17, 1836, in Colchester.

286.

JOHN RICHARD WORTHINGTON of Cooperstown, N. Y., married. Sept. 13, 1837, Marv Alice Dorrance (b. Jan. 20, 1806, in Dalton, Mass.), daughter of Trumbull Dorrance, M.D., and Chloe Fuller of Dalton, Mass. Mr. John R. Worthington died Jan. 15, 1878, at Cooperstown.

CHILDREN.

610. ALICE TRUMBULL, born June 18, 1838, in Cooperstown;
married, July 28, 1863, at Coop-
erstown, Rev. Stephen Henry
Synnott of Ithaca, N. Y. (b.
Sept. 10, 1836, in St. John, N.
B.), son of Stephen Synnott and
Margaret S. .Viets.

CHILDREN.

1. Margaret Viets Synnott, b.
Sept. 8, 1864; married, May
25, 1887, Edward Ashton
Patterson of Troy, N. Y.

Ch.

1. Julia Dauchy Patterson, b.
May 20, 1888.
ɔ   Mary Trumbull Patterson,
b. Nov. 28, 1889.

2. Richard Henry Synnott, b.
Dec. 19, 1865; d. Dec. 20,
1865.
3. Mary Alice Synnott, b. April
26, 1868; d. June 29, 1868.

†611. JOHN,   born Oct. 25, 1840, in Cooperstown.
612. KATE DORRANCE, born Aug. 14, 1842, in Cooperstown;
married, May 26, 1864, Archi-
bald McIntyre Gregory, M. D.,
of Jersey City, N. J., son of Dud
ley S. Gregory and Anna Maria
Lyon.

Mrs. Kate Gregory died Oct. 4, 1865, at Jersey City. Mr Gregory died June 4, 1874, at Hammersmith, England.

CHILDREN.

1. Kate Worthington Gregory, b. Oct. 4, 1865, in Jersey City; m., June 12, 1890, at Malta, Herbert Whitmore Savory, R. N., 1st Lieut., H. M. S. "Scout," second son of Charles Harley Savory of London, England.

613. RICHARD   born Oct. 2, 1844, in Cooperstown.

614. MARY,   born Aug. 10, 1847, in Cooperstown; unmarried.

615. MARGARET CARY, born March 18, 1850, in Cooperstown; married, Oct. 5, 1881, George William Graham Bonner of Montreal, Canada.

CHILDREN.

1. John Richard Worthington Bonner, b. Dec. 5, 1882.
2. Mary Graham Bonner, b. Sept. 5, 1889.

†616. HENRY   born May 4, 1852, in Cooperstown.

287.

REV. ALBERT WORTHINGTON of Ambler, Pa., was graduated from Hamilton College, N. J., and from Princeton Theological Seminary in 1830. Was home missionary in Michigan from

1830 to 1840; his last pastorate was at New Gretna, N. J.; is connected with the West Jersey Presbytery, and although now (1892) in his 87th year, he occasionally preaches. Rev Mr. Worthington married, July 1, 1835, at Ypsilanti, Michigan, Ruth Parker (b. Oct. 2, 1808, in Holden, Mass.). Mrs. Ruth Worthington died April 17, 1871, in Vineland, N. J. Rev. Albert Worthington died May 16, 1893.

CHILDREN.

617. CLARA,   born Feb. 12, 1837, in Milford, Mich., married, May 27, 1867, at Vine land, N. J., Isaac N. Wilson. Mrs. Clara Wilson died Jan. 27, 1872, at Vineland.

CHILDREN.

1. Clara May Wilson, b. May 11, 1868, in Philadelphia.
2. Florence Newcomb Wilson, b. Sept. 4, 1869, in Philadel phia; d. Oct. 3, 1869, at Philadelphia.

618. ELIZABETH   born March 30, 1840; married, May 13, 1868, Joseph Dennis Harris, M. D. Dr. Harris died Dec. 25, 1884.

CHILDREN.

1. Worthie Dennis Harris, b. March 11, 1871.
2. Thoro Dennis Harris, b. March 31, 1874.

†619. ALBERT PAYSON, born July 5, 1842, at Milford, Mich.

288.

RALPH HENRY WORTHINGTON of New York, married Aug. 13, 1860, Josephine S. Peake (b. May 8, 1838), daughter of William Peake and Ann D. Merwin.

Mr. Worthington died in the spring of 1892.

CHILDREN.

620. CLARA MERWIN, born July 15, 1862.
621. KATE AUGUSTA, born March 15, 1866 in Nyack, N. Y.; married, June 9, 1885, Richard de Treville of Charleston, S. C. (b. Nov. 19, 1863), son of Richard de Treville and Marcia Jacoby.

290.

GEORGE WORTHINGTON, merchant and banker, of Cleveland, Ohio, was born in Cooperstown, N. Y., Sept. 21, 1813, and died at Cleveland, Nov. 9, 1871

"He commenced his business career at Utica, N. Y., in 1830, by entering the hardware store of James Sayer. There he remained four years when, having acquired a thorough knowledge of the business, he removed to Cleveland, where he established himself in business in 1835. Cleveland at that time was but a village, with a population of about seven hundred persons." His first store occupied the ground on which now stands the Bethel building; afterwards he purchased the stock of Cleveland, Sterling & Co., on the corner of Water and Superior streets, where the National bank buildings now stand, and associated with himself as business partner Mr. William Bingham. In 1841 Mr. Bingham sold out his interest. A few years later Mr. Worthington associated with himself Mr. James Barnett (his cousin) and Mr. Edward Bingham. About 1862 Mr. Worthington projected the Cleveland Iron and Nail works, and, in connection with Mr. William Bingham, matured the plans and in a year got the machinery into successful operation. Shortly after they built works for the manufacture of gas pipe. He was also largely interested in blast furnaces. On the passage of the "National Bank Law" Mr. Worthington, with other capitalists, organized the First National Bank of Cleveland. The bank was incorporated in 1863, and at the first meeting of the stockholders, held in June of that year, he was chosen one of the directors and elected president of the bank. This position he held until his death. He was one of the directors of the Ohio Savings and Loan bank, and largely interested in local insurance interests. He was for some years a director of the Cleveland, Columbus, Cincinnati & Indianapolis Railway Company, and was also president of the Cleveland Iron Mining Company. In the development of the iron interests of Cleveland, which from a small beginning have since assumed such immense proportions, he was one of the pioneers. He also did much in the way of building up the city, especially the business portions. He did much toward converting the village, as he found it, into the great city of to-day, being a man whose activity always led him to feel a great pride in building up the town and setting men to work to improve his property. He strove, in many instances, to improve and advance the interests of the city, rather than his personal or pecuniary interests. A man of large comprehension, bold and fearless in going into large operations, and liberal in his ideas in carrying them out—he was peculiarly adapted to enterprises of that character. He would often go in where others quailed, and was always bound to carry them to a successful issue. All in which he was engaged have grown to be of great magnitude. The wholesale hardware business, which still bears his name, has become one of the largest in the West. As a business man he possessed superior qualifications, being a hard worker, shrewd yet liberal, clear, positive, and of good judgment. A man well read, thoughtful and intelligent, he could comprehend and go into the detail of all matters most thoroughly. As a companion he was agreeable, well versed in politics (in which his sentiments were strongly anti-slavery). During the war he was an active worker in everything that would tend to insure success to Union arms. To the cause he gave freely of his means and sacrificed both time and personal convenience. In his commercial transactions he was a man of justice, correctness, equity and high personal virtues. Kindly in his nature, he endeared himself to his business associates and intimate friends.

At the time of his death he was a member of the Third Presbyterian Church of Cleveland, having been one of the thirteen who were set off from the Stone, or First Presbyterian Church, to build up the new church. The west window of the Third Presbyterian Church is a memorial to Mr. Worthington, put there by his widow and children who survived him. He came to the Stone church by letter from the Presbyterian church of Utica, N. Y., with which he had united during his clerkship in Utica. To the support of the church of his choice he gave liberally, and in her prosperity he took delight. He was a man of warm and generous domestic feelings, greatly attached to his family and fondly beloved by them.—*Historical and Biographical Cyclopædia of the State of Ohio.*

Mr. Worthington married, Nov. 16, 1840, at Cleveland O., Maria Cushman Blackmar (b. Sept. 14, 1817, in Dorset, Vt.), daughter of Reuben Harmon Blackmar of Cleveland (b. Aug. 1793; d. March 3, 1862, at Cleveland, son of Dr. Jonathan Blackmar of Dorset, Vt.), and Amanda Cushman (b. 1797; d. Dec. 16, 1847, at Cleveland, who was a direct descendant of Thomas Cushman and his wife, Mary Allerton, the Pilgrims). Mr. Reuben Blackmar and his family came to Cleveland in 1837 from Bennington, Vt.

CHILDREN.

†622. RALPH,   born Dec. 4, 1841, in Cleveland.
623. ABIGAIL MARIA, born Sept. 27, ——, in Cleveland married, Oct. 18, 1866, at Cleveland, George Hoyt of Cleveland (b. Aug. 20, 1838, in Chardon, Ohio), son of Sylvester Hoyt and Eleanor Converse of Chardon, Ohio.

CHILDREN.

1. Worthington Hoyt, b. Oct. 28, 1867, in Cleveland.
2. Eleanor Hoyt, b. Feb. 22, 1870, in Cleveland; m., Feb. 14, 1893, Augustus Wells Kilbourne of Cleveland, O.
3. George Hoyt, born Aug. , 1871, in Cleveland.

624. CHARLES CUSHMAN, born Jan. 15, 1846, in Cleveland; died June 5, 1846.

625. GEORGIANA, born March 29, 1847, in Cleveland; died Aug. 15, 1848.

626. MARY BEADLE, born Sept. 28, —, in Cleveland; married, Nov. 9,.1871, at Cleveland Clark Irving Butts of Cleveland son of Freeman Butts and Mary Jane Ballard.

CHILDREN.

1. Freeman Worthington Butts, b. Aug. 13, 1872, in Cleveland.
2. Alice Maude Butts, b. Nov. 8, 1876, in Cleveland.
3. Mary Butts, b. Oct. 6, 1879, in Cleveland.

627. CLARISSA CLARK, born January 15, in Cleveland; married, Oct. 9, 1873, at Cleveland, Willis Benjamin Hale of Cleveland (b. June 17, 1849), son of Edwin Butler Hale and Susan

Hoyt (dau. of Sylvester Hoyt
and Eleanor Converse of Chardon, Ohio).

CHILDREN.

1. Cara Hale, b. Sept. 19,
1875, in Cleveland.
2. Edwin Worthington Hale,
b. Jan. 9, 1878, in Cleveland.
3. Nellie Hale, b. Jan. 9, 1878
in Cleveland.
4. Willis Worthington Hale, b.
May 23, 1886, in Cleveland.

†628. GEORGE, born Aug. 8, 1854, in Cleveland.

629. ALICE, born Feb. 14, 1857, in Cleveland;
married, Aug. 26, 1877, at
Cleveland, Martin James Pendle-
ton of Cleveland, son of Charles
Henry Pendleton and Charity
Sears.

Mr. Martin Pendleton died
June 20, 1892, in Cleveland,
Ohio.

CHILDREN.

1. Edward Pendleton, b. Feb.
26, 1878, in Philadelphia.
2. George Worthington Pendle
ton, b. June 21, 1881, in
New York.
3. Alice Pendleton, b. Oct. 20,
1882, in Iowa City, Io.

  4. James Pendleton, b. June 21,
    1883, in Iowa City, Io.; died
    in infancy in Iowa City, Io.
  5. Eugenie Pendleton, b. Nov.
    22, 1887, in Cleveland, O.

293.

JOHN WORTHINGTON of Irasburgh, Vt., married, Nov. 9
1831, Catharine Bassett, daughter of Benoni Bassett and
Anna Rice.

Mr. Worthington died Jan. 20, 1869, in Irasburgh.

CHILDREN.

†630. GEORGE,   born June 17, 1832, in New York.

304.

DAN LEANDER WORTHINGTON of East Bethany, N. Y.,
married, June 26, 1836, at East Bethany, Indiana, Louise
Pierson (b. Sep. 6, 1816, in East Bethany), daughter of
Richard Pierson (b. Jan. 9, 1783; d. Dec. 20, 1853) and
Indiana Lavina Comstock (died Feb. 21, 1861).

CHILDREN.

†631. RICHARD PIERSON, born Jan. 1, 1838.
†632. ROBERT CONE, born Dec. 15, 1839.
†633. CHARLES GAD, born Nov. 6, 1841.
 634. GEORGE,   born March 18, 1844, in East
           Bethany, N. Y.
 635. DAN,   born April 24, 1849; d. Dec. 20, 1879;
           unmarried.

305.

GAD BELDEN WORTHINGTON of Batavia, N. Y., married, 1st, June 2, 1841, Anna Maria Dixon (b. 1819, in Bethany), daughter of Edward Dixon and Amanda Comstock

Mrs. Anna Worthington died May 20; 1854, and Mr Worthington married, 2nd, Sept. 8, 1856, Olive Susan Towner (b. Aug. 17, 1816, in Batavia), daughter of Ephraim Towner and Anna Kellogg.

CHILDREN BY 1ST WIFE.

636. AMANDA COMSTOCK, born April 17, 1842.

637. MARY,   born June 29, 1847, in Batavia; died Aug. 29, 1848.

638. SARAH,   born June 29, 1847, in Batavia; married, Sept. 19, 1876, Edward De Lancey Palmer of Albany, N. Y. (b. March 19, 1848, in Newtonville, N. Y.), son of Amos P. Palmer and Hannah B. Crafts.

CHILDREN.

1. Worthington Palmer, b May 29, 1878.
2. Florence Palmer, b. Nov. 14, 1879.
3. De Lancey Palmer, b. July 22, 1885.

639. GAD DIXON,   born Oct. 24, 1852, in Batavia.

†640. EDWARD WILLIAM, born May 10, 1854, in Batavia.

307.

SAMUEL KELLOGG WORTHINGTON of Buffalo, N. Y., married, Sept. 13, 1855, Rachel Woods, daughter of John Woods and Sarah Lynch (of Columbia, S. C.), of Hamilton, Ohio.

CHILDREN.

641. ROBERT HOLLISTER, born Sept. 13, 1856, in Buffalo
                   N. Y.; lawyer.
†642. ARTHUR WOODS, born June 27, 1858, in Buffalo, N. Y.
643. FLORENCE,   born April 3, 1860, in Buffalo, N. Y.
644. LOUISE,   born Jan. 2, 1862, in Buffalo, N. Y.
645. SARAH FRANCES, born Sept. 16, 1868, in Buffalo, N. Y.
646. EDITH,   born Dec. 10, 1872, in Buffalo, N. Y.

308.

JOHN WORTHINGTON, ———, married, Sept. 21, 1852, Mary H. Kimberly of Batavia, N. Y.

  Mr. Worthington died Apr. 15, 1870, at Hastings, Minn.

CHILDREN.

647. JOHN FRANCIS, born May 18, 1854, in Batavia,
                 N. Y.; died April 8, 1859.
648. MARY ELIZABETH, born Sept. 7, 1856; died Aug. 18,
                 1859.
†649. FREDERICK,   born Feb. 6, 1861, in East Bethany,
                 N. Y.
650. MARGARET,   born June 20, 1867; died Aug. ɩ
                 1867.

RT. REV. GEO. WORTHINGTON, Bishop of Nebraska.

310.

Robert Worthington of Oakland, Cal., married, Dec. 29, 1859, Jane A. Bristol (b. Jan. 31, 1836, in Canaan, N. Y.), daughter of George Bristol and Sally Hutchinson.

Mr. Robert Worthington died Aug. 13, 1862, in Oakland, Cal.

CHILDREN.

651. Fannie,   born Nov. 8, 1861.

313.

Right Rev. George Worthington, D. D., LL. D., Bishop of Nebraska, residing at Omaha. Bishop Worthington was graduated from Hobart College, Geneva, N. Y., in 1860, and from the General Theological Seminary in New York in 1863, at which time he was ordained deacon and became assistant to the Rev. T. W. Coit, D. D., rector of St. Paul's Church of Troy, N. Y. In 1865 Bishop Worthington was advanced to the priesthood by Bishop Horatio Potter of New York, and became rector of Christ Church at Ballston Spa, N. Y.; where he remained until 1868, when he became the rector of St. John's Church at Detroit, Mich. While there he was elected Missionary Bishop to China by the General Convention in 1883, which he declined. Two years later, on Feb. 24, 1885, he was consecrated Bishop of Nebraska, to which episcopate he was twice elected. From his *alma mater* he has had conferred upon him the degrees of B. A., A. M., D. D., LL. D. Bishop Worthington married, April 21, 1892, at the Church of the Heavenly Rest, in New York City, Amelia Thibault Milton, daughter of W. H. Milton of Boston, Mass.

315.

HENRY SHERRILL WORTHINGTON of Batavia, N. Y., married, May 6, 1852, Elizabeth Foote of Batavia.

Mr. Worthington died Jan. 22, 1853, in Batavia.

CHILDREN.

652. LIBBIE SHERRILL, born May 7, 1853; died March 5, 1856.

320.

AMOS WORTHINGTON of College Hill, Ohio, married, 1st. Dec., 1831, Frances Blatchly Wood, daughter of Dr. Stephen Wood and Catharine Freeman of Cleves, O. Mrs. Frances Worthington died May 2, 1840, and Mr. Worthington married, 2nd, July, 1842, Jane C. Wilson of Cincinnati, Ohio

Mr. Amos Worthington died at College Hill, Ohio, Feb. 18, 1882·

CHILDREN BY 1ST WIFE.

†653. AMOS FRANCIS,   born Aug. 27, 1832, in Cleves, O.

654. CATHARINE DEZIER, born, 1834, in Cleves, O.; died 1851.

†655. STEPHEN WOOD, born, 1835, in Cleves, O.

†656. JAMES GALLUP, born Aug. 3, 1837, in Cleves, O.

657. LUCY,   born, 1839, in Cleves, O.; died 1839.

CHILDREN BY 2ND WIFE.

658. WILLIAM WILSON, born June 5, 1843.

659. MARY LOUISE, born, 1847, in Cincinnati, O.

660. JENNIE MARIA, born Dec. 5, 1852, in Cincinnati, O.; married, June 9, 1881, Albert H. Mitchell of Avondale, O.

661. LILLIAN, born Feb. 22, 1856, in Cincinnati;
        married, June 3, 1884, Spencer
        B. Dodd of College Hill, O., son
        of George S. Dodd and Annie
        Bowme.

CHILDREN.

1. Lewis Worthington Dodd,
   b. April 17, 1885, in College
   Hill, Ohio.
2. Margorie Louise Dodd, b.
   Jan. 14, 1889, in College
   Hill, Ohio.

662. GEORGE WASHINGTON, born July 4, 1858, at College Hill.
663. LIZZIE M., born —, 1860; died —, 1863.

324.

LEWIS WORTHINGTON of Cincinnati, O., removed from Agawam, Mass., Dec., 1823, to Genesee Co., N. Y. (now Orleans
Co.), where he entered the employ of a mercantile firm, residing part of the time at Albion and part of the time at Batavia,
until 1829, when he removed to Cincinnati, Ohio, and entered
the grocery business, in which he continued until 1846, when
he purchased the Globe Iron Works, which he conducted for
many years in partnership with his nephew, William Watson
Worthington. Married, Oct. 3, 1837, Sally Ann Pierce (b.
Sept. 23, 1821), daughter of Joseph and Sally Ann Pierce of
Cincinnati. Mrs. Sally Worthington died April 1, 1876. Mr.
Lewis Worthington died April 12, 1879, in Paris, France.

CHILDREN.

†664. LEWIS SEDAM, born March 21, 1839, in Cincinnati.

326.

EDWARD WORTHINGTON of Winona, Minn., where he settled in 1857, having removed, when quite young, from Agawam to Hartford and subsequently to Mobile, New Orleans, New York, and Norwich, Conn. Married, Nov. 24, 1841, Jane Maria Shepard (b. Sept. 1, 1821, in New Rochell, N. Y.), daughter of John Shepard and Jane Maria Labagh of New York. Mrs. Jane Worthington died Jan. 15, 1871, in Winona. Mr. Edward Worthington died Sept. 20, 1884, in Winona.

CHILDREN.

665. MARIA LOUISE, born Dec. 9, 1842, in New York; married, Nov. 24, 1869, Philo Good man Hubbell of Winona, Minn. (b. Dec. 14, 1843, in Bath, N. Y.), son of Philo Patterson Hubbell and Elizabeth Bachus.

CHILDREN.

1. Theodore Worthington Hub bell, b. Aug. 12, 1871; d. Dec. 9, 1873.
2. Max Berry Hubbell, b. June 21, 1874.
3. Francis Edward Hubbell, b. Jan. 1, 1877; d. Nov. 14, 1886.
4. Annie Louise Hubbell, b. Sept. 26, 1878.
5. May Eliza Hubbell, b. Jan. 9, 1883.

†666. JOHN SHEPARD, born April 17, 1844, in Norwich, Conn.
667. JANE ELIZABETH, born May 18, 1846; married, Sept.
       23, 1868, in Winona, Minn.,
       Oliver D. Adams. · Mrs. Jané
       Adams died Oct. 20, 1869, at
       Winona.
668. AMOS EDWARD, born Sept. 10, 1848.
669. MARY COLEBROOK, born Feb. 11, 1853, in Norwich,
       Conn.; married, Jan. 10, 1884,
       Judson Keith Deming of Du-
       buque, Iowa (b. Sept. 18, 1858,
       in Shelden, Vt.), son of Anson
       Harrington Deming and Han--
       nah Keith Judson.

CHILDREN.

       1. Elsa Louise Deming, b. Dec.
           6, 1885.
       2. Keith Worthington Deming,
           b. June 29, 1886.
670. WILLIAM FISKE, born Oct. 23, 1850, in Norwich, Conn.·
       d. March 16, 1878; unmarried.
671. LEWIS WATSON, born Aug. 5, 1855, in Norwich, Conn.
672. LUCY FRANCES, born Feb. 15, 1860.
673. CHARLES BUCKINGHAM, born June, 1861; died Aug.,
       1862.
674. HENRY APPLETON, born March 14, 1867, in Winona.

330.

AMBROSE WORTHINGTON of West Bloomfield, N. Y., married,
1st, about 1823, Clemanthe Larned, who died about 1828, in
Suffield, Conn. Mr. Worthington removed to Western New

York and married, 2nd, in 1832, at Geneseo, Abby Leach (b. 1807, in West Bloomfield, N. Y.), daughter of Payne Leach and Joanna Clark (b. Jan. 15, 1781, in Lyme, Conn.).   They lived at Geneseo for about five years, then removing to Canandaigua in 1845. " Mr. Worthington was one of the oldest and most respected citizens of West Bloomfield; he was at one time landlord of the old American Hotel in Geneseo, when the stage lines were the only public conveyances, and, together with his wife, made his house a favorite stopping-place for many weary travelers.   He afterwards kept the Canandaigua House, and made it famous far and near as a model hotel."

Mrs. Abby Worthington died Oct. 31, 1875, at West Bloomfield.

Mr. Ambrose Worthington died Jan. 29, 1888, at West Bloomfield.

CHILDREN BY 1ST WIFE.

†675.   WILLIAM WATSON, born March 16, 1825, at Agawam, Mass.

CHILDREN BY 2ND WIFE.

†676.   EDWARD FULLER, born March 18, 1845, in Geneseo, N. Y.

331.

JAMES WORTHINGTON, of Springfield, Mass., removed from Agawam, Mass., to Springfield, Mass., and married Mary Bouticon of Springfield.   They removed to Worcester, Mass., where he kept a hotel for several years, and then, returning to Springfield, he kept the Hampdon House.   Mr. Worthington died Dec. 15, 1838, at Springfield.   Had no ch.

335.

ROBERT WORTHINGTON of West Bloomfield, N. Y., where he removed, with his father, from Agawam, Mass., and succeeded him on the farm; married, Oct. 16, 1836, Louisa P. Rexford of Lima, N. Y. (b. March 10, 1809, in Lima, N. Y.), daughter of Micah Rexford and Pauline Holden.

Mr. Worthington died March 12, 1849.

Mrs. Louisa Worthington died Feb. 23, 1879.

CHILDREN.

677. MARY LOUISE, born Aug. 24, 1837; died April 24, 1854.

678. JAMES REXFORD, born Dec. 7, 1843, a farmer of West Bloomfield, N. Y.

339.

HENRY WORTHINGTON of Agawam, Mass., married, May 6, 1835, Henrietta Renton (b. Aug. 13, 1814, in Oxford, England), daughter of William Renton and Henrietta Rayne. Both Mr. and Mrs. Worthington are living (1892), and reside in the old homestead at Agawam. The land came to the grandfather of Henry Worthington upon the division of lands in West Springfield (now Agawam).

CHILDREN.

679. LASEVIRA JANE, born July 27, 1837, in Springfield, Mass.; married, May 16, 1861, John N. Cook, son of Ansel Cook and Saphionia Egleston.

CHILDREN.

1. Henry Ansel Cook, b. April 8, 1864.
2. Carrie Louise Cook, b. Feb. 24. 1871.
3. Frank Newton Cook, b. April 18, 1872; d. Dec. 15 1878.

680. HENRIETTA PHEBE, born March 26, 1839; died Oct. 18, 1840.

†681. HENRY ROLAND, born June 30, 1842, in Springfield, Mass.

682. ELLEN MARIA,   born June 21, 1847, in Springfield, Mass.; married, Nov. 24, 1870, Charles H. Woodsum (b. June 14, 1848, in Livermore Falls, Ma.), son of John Woodsum and Mary J. Harvev. Have no ch.

†683. ALBERT EDWIN, born Oct. 18, 1849.

340.

MINER WORTHINGTON of Westfield Mass., married, May 30, 1838, Nancy I. Flower (b. April 5, 1813).
Mrs. Nancy Worthington died May 9, 1883.

CHILDREN.

684. FANNY H.,   born June, 1840; married William C. Hatch, and died October 15, 1886.

685. EDWARD S.,   born Jan. 18, 1842; died Sept. 12, 1861, unmarried.

†686. CLARENCE M.,   born Sept. 17, 1844.
687. JULIA P ,   born Aug. 17, 1847; married, April
19, 1871, E. Hamilton Hills of
Hartford, Ct.

341.

JOB WORTHINGTON of Norwood, Mass. married, Sept. 16, 1846, Eliza J. Warner of Groveland, N. Y. (b. 1822, in Geneseo), daughter of David Warner and Hannah Welton.

Mr. Job Worthington died March 30, 1878. Had no children.

342.

HON. ROLAND WORTHINGTON of Boston, Mass.; married, April 25, 1854, Abbie Bartlett Adams (b., 1825, in Roxbury, Mass.), daughter of James Adams and Mary Williams.

Mr. Worthington was collector of the Port of Boston under President Garfield; has been member of the House of Representatives of Massachusetts, and is the principal owner of the Boston *Evening Traveller*.

CHILDREN.

688. JULIA HILL,   born March 5, 1854.
689. ROLAND, JR.,   born Nov. 10, 1858.
690. EDWARD ADAMS, born 1860; died 1862.
691. FANNIE SMITH,   born 1862.

343.

SOLOMON WORTHINGTON of Springfield, Mass., president of the "S. Worthington Paper Co." of Holyoke, Mass., married,

1st, Oct. 16, 1850; in Groveland, N. Y., Nancy L. Pray (b.
1826, in Groveland), daughter of James Pray of Groveland.
Mrs. Nancy Worthington died, Aug., 1852, and Mr. Worth
ington married, 2nd, April 18, 1854, in New York, Matilda
W. Westfall (b., 1829, in New York), daughter of George
Westfall of New York.

CHILDREN BY 1ST WIFE.

†692. JAMES ROLAND, born Aug. 11, 1851, in Brooklyn,
        N. Y.

CHILDREN BY 2ND WIFE.

693. CLARA MATILDA ,born Aug. 10, 1856; married, Sept.
        23, 1877, John Atwater of
        Brooklyn, N. Y

CHILDREN.

        1. Albert W. Atwater, born
            Dec. 23, 1880, in Brooklyn.

'694· ALBERT EDWARD born Oct. 15. 1860, in Brooklyn,
        N. Y.

347.

CAPTAIN RANSFORD WORTHINGTON of Agawam, Mass.,
married, Jan. 24, 1822, Betsey Roberts (b July 25, 1796, in
Middletown, Ct.), eldest daughter of William Roberts and
Beulah Hedges.

Captain Worthington died Oct. 15, 1878.

Mr. William Roberts was a Connecticut farmer, removing
from Middletown to Pittsfield, Mass., when his daughter
Betsey was quite young. After remaining there a short time,

they removed to Feeding Hills: in March, 1803, to the property still owned by the Roberts family. Mrs. Roberts and one of Mr. Roberts' sisters lived to the age of one hundred years. Betsey Roberts' early life was spent mostly at home and teaching school until 1822, when she married Captain Worthington, a builder in Agawam. The ceremony was performed by Squire David Worthington, father of Ransford, for the reason that.the pastor of the Baptist Church was away from home, and Ransford, being such a strong Baptist, would not consent to having a pastor of any other denomination. Ransford was a militia-man of the War of 1812, and also captain of a militia company, from which fact he was known in after years as Captain Ransford. Mrs. Betsey Worthington joined the Baptist Church in Agawam in 1826, and upon the celebration of her ninety-fifth birthday, on July 25, 1891, she was the only living member of that time.

Mrs. Betsey Worthington died May 11, 1892.

CHILDREN.

†695. SOLON ROBERTS, born Jan. 2, 1823.

†696. RANSFORD, 2ND, born Jan. 18, 1827, in Agawam.

697. LAURA JANE, born Jan. 2, 1825, in Agawam; married William H. Wheeler.

Mrs. Laura Wheeler died March 6, 1845.

Mr. Wheeler died Jan. 14, 1849, aged 28 years.

698. ADONIRAM JUDSON, born Oct. 1, 1831; died May 27, 1853.

†699. WILLIAM HENRY, born Jan. 3, 1839.

348.

DAVID WORTHINGTON, 2nd, of Suffield, Ct., married, April 6, 1824, Orpha Warriner (b. Dec. 25, 1798, in West Springfield, Mass.), daughter of Gad Warriner and Eunice Worthington, and granddaughter of Jonathan and Mary Purchase Worthington of Agawam.

Mrs. Orpha Worthington died Aug. 20, 1883.

Mr. David Worthington died Jan. 5, 1871.

CHILDREN.

700. ORPHA WARRINER, born Jan. 6, 1825; married, Sept. 12, 1844, Joseph Creighton Hastings (b. Oct. 5, 1822, in Suffield), son of William Hastings and Lydia Remington.

Mrs. Orpha Hastings died Nov. 12, 1866, in Suffield.

CHILDREN.

1. Judson Worthington Hastings, b. June 13, 1853, in Suffield; removed to Feeding Hills, Mass., and married, Nov. 18, 1880, Mary Matilda Thomson (b. March 30, 1852, in Monterey, Mass.), dau. of Lyman Thomson and Mary Lucinda Turner.

Mrs. Mary Hastings died June 2, 1892, in Feeding Hills, Mass.

DAVID WORTHINGTON.

Ch.

1. William Thomson Hastings, b. Dec. 2, 1881.
2. Joseph Remington Hastings, b. Oct. 17, 1883.
3. Percival Vining Hastings, b. Feb. 27, 1885.
4. Philip Worthington Hastings, b. March 4, 1887.
5. Creighton Hastings, b. Oct. 5, 1888; d. Oct. 10, 1888.
6. Helen Matilda Hastings, b. Oct. 16, 1891.

2. Charles William Hastings, b. July 27, 1855, in Suffield; m., May 5, 1879, Ellen Melinda Thomson (b. March 19, 1855, in Monterey, Mass.), dau. of Lyman Thomson and Mary Lucinda Turner.

Ch.

1. Henry Worthington Hastings, b. Feb. 1, 1883.
2. George Thomson Hastings, b. Aug. 11, 1885.
3. Mary Orpha Jane Hastings, b. Jan. 17, 1890.

701. HARRIET ANN, born Nov. 15, 1829, in Agawam, Mass.; died March 28, 1837.

349.

ALBERT WORTHINGTON of Amherst, Mass., married, July 31, 1821, Lucinda Moore (b. April 2, 1803, in Stafford, Ct.), daughter of Alexander Moore and Lavina Colburn.

Mr. Albert Worthington died Dec. 6, 1826, at Amherst.

Mrs. Lucinda Worthington died Feb. 27, 1884, at Wales.

CHILDREN.

702. MARY M.,   born Aug. 14, 1822, in Amherst;
married, Nov. 15, 1843, Abner
Needham of Stafford, Ct. (b.
Jan. 31, 1817, in Stafford), son
of Daniel Needham and Lucy
Green.

Mrs. Mary Needham died July
29, 1873. .

CHILDREN.

1. Adelbert Needham, b April 5,
1847, in Stafford, Ct.;
m., Aug. 6, 1872, Josephine
Turner (b. July 8, 1850, in
Coventry, Ct.), dau. of
Rufus Turner and Laura
Woodworth. Have no ch.
2. Isabella Needham, b. Oct.
9, 1848, in Stafford; d.
Aug. 22, 1849.
3. Arabella Needham, b. Oct.
9, 1848, in Stafford; m.,
Feb. 19, 1873, Chauncey
Orcutt (b. Dec. 13, 1840, in
Stafford), son of Harvey
Orcutt and Mary Ann
Billings. 1 dau.

703. ANGENE,   born April 14, 1827, in Amherst;
married, March 18, 1851, John

Tavlor of Stafford Springs, Ct. (b. March 26, 1830, in Cumberland, England), son of James Tavlor and Jane Heatherington.

Mrs. Angene Taylor died April 8, 1861.

CHILDREN.

1. George F. Taylor, b. March 18, 1853; d. Jan. 20, 1859.
2. John William Taylor, b. November 11, 1856; m., Aug. 10, 1881, Elizabeth Kinney, dau. of William Kinney and Sabina Monroe. 3 ch.
3. Albert Edward Taylor, b. March 13, 1859; d. Aug. 5, 1866.
4. Charles H. Tavlor, born March 28, 1861; d. April 20, 1861.

†704. ALBERT   born Nov. 8, 1823.

358.

LYNUS PERSONS WORTHINGTON of Grafton, N. Y., married, 1st, Betsey Ann Burdick (b. June 7, 1808, in Grafton).

Mrs. Betsey Worthington died July 1, 1837, and Mr. Worthington married, 2nd, Melinda Hall (b. May 28, 1818).

Mrs. Melinda Worthington died Aug. 12, 1843, and Mr. Worthington married, 3rd, Mrs. Hannah Louisa Haner Coonrad, widow of George Coonrad.

CHILDREN BY 1ST WIFE.

705. JERUSHA ANN,   born March 6, 1830; married James
                    Mills of Grafton, N. Y.; settled
                    at Janesville, Wis. Had a dau.,
                    Emma L. Mills, who m. Eugene
                    Le Clair, and settled at Black
                    River Falls, Wis. James and
                    Jerusha Mills are both deceased.
                    Eugene Le Clair and a child of
                    his died recently.
706. JULIA AUGUSTA, born March 29, 1832; died March
                    23, 1851.
707. LOVISA BUELAH, born July 18, 1833; died Oct. 8,
                    1867; unmarried.
708. LYNUS MELVIN, born Oct. 29, 1835,; died Aug. 6,
                    1836.
709. BETSEY ANN,   born Aug. 13, 1836; died May 5, 1837

CHILDREN BY 3RD WIFE.

†710. ALBERT   born Dec. 28, 1847, in Troy, N. Y.
711. EDGAR,   born Jan. 4, 1850; died Sept. 12,
                    1874.
712. ALICE AUGUSTA born Aug. 22, 1852; married, Dec. 2,
                    1874, Frederick A. Sharp of
                    Greenbush, N. Y. (b. May 21,
                    1852), son of Columbus Sharp
                    and Rachel Lancing.
                        Mrs. Alice Sharp died March
                    26, 1888.

CHILDREN.

1. Stella Mav Sharp. b. Jan.
   12, 1876.

2. Edna Lancing Sharp, b. Aug. 31, 1878.
3. Louisa Albertine Sharp, b. July 31, 1880.
4. Columbus Alexander Sharp, b. April 6, 1882; d. Nov. 28, 1882.
5. Marv Georgiana Sharp, b. May 11, 1884.

361.

DAVID FERRY WORTHINGTON of Troy, N. Y., married, Oct. 3, 1839, Elizabeth Hill (b. Jan. 20, 1819, in Grafton, N. Y.), daughter of James Hill and Lucretia Trumbull of Grafton.
Mr. David Worthington died Nov. 7, 1872, in Troy, N. Y.
Mrs. Elizabeth Worthington died March 3, 1884.

CHILDREN.

†713. JOHN,   born Aug. 1, 1840.

367.

AARON FERRE WORTHINGTON of Petersburgh, N. Y. married, Sept. 22, 1851, Harriet Chapman (b. Aug. 28, 1828, in Troy, N. Y.), daughter of Aaron Chapman.
Mr. Aaron Worthington died Oct. 25, 1868, in Petersburgh, N. Y
Mrs. Harriet Worthington died July 4, 1890.

CHILDREN.

714. HELEN FRANCES, born Sept. 30, 1852; married Niles Thurber.

CHILDREN.

1. Dollie Thurber, b. Sept. 8, 1877.

368.

DAVID ROSS WORTHINGTON of Petersburgh, N. Y., married, April 1, 1836, Roxana Allen (b. Aug. 31, 1813), daughter of Jeremiah Allen and Martha Jones.

Mr. David Worthington died Dec. 19, 1844, and his widow married, in 1856 or 7, Thomas Johnson, and had two children:

> Francis Allen Johnson, b. March 1, 1859.
>
> Addison J. Johnson, b. Sept. 1, 1861.

Mrs. Roxana Worthington Johnson died June 11, 1873.

CHILDREN.

715. PAULINA ABIGAIL, born Jan. 1, 1837.
716. DELIGHT   born April 3. 1838; died Feb. 20, 1841.
717. AARON FERRE,   born Jan. 4, 1840; died June 25, 1840.
718. MARTHA PRISCILLA, born Sept. 15, 1841; married, May 15, 1863, Durham O. Abel of Hoosic Falls, N. Y., son of James Abel and Anna Sherman.

CHILDREN.

1. Arthur Worthington Abel, b. Feb. 16, 1864.
2. Charles D. Abel, b. June 13, 1865.

3. Albert F. Abel, b. Oct. 6, 1866.
4. Mattie Pauline Abel, b. Feb. 14, 1868.
5. Fernie Abel, b. March 7, 1870.
6. Anna D. Abel, b. Aug. 27, 1872.
7. Solon H. Abel, b. Feb. 27, 1873.
8. Edric R. Abel, b. Nov. 2, 1876.
9. Anson Abel, b. July 11, 1878.
10. Frank S. Abel, b. Dec. 29, 1880.

719. CALPHURNA MALINE, born April 19, 1844, in Petersburgh, N. Y.; married, March 25, 1884, J. W. Hiney of Southington, Ct. (b. Aug. 2, 1829, in Albany, N. Y.), son of William F. Hiney and Edith Hollenbeck.

CHILDREN.

1. Worthington L. Hiney, b. Nov. 6, 1885; died Aug. 25, 1886.

369.

WILLIAM CHAPIN WORTHINGTON married Eunice Veren, daughter of Joseph?

Mr. Worthington died Aug. 6, 1856. Had no children.

371.

WINFIELD SCOTT WORTHINGTON of Petersburgh, N. Y.,
married, July 4, 1846, Miranda Tifft (b. March 21, 1829, in
Petersburgh), daughter of William V. Tifft and Sally Mitchell.

CHILDREN.

720. SEDINIA D.,   born March 6, 1847, in Petersburgh ·
                        died March 8, 1848.
†721. AARON AMBROSE, born June 19, 1850, in Petersburgh.
722. MARY M   born Feb. 5, 1854, in Petersburgh;
                        died Aug. 3, 1854.
723. ANN CHELENE,   born Nov. 28, 1858, in Farmington
                        Ill.; married, Dec. 25, 1883,
                        Myron E. Clark (b. Feb. 24,
                        1857, in Grafton, N. Y.), son of
                        Edwin R. Clark and Lois J.
                        Brock.

CHILDREN.

                        1. Ruthven Scott Clark, b.
                        Feb. 1, 1885; d. Dec. 28,
                        1889.

724. ABIGAIL ROSS,   born Dec. 18, 1860, in Trivoli, Ill.;
                        married, Jan. 7, 1880, Henry
                        B. Harra (b. March 9, 1860, in
                        New York), Son of Charles
                        Harra and Sarah Blott.
†725. WINFIELD SCOTT, 2ND, born May 26, 1864, in Trivoli,
                        Ill.

372.

JOHN MAIN WORTHINGTON of Petersburgh, N. Y., married 1st, Judith Ann Rowland of Pittstown, N. Y., and, 2nd, Mrs. Allen Surdam.

Mr. John Worthington died Oct. 3, 1875.

CHILDREN.

726. SARAH FRANCES, born Sept. 6, 1845; married a Mr. Card of Dakota Territory

727. MARVETTE, born May 13, 1845, in Pittstown, N. Y.; married, Aug. 31, 1865, Amaziah A. Fillmore of Rural Hill, N. Y. (b. in Ellisburgh, N. Y.), son of Orsen B. Fillmore and Susan Ann Lyons of Rural Hill, N. Y.

CHILDREN.

1. Orsen D. Fillmore, b. Nov. 23, 1867.

728. EMERLINE, born ———; died Apr. 11, 1890; married Hiram Jones of Petersburgh, N Y

†729. ELLIOT HOAGE, born Aug. 2, 1848, in Petersburgh, N. Y.

374.

HARVEY REYNOLDS WORTHINGTON of Grafton, N. Y., married, July 8, 1847, Sally Jane Beckwith (b. in 1826, in Pownal, Vt.), daughter of Henry V. Beckwith of Troy, N. Y.

Mrs. Sally Worthington died Oct. 30, 1888.

CHILDREN.

†730   JOHN LINUS,   born April 11, 1826, in Pownal, Vt.

377.

DAVID MORTIMER WORTHINGTON of Rural Hill, N. Y., married, Oct. 12, 1856, Abigail Thompson (b. March 7, 1836, in Ellisburgh, N. Y.), daughter of William Thompson.

CHILDREN.

†731.   THOMAS SETH,   born Dec. 23, 1856, in Ellisburgh, N. Y.

732.   HATTIE ELIZABETH, born Oct. 17, 1858; died Aug. 3, 1880; unmarried.

733.   MARY ANN,   born July 31, 1862, in Woodville, N. Y.; married, Nov. 21, 1880, John Hagadone (b. June 30, 1855, in Ellisburgh, N. Y.), son of Martin C. Hagadone and Anna B. Curtis.

CHILDREN.

1. Ethel Loberta Hagadone, b. Dec. 25, 1881, in Belleville, N. Y.
2. David Martin Hagadone, b. March 9, 1884, in Woodville, N. Y.
3. Mvstie Eula Hagadone, b. Feb. 19, 1888, in Rural Hill N. Y.

381.

HARVEY WORTHINGTON of Concord, N. H., married, 1st, Rosa Hyland, who died Oct., 1869. Married, 2nd, Aug. 5, 1870, Julia Howes, widow of William F. Carr. She was b. Dec. 20, 1829, in Norwich, Vt., daughter of David Howes and Lucinda Blaisdell.

CHILDREN BY 1ST WIFE.

734. GEORGE THOMAS, born May 27, 1860.

CHILDREN BY 2ND WIFE.

735. ESTELLA, born Dec. 2, 1873.

382.

THOMAS E. WORTHINGTON of New Haven, Ct., married, Sept, 3, 1867, Mary Jane Pardee (b. Aug. 25, 1847, in Oxford, Ct.), daughter of William L. Pardee and Sarah E. Sacket.

CHILDREN.

736. MARY EVALINA, born Feb. 6, 1872; died July 8, 1872. An adopted daughter.

383.

GEORGE WORTHINGTON of Gilmanton, N. H., married, Feb. 13, 1867, Sarah Abbie Loche (b. Dec. 20. 1845, in Gilmanton, N. H.), daughter of Reuben Loche and Eliza Shaw.

CHILDREN.

737. HARVEY JAMES, born Nov. 28, 1867; died March 22, 1873.

738. GEORGE THOMAS, born Sept. 28, 1869.
739. GRACE BELLE,   born Aug. 3, 1878.
740. ETHEL MAY   born July 18, 1883.

393.

WATSON ALFRED WORTHINGTON of Hinsdale Mass., married, Nov. 26, 1857, Martha Jane Lyons (b. Aug. 22, 1831, in Wales, Mass.), daughter of Lyman Lyons and Lydia Eaton.

Mr. Worthington died June 16, 1884, and his widow married, Aug. 11, 1886, Rev. A. A. Robinson of Packerville, Ct.

CHILDREN.

741. CHARLES SPURGEON, born Jan. 30, 1859, in Hinsdale; died July 30, 1873.
742. EVA CARRIE,   born April 3, 1863, in W. Woodstock, Ct.; died June 1, 1866.

394.

LEWIS NELSON WORTHINGTON of Agawam, Mass., married, Aug. 20, 1863, Alice Sophia Cowles (b. Oct. 28, 1838, in Palermo, N. Y.), daughter of Samuel Cowles and Sally Perkins of Oswego, N. Y.

CHILDREN.

†743. FREDERICK ALFRED, born Sept. 1, 1864.
744. ALICE ROAE,   born Feb. 12, 1877.

401.

WILLIAM LESTER WORTHINGTON of Centreville, Mich.; married, Sept. 6, 1846, Catherine Hale (b. July 18, 1823, in Wayne Co., N. Y.), daughter of Chester Hale and Susan ——.

Mrs. Catherine Worthington died Jan. 8, 1876, and Mr. Worthington married for his second wife, on May 10, 1883, Sarah J. Strong (b. Jan. 9, 1840), daughter of Gager Strong and Laurinda Fuller.

CHILDREN BY 1ST WIFE.

745. CAROLINE MERRILL, born July 16, 1847, in Flowerfield, Mich.; married, Jan. 1, 1867, John J. Hasbrouck of Centreville, Mich. (b. Jan. 25, 1842, in N. Y. State), son of John Hasbrouck and Rachel Ann Ostrander.

CHILDREN.

1. Jennie B. Hasbrouck, b June 22, 1874.
2. Hugh Earl Hasbrouck. b. Aug. 17, 1881.
3. Edward Hasbrouck, b. July 31, 1883.

746. HENRY WHITED born December 23, 1849.
747. FLORILLA, born June 3, 1852.
†748. CHARLES EDWARD, born Oct. 24, 1854, in Flowerfield, Mich.
749. ELVA LUELLA, born Oct. 11, 1856; died Oct. 20, 1875.
750. GEORGE BARTLETT, born Aug. 5, 1859.
751. WILLIAM BARTLETT, born Sept. 5, 1861, in Flowerfield, Mich.
752. SARAH JANE, born Jan. 10, 1864, in Centreville, Mich.; married, Dec. 9, 1885, Charles Hovev of Centreville

(b. March 30, 1861, in Marcel-
lus, N. Y.), son of Charles
William Hovey and Rachel Ann
Hopper.

CHILDREN.

1. Vera Genevie Hovey, b. Jan.
    13, 1887.

753. CATHERINE HARRIET, born Jan. 20, 1867, in Centreville, Mich.; married, March 10,
1884, Clifford Dougherty of
same place (b. May 17, 1864, in
St. Joseph Co., Mich.), son of
Robert Henry Dougherty and
Mary Louise Thomas.

CHILDREN.

1. Hazel Dougherty, b. Aug. 4,
    1889, in Centreville.

754. LAURA IRINE,   born ——; married, April 16, 1891
Olio A. Wilson.

402.

WARREN SYLVESTER WORTHINGTON of Webster City, Iowa.
Can learn nothing of him.   Is said to have married and had
one child, who died young.

405.

THEODORE WORTHINGTON of Texas, Mich., married, March
9, 1859, Sarah E. Nelson (b. June 23, 1842, in Cass Co.,
Mich.), daughter of Asahel Nelson and Marium Bates.
Mrs. Sarah Worthington died Jan. 3, 1883.

CHILDREN.

755. GEORGE FRANKLIN, born Aug. 11, 1861; died Sept. 30
1861.
†756. HARRY A.,   born Dec. 27, 1866.

408.

WILLIAM WORTHINGTON of Rockford Ill., son of Joel and
Rachael (Warriner) Worthington of Enfield, Ct., and Springfield, Mass., was born July 5, 1813, in Enfield, Ct. When
quite young his parents, with their two sons, William and
Henry, removed to Ohio, where they remained some years, and
where his father died, and his mother married Joshua Howes.
In the spring of 1838 the family again moved westward, and
settled in Rockford, Ill. There, for forty-eight years, and
until his death, on April 11, 1886, William Worthington con-
tinned to reside. A long residence of nearly half a century of
continual business activity and prominence as a member of
the Methodist church, had made him better known through
out the town and county than most citizens not before the
public in an official capacity. He was closely identified with
the early history of the bustling city. Coming when but a
mere handful of pioneers had settled on the banks of the Rock
river, the enterprising young man was warmly welcomed in
the settlement. Though the new arrival had but seven dollars
in his pocket, his push and enterprise soon made a place for
him in Rockford. For some years he was a clerk for Daniel
S. Haight, who was postmaster and kept a general store.
Subsequently he went to farming, and in later years often
related how he used to cultivate corn where the business
blocks of the East Side now stand. It was after this experience that he appeared in the community as the village
blacksmith, and the first smith to set up an anvil in Rockford.

His shop was located at the corner of what is now East State and First streets, where he owned two lots. The street then sloped, by a steep incline, to the river edge. Subsequently it was graded up ten or twelve feet, and the site of the first smith's shop was buried. He gave up the business in 1843 and sold the two lots for $450. A few feet was sold from them in 1883 for $10,000. During 1843, Dr. Searl and Mr. Worthington opened the first drug store in Rockford. They continued the business under the firm name of Searl & Worthington until 1850, when Dr. Searl retired and Mr. John Thurston was taken into partnership. Worthington & Thurston were the first owners of the stone quarry located on the river bank south of the city. They opened the quarry, which has been in constant use ever since. The first stone quarried on the East Side was used in erecting their large block on East street. There the drug store was enlarged and the business increased. At the drug store, in that day, the politicians met and talked up the questions of the day; there the local sages congregated, and it was in their store that the campaign against the Driscolls and their band of marauders was planned. In 1868 Mr. Worthington sold out to Mr. Robert Rowland and spent the winter in Florida. Three years later he purchased the drug store of Currier & Morton on East Main street, where he remained until moving into the present store in the new block, built in 1885 by his son William Henry Worthington. In 1881 he had taken into partnership his two sons, William H. and Frank Harrison, who still conduct the business under the firm name of W. H. Worthington & Co.

Mr. William Worthington was a prominent Methodist, and helped build the " First Church " that stood on South Second street, where the " Centennial Church " now stands.

He married, Oct. 27, 1844, at Little Fort, now Waukegan, Ill., Maria Baker (b. Nov. 30, 1824), who died Oct. 2, 1846, and Mr. Worthington married his second wife, Aug. 3, 1847, Eliza Kellogg (b. June 14, 1823), daughter of Roderick Kellogg and Sarah Taylor of Clarendon, Ohio.

Mr. William Worthington died April 11, 1886, at Rockford, Ill.

CHILDREN BY 1ST WIFE.

757. ALBERT,   born Sept. 11, 1845, in Rockford; died Sept. 26, 1846.

CHILDREN BY 2ND WIFE.

758. ELLA,   born June 20, 1848, in Rockford; died May 2, 1852, in Rockford.
759. JULIA LENA,   born Nov. 29, 1852, in Rockford.
†760. WILLIAM HENRY, born Nov. 4, 1854, in Rockford.
761. FRANK HARRISON, born Aug. 23, 1856, in Rockford.
762. CHARLES READE, born Sept. 17, 1858, in Rockford.
763. IDA,   born Jan. 6, 1865, in Rockford; died Dec. 10, 1865, in Rockford.

409.

REV. HENRY WORTHINGTON of Douangiac, Mich., married, 1st, in 1839, Jane Mills (b. Aug. 23, 1821, in Victory, N. Y.), daughter of Ammon Mills and Betsey McIntyre.

She died in 1861, and Rev. Mr. Worthington married, 2nd, in 1862, Mary Clower (b. Sept. 21, 1829, in Monroeville, Ohio), daughter of Eber Root and Mary Gamble.

Rev. Henry Wortbington died July 10, 1881, in Douangiac, Mich.

CHILDREN BY 1ST WIFE.

764. RACHAEL,   born 1842, in West Leroy, Mich.; married, Jan. 6, 1869, Vernon

Horace Smith of Ionia, Ill. (b.
Dec. 29, 1838, in Canada), son
of Ansel Smith and Phebe Cross.

CHILDREN.

1. Henry Horace Smith, b.
   Mav 1, 1873.
2. Arthur Maurice Smith, b.
   Feb. 16, 1875.
3. Bertha Lucy Smith, b. April
   12, 1877; died July 30, 1877.
4. Laurence Smith, b. June
   25, 1881.
5. Jessie Smith, b. Aug. 12,
   1883.

†765. WILLIAM HENRY, born Sept. 1, 1846.
†766. MELVIN,   born Feb. 26, 1852, in Utica, Mich.
†767. ALBERT ARTHUR, born Mav 1, 1857, in Battle Creek,
          Mich.

410.

GEORGE WASHINGTON WORTHINGTON of Shelter Island L. I.,
married, Dec. 28, 1859, Mary C. Raynor (b. Dec. 31, 1836),
daughter of Edward Ravnor and Mary Danes of Shelter
Island.

Mr. George Worthington died May 23, 1867.
Mrs. Mary Worthington died Jan. 25, 1885.

CHILDREN.

768. WILLIS WOODFORD, born Nov. 14, 1860, in Shelter
          Island.

413.

JOHN TYLER WORTHINGTON of Lawrence, L. I., married, March 14, 1867, Julia A. Robinson (b. June 12, 1848), daughter of John Robinson and Rebecca Barteau of Moriches, L. I.

CHILDREN.

769.	HENRY C.,	born Dec. 31, 1869.
770.	EMMA M.,	born Sept. 28, 1870; died July 16, 187?
771.	ROBERT T.	born June 10, 1873.
772.	REGINALD,	born Aug. 4, 1878.
773.	JOHN BARTEAU,	born June 25, 1880.

417.

JONATHAN BRADFORD WORTHINGTON of Middle Island, L. I., married, April 17, 1876, Mrs. Ellen Terry of Riverhead, L. I. (b. June 6, 1850, in New York), widow of Silas Terry; her mother's maiden name being Ellen Burns.

CHILDREN.

774.	CLIFFORD,	born Feb. 22, 1879.
775.	BLANCH,	born Feb. 14, 1882; died Dec. 3, 1887.
776.	BRADFORD,	born June 18, 1886.

432.

JAMES BURKE WORTHINGTON of Bridge Hampton, L. I., N. Y., married, June 25, 1868, Mary Cook (b. May 21, 1847, in Bridge Hampton, L. I.), daughter of Samuel Cook and Hannah E. Dimon.

CHILDREN.

777. EDITH G.,   born May 29, 1874, in Bridge Hamp-
                        ton.
778. LEROY C.,   born Jan. 28. 1877, in Bridge Hamp-
                        ton ; died Jan. 23, 1883.
779. MARY FLORENCE, born Feb. 20, 1884, in Bridge Hamp-
                        ton.

435.

JOHN ALONZO WORTHINGTON of Riverhead, L. I., N. Y., mar-
ried, 1st, June 15, 1875, Winifred Terry (b. 1854, in Moriches,
L. I.), daughter of Captain Charles B. Terry and Maria
Osborne. She died Jan. 1879, and Mr. Worthington married,
2nd, Jan. 31, 1885, Ida Cook (b. Feb. 28, 1857, in Brooklyn,
N. Y.), an adopted daughter of her uncle, Rev. Mr. Cook of
Riverhead, L. I., and daughter of Edward and Sarrissa Cook.

CHILDREN BY 1ST WIFE.

780. CALVIN,   born ——, 1876; died at 3 weeks old.
No children by 2nd wife.

438.

WILLIS COLEMAN WORTHINGTON of Rochester, N. Y., married, Oct. 23, 1890. Josephine A. Ron.

CHILDREN.

781 MARJORIE LOUISE, born Aug. 13, 1891, in Rochester.

445.

THADDEUS WORTHINGTON of Yorkshire Centre, N. Y., married, Feb. 24, 1830, Sally Ann Wilkes (b. June 9, 1808).

Mr. Thaddeus Worthington died Sept. 23, 1867, in Yorkshire, N. Y.

Mrs. Sally Worthington died Jan. 10, 1889, in Farmersville, N. Y.

CHILDREN.

782. JAMES,   born Dec. 20, 1830; died April 5, 1835.
†783. MYRON,   born Dec. 3, 1832.
†784. JOHN,   born June 9, 1834, in Freedom, N. Y.
785. OLIVE,   born April 20, 1836; died Sept. 6, 1865.
786. AMANDA,   born March 20, 1838, in Freedom, N. Y.; married, April 1, 1861 Russell Worthington of Farmersville, N. Y. (b. March 8, 1839), son of Samuel Worthington and Comfort Osborn.
†787. CHARLES,   born Jan. 25, 1840, in Freedom, N.Y.
788. LYDIA J.,   born Jan. 20, 1842, in Freedom, N. Y.; married, Dec. 4, 1866, H. W. Huyck of Arcade, N. Y. (b. Oct. 27, 1844, in Franklinville, N.Y.), son of M. H. Huyck and J. A. Greenwood.

CHILDREN.

1. Ada J. Huyck, b. March 19, 1870.

2. George M. Huyck, b. Dec. 17, 1873.

789. SALLY ANN,   born October 4, 1843, in Freedom, N Y.; died July 16, 1864.

790. MARIA M.,   born Dec. 16, 1845, in Sandusky, N. Y.; married, March 13, 1865, George S. Romley of Paxico, Kansas (b. Nov. 30' 1842, in Farmersville, N. Y.), son of Nathaniel S. Romley and Hannah Carpenter.

CHILDREN.

1. Charles W. Romlev, b. July 9, 1867.
2. May M. Romley, b. Nov. 17, 1878.

791. MARY N.,   born Nov. 19, 1847; married, in 1869, in Arcade, N. Y., Walter Roe, and died July 11, 1873, in Pennsylvania.

CHILDREN.

1. Bertha A. Roe, b. Sept. 21, 1870, in Yorkshire, N. Y.

447.

SAMUEL WORTHINGTON, a farmer of Farmersville, N. Y.; married Comfort Osborn (b. May 14, 1799).

Mr. Samuel Worthington died May 3, 186/.

Mrs. Comfort Worthington died July 18, 1881.

CHILDREN.

792. HANNAH,   born Oct. 30, 1832.
793. SALLY,   born Aug. 15, 1834, in Freedom, N. Y.
794. JACOB,   born July 14, 1837.
†795. RUSSELL,   born March 8, 1839.
796. GILES,   born Sept. 1, 1841.
†797. MILES,   born Jan. 13, 1844, in Farmersville, N. Y.

448.

JOHN WORTHINGTON, 2nd, of Farmersville, N. Y., a local preacher of the Methodist Episcopal Church, married, Sept. 27, 1829, Maria Cornwell (b. March 26, 1808), daughter of Israel Cornwell and Mary Mason.

Mr. John Worthington died Nov. 6, 1865.

Mrs. Maria Worthington died June 30, 1864.

CHILDREN.

†798. DE BIAS,   born June 27, 1830, in Freedom, N.Y.
†799. GEORGE WASHINGTON, born Aug. 7, 1833, in Freedom, N. Y.
†800. RANDOLPH,   born July 26, 1834, in Wales, N. Y.
†801. WILLIAM FRANK, born Dec. 18, 1836, in Farmersville N. Y.
†802. IRA CATLIN,   born July 16, 1841; in Farmersville, N. Y.
†803. LEONARD MASON, born April 12, 1844, in Farmersville, N. Y.

450.

SQUIRE WORTHINGTON, a farmer of Farmersville, N. Y., married, Jan. 29, 1834, Annise Preston (b. April 8, 1808, in Mass.), daughter of Jacob Preston.

Mr. Squire Worthington died July 20, 1890.
Mrs. Annise Worthington died April 10, 1872.

CHILDREN.

†804. SYLVESTER B., born Nov. 28, 1836, in Farmersville, N. Y.

†805. HENRY, born Sept. 21, 1838, in Farmersville, N. Y.

806. LUCINA M., born July 5, 1840, in Farmersville, N. Y.

807. LOIS ANN, born Jan. 22, 1842, in Great Valley N. Y.; married, Oct. 29, 1873, David R. Watson (b. March 5, 1806, in Washington Co., N. Y.), son of Andrew Watson and Hannah Worthington of York, N. Y.

Mr. David Watson died Oct. 6, 1890.

CHILDREN.

1. Walter D. Watson, b. Jan. 25, 1875, in York, N. Y.

459.

HERMAN WORTHINGTON of Fulton, Whiteside Co., Ill., married, April 5, 1865, Mary Hollinshead (b. July 21, 1839, in Whiteside Co., Ill.), daughter of John Hollinshead and Elizabeth Rush.

CHILDREN.

808. SARAH ELIZABETH, born Sept. 26, 1873, in Ustick, Ill

809. MARY   born Nov. 18, 1876, in Ustick, Ill.

460.

SOLOMON FISK WORTHINGTON of Winfield, Queens Co., L. I., N. Y., married, Nov. 10, 1890, Elizabeth Merrifield.

SEVENTH GENERATION.

466.

ELIAS MORGAN WORTHINGTON of Monroe, Mich., married, Nov. 8, 1832, Emily Pierce (b. March 28, 1809), daughter of Azel Pierce and Eliza Brewster of Lebanon, Ct.

Mr. Elias Worthington died Aug. 30, 1840, in Monroe, Mich.

CHILDREN.

810. MARGARET ELIZA, born Sept. 16, 1834, in Colchester, Ct.; married Deacon Alden A. Baker of Colchester.

CHILDREN.

1. Arthur Pierce Baker, b 1861.
2. Lillias Harriet Baker, b 1865.

†811. CHARLES ALFRED, born Aug. 4, 1837, in Monroe.

812. ELIAS,   born Nov. 8, 1840, in Monroe; died in 1849.

470.

OLCOTT WORTHINGTON of Colchester, Ct., married, May 19, 1836, Sophia Welles, daughter of John Welles of Colchester. Mrs. Sophia Worthington died Dec. 19, 1864, in Colchester. Mr. Olcott Worthington died Jan. 18, 1884. No children.

482.

HENRY ROSSITER WORTHINGTON of Irvington on Hudson, N. Y., married, Sept. 24, 1839, Laura I. Newton, daughter of Commodore John Thomas Newton of Alexandria, Virginia.

Mr. Worthington died Dec. 7, 1880, in New York City

Mrs. Laura Worthington died March 1, 1893.

Mr. Worthington was vice-president of the American Society of Mechanical engineers and "had earned a high place as an ingenious inventor and a successful engineer, and his work will leave an indelible impress upon professional practice; but the influence and traditions of him as a man and a friend will outlive generations of engineers.

"The foundation of this mingled esteem and affection was his intense and abiding love of the truth; the foundation was built upon by scientific methods, and the structure was adorned by personal graces and accomplishments. The love of truth, that came to him from a high-minded ancestry, was nurtured by his professional pursuits—for his profession, unlike some other professions, and this is their misfortune, not their fault, has one inevitable criterion, and that is the truth. This sentiment—for it grew in him from a conviction to a sentiment—not only controlled his professional and private conduct, but it stimulated in him an honest skepticism regarding those beliefs in general which have come down to us with no higher authority than that they are an inheritance. He

HENRY ROSSITER WORTHINGTON.

was a willing and valiant assailant of "humbug" in every form; and, nobler than this, he was the patient iconoclast who dispelled the phantoms in the mind of many an inventor, and who saved many a plodding experimenter—not in applied science alone—from impending disaster.

"But he was also endowed with a grand humanity, which practice perfected. Nor were his friends, so called, the sole beneficiaries; only a long and intimate fellowship with him has discovered many of his private charities, and the half of them will probably never be known.

"These attributes found apt and eloquent expression in his scholarly culture, and brilliancy in his spontaneous and perennial wit. As the patient, but not generally unimpassioned, advocate of a truth, or as the exposer of a fallacy or an imposture, by analysis, by analogy, by ridicule, he had few equals."

"Mr. Worthington was undoubtedly the first proposer and constructor of the direct steam-pump. The duplex system in pumping-engines—one engine actuating the steam valves of the other, causing a pause of the pistons at the end of the stroke, so that the water-valves can seat themselves quietly and preserve a uniform water pressure, thus being a vast improvement on the Cornish engine—is generally admitted to be one of the most ingenious and effective, and certainly one of the most largely applied advances in modern engineering.

"Mr. Worthington was chiefly known as a hydraulic engineer, but apart from this specialty his experimental and practical contributions to other departments of engineering, such as canal steam navigation, compound engines, instruments of precision and machine tools, would entitle him to a high position in the profession."

CHILDREN.

†813. HENRY FRAZER.
†814. CHARLES CAMPBELL.
815. AMALIE STUART NEWTON, married, 1st, Edward M.
Whitehouse, 2nd, Thomas
Whiteside Rae.

CH. BY 1ST HUSBAND.

1. Worthington Whitehouse.
2. Edward Whitehouse.

CH. BY 2ND HUSBAND.

1. Zard Newton Rae.

816. SARA NEWTON,   married William Lauman Bull.

CHILDREN.

1. Frederick Bull.
2. Henry Worthington Bull.
3. Lauman Bull.

487.

ROBERT HÉRBERT WORTHINGTON, M. D., of Berkley, Va.,
was assistant surgeon in Pickett's Division C. S. A.; married,
April 13, 1869, at Ingleside, Princess Ann Co., Va., Sarah J
B. Scott (b. Oct. 11, 1840, in Perquimans Co., N. C.), daughter
of William Copeland Scott and Mary Elizabeth Brown of
Princess Ann Co.   Mrs. Mary Elizabeth Scott was a
daughter of Joseph Armitt Brown of Philadelphia and niece
of Charles Brockden Brown, the first American novelist.
Dr. Robert Worthington died May 12, 1886, in Berkley, Va.

817. MARY ELIZABETH, born Sept. 4, 1871, in Ingleside, Va.; married, Dec. 15, 1891, in Berkley, Va., William Spencer Grinalds (b. Sept. 14, 1857, in Norfolk Co., Va.), son of Henry Clay Grinalds and Sarah Fletcher.

488.

GEORGE WASHINGTON WORTHINGTON married Mrs. Katherine Howlett. Mr. Worthington died Feb. 22, 1885.
No children.

490.

DENISON WORTHINGTON, a lawyer of Rockey Mount, North Carolina, married Mrs. Julia Monroe (Wheeler) Mebane of Murfreesboro, N. C., niece of Hon. John H. Wheeler, who was U. S. Minister to Nicaragua, and of Junius B. Wheeler, Col., U. S. Engineer, Professor at West Point.

818. ALICE ELIZABETH.
819. SAMUEL WHEELER.

491.

HERBERT LIVINGSTON WORTHINGTON, a lawyer of Norfolk, Virginia, married, Nov. 18, 1883, Mrs. Elizabeth DeFerris (Kimberly) Benbury.
No children.

495.

DANIEL CHARLES WORTHINGTON of Norfolk, Virginia, married, Oct. 21, 1884,. Lydia Sylvester (b. Aug. 22, 1853, in Norfolk Co., Virginia), daughter of Miles Wilson Sylvester and Charlotte Old.

CHILDREN.

820. ALICE JULIA,   born Oct. 17, 1885; died Nov. 16, 1885.
821. WILLIAM WILSON, born April 27, 1890.

498.

ROBERT SEARING WORTHINGTON of Oak Park, Chicago, Illinois, assistant secretary of Board of Trade and manager of Board of Trade building, Chicago; married, Feb. 12 1861, Elnora Esther Cobb (b. July 13, 1839, in Eaton, N.Y.), daughter of Nathan Cobb and Esther DeLoss.

CHILDREN.

822. MARTHA ELNORA born Nov. 17, 1865; married, Dec. 5, 1888, Henry Bogart Richardson of Oak Place, Ill., son of William Richardson and Mary A. C. Bogart.

CHILDREN.

1. Robert Worthington Richardson, b. Oct. 18, 1890, in Oak Place.

501.

DENISON LA GRANGE WORTHINGTON. Lived at Summit, Wis.; Madison, Wis., and Oak Park, Illinois. Married, in 1882, Edith Harrison. •
Mr. Worthington died May 10, 1885, in Oak Park.
No children.

502.

WILLIAM HENRY WORTHINGTON. Lived at Summit and Madison, Wis.; Chicago, Ill.; and Denver, Colorado. Married, Nov. 17, 1868, Jennie Thompson (b. April 19, 1846, in Cincinnati, Ohio), daughter of Oliver Hopkins Thompson and Emma Ann Hearth.
Mr. William Worthington died July 20, 1881, in Denver, where he had been a dealer in real estate.

CHILDREN.

823.	MARY,	born April 16, 1872.
824.	DENISON,	born May 11, 1875.
825.	BESSIE,	born Aug. 25, 1877; died Feb. 23, 1882.

505.

JAMES LA GRANGE WORTHINGTON, a merchant in Chicago. Lived at Summit and Madison, Wis., and now at Oak Park, Ill. Married, Oct. 26, 1882, Ella Louise Anderson (b. Feb. 7, 1857, in Philadelphia, Pa.), daughter of William Harkness Anderson and Hannah Y. Pickands.

CHILDREN.

826· ETHEL,   born Jan. 8, 1884.
827. MIRIAM,   born March 4' 1888.

506.

GERRIT HAZARD WORTHINGTON of Madison, Wis., and Oak Park, Ill.; manager Western Department of Continental Fire Insurance Co.; married, April 16, 1884, Susie Maude Ingman (b. Aug. 10, 1863, in Madison, Wis.), daughter of Lucius Smith Ingman and Sarah Jane Bowen.

CHILDREN.

828· LA GRANGE,   born Jan. 15, 1885.
829. VIRGINIA,   born Nov. 11, 1886.
830. ROBERT INGMAN born Dec. 9, 1888.

508.

ELLIS WORTHINGTON of Hartford, Ct., married, 1st, Oct. 9 1844' Gertrude Catherine H. De Lamater (b. Aug. 22, 1817, in Sheffield, Mass.), daughter of Professor John De Lamater M.D., of Cleveland, Ohio, and Ruth Angell. Mrs. Gertrude Worthington died Feb. 14, 1866; and Mr. Worthington married, 2nd, March 5, 1867, Sophia Beckwith, daughter of George Beckwith and Ruth Matson Beckwith of Palmyra, N. Y

Mr. Ellis Worthington died Nov. 28, 1871, at Palmyra, N. Y.

CHILDREN.

†831. CHARLES ELLIS, born Jan. 4, 1849, in Cleveland, O.
832. FREDERICK FISHER, born Dec. 9, 1855.

509.

ALBERT WORTHINGTON of Norwood, Mass., married, Feb., 1850, Caroline Leonard, daughter of Zadolk Leonard and Caroline Blackman.

Mr. Albert Worthington died Feb. 12 1889.

CHILDREN.

†833.	GEORGE,	born Feb. 27, 1851.
834.	ALBERT,	born March 25, 1853; died Oct. 29, 1859.
835.	ELLIS,	born Dec. 7, 1855.
†836.	LUCIUS,	born Sept. 21, 1858.
837.	LYDIA MAY,	born Oct. 19, 1863; died May 6, 1881.

510.

ERASTUS WORTHINGTON, a lawyer of Dedham, Mass., married, Nov. 25, 1861, Elizabeth Foster Briggs (b. Aug. 2, 1830, in Boston, Mass.), daughter of Robert Briggs and Caroline Morton.

CHILDREN.

838. CAROLINE MORTON, born Nov. 4, 1862.
839. ERASTUS. born Dec. 12, 1863.
840· ROBERT BRIGGS, born July 22, 1866.
841. ALVAN FISHER, born Nov. 29, 1867.
842. ARTHUR MORTON, born March 30, 1870.
843. JOHN WINTHROP, born Nov. 28, 1872.

511.

DAVID SAMUEL WORTHINGTON of Sandusky, Ohio, married, March 27, 1842, in Niagara Co., N. Y., Emily Temperance

Spalding (b. Nov. 30,1815, in Berkshire Co., Mass.), daughter
of Harvey Spalding and Temperance Worthington of Royalton, N. Y.

Mrs. Emily Worthington died March 1, 1887

Mr. David Worthington living (1892) near Sandusky, Ohio.

CHILDREN.

844. ELIZABETH TEMPERANCE, born Nov. 30, 1842, in
Royalton, N. Y.; died March
24, 1860, in Sandusky, O

845. MARTHA GERTRUDE, born August 9, 1845, in Royalton, N. Y.; died March 30, 1865
in Sandusky, O.

846. NETTIE,   born Aug. 10, 1857, in Royalton, N.
Y.; married Oct. 8, 1879,
Charles Henry Wilson of San
dusky, O. (b. Nov. 13, 1854, in
Margaritta, O.), son of William
H. Wilson and Julia Bardshar.

CHILDREN.

1. Henry Worthington Wilson
b. March 11, 1880.
2. Jay Charles Wilson, b. Aug·
6, 1882.

513.

LORENZO WORTHINGTON, a farmer of Bloomingville, Erie
Co., Ohio, married, May 29, 1848, Sarah Catherine Meech (b.
Sept. 25, 1825, in Geneva, N. Y.), daughter of John Meech and
Elizabeth J. Newton.

CHILDREN.

847. ALICE JANE,   born March 8, 1849, in Perkins, Ohio·
                    died July 20, 1854, in Perkins,
                    Ohio.
848. FRANCES SOPHIA, born Nov. 30, 1850, in Perkins, Ohio·
                    married, June 13, 1871, Stephen
                    Moos of Sandusky, O., (b. Dec
                    4, 1847, in Prussia), son of
                    Adam and Barbara Moos.

CHILDREN.

        1.   Frederick Samuel Moos, b.
             May 20, 1872.
        2   Charles Worthington Moos,
             b. April 4, 1880.
849. SAMUEL EDWARD, born Nov. 7, 1852, in Perkins, O.;
                    died Aug. 21, 1854, in Perkins.
†850. CHARLES EDWARD, born Aug. 21, 1855, in Perkins, O.
†851. DAVID LORENZO, born Aug. 18, 1857, in Perkins, O.
852. ALMIRA VANTINE, born July 13, 1859, in Perkins, O.
                    married, Dec. 14, 1887, John
                    Nathan Ramsdell (b. Dec. 25
                    1850, in Weavers Corners, Ohio),
                    son of William Bradley Ramsdell
                    and Emily Webster Ladd.
                    Mrs. Almira Ramsdell died
                    Dec. 22, 1888. No children.
853. EMILY ELIZABETH, born Oct. 23, 1861.

517

RALPH CUSHMAN WORTHINGTON of Centralia Wisconsin,
married, Nov. 11, 1856, Susan Hall Compton (b. June 14

1834, in Seneca Co., N. Y.), daughter of John Compton and Ivah Hall.

Mrs. Susan Worthington died June 27, 1884.

CHILDREN.

854. HARRY CUSHMAN, born April 25, 1860.
855. BRAINARD TAYLOR, born July 20, 1861; died June 23, 1862.
856. DAVID,   born Oct. 10, 1865.
857. EDITH C.,   born Feb. 14, 1867; died Jan. 24 1870.
858. MAY,   born April 6, 1871; died Oct. 13, 1873.

521.

BRAINARD TAYLOR WORTHINGTON of Centralia, Wisconsin, married, Dec. 14, 1868, Mary White (b. Feb. 28, 1848, in Glen Falls, N. Y.), daughter of James M. White and Charlotte Cole.

CHILDREN.

859. HENRY CUSHMAN, born Oct. 2, 1869; died Feb. 28, 1880.

523.

GEORGE GARY WORTHINGTON, merchant of Shreveport, La., married, Nov. 28, 1861, at Black Hawk Co., Iowa, Lucretia Maxwell (b. ——, 1838, in Mass.), daughter of James Maxwell.

Mrs. Lucretia Worthington died June 24, 1870, in Black Hawk Co., Iowa.

CHILDREN.

860. HERBERT M.,   born Feb., 1865.
861. STELLA MARY,   born Dec. ⁱ, 1868.

525.

AMASA WORTHINGTON of Brooklyn, N. Y., married, Oct. 26, 1886, Margaret A. Cole (b. Jan. 22 1849, in Hamilton, Ontario), daughter of Samuel Cole and Charlotte Macdude.

CHILDREN.

862. PEARL,   born Aug. 14, 1887; died Oct. 4, 1887.
863. JOHN JEWETT,   born July 12, 1889.

528.

FRANCIS ELIJAH WORTHINGTON, a farmer of Western Union Junction, Wisconsin, married, Dec. 28, 1863, Eliza Jane Mc Intyre (b. Aug. 18, 1839, in Bayham, Canada), daughter of John McIntyre and Hannah Edison.

CHILDREN.

864. JAY COOK,   born Jan. 26, 1865, in La Grange, Wis.; died Aug. 23, 1867.
865. SHIRLY FRANK   born April 26, 1866, in La Grange, Wis.
866. DON CLAIR,   born Jan. 2, 1870, in La Grange, Wis.
867. OTTO EDISON,   born April 23, 1871, in La Grange, Wis.
868. GUY McINTYRE, born Aug. 15, 1872, in La Grange, Wis.

869. ROY ELIJAH,   born Dec. 17, 1873, in La Grange,
                        Wis.
870. GERTRUDE,   born Nov. 24, 1876, in Mt. Pleasant,
                        Wis.

530.

GEORGE L. WORTHINGTON of Brooklyn, Michigan, married,
Dec. 17, 1867, Hattie Townson (b. Nov. 24, 1843, in
Brooklyn, Mich.), daughter of Joseph Townson and Mary
White.

CHILDREN.

871. JOSEPH,   born Nov. 8, 1873; died Aug. 21
                       1883.
872. GEORGE,   born Jan. 11, 1879.

531.

CHARLES WORTHINGTON of Miami Co., Kansas, married,
May 13, 1868, Anna Sage (b. June 26, 1849, in Huntington,
Ohio), daughter of Charles R. Sage, Jr., and Martha Twitchell.

CHILDREN.

873. CLARA,   born Feb. 25, 1869.
874. GEORGE,   born Aug. 19, 1871.
875. FREDERICK,   born Sept. 30, 1873.
876. NELLIE,   born Oct. 6, 1875.
877. ALVIRA,   born Dec. 1, 1877.
878. CLYDE,   born Dec. 30, 1879.
879. LUTIE,   born Feb. 20, 1884.
880. ALDULA,   born May 21, 1887.
881. ELIZABETH,   born June 8, 1890.

537.

Dr. DAVID HENRY WORTHINGTON of Fairfield, Iowa, married 1st, April 26, 1881, Clara L. Sharpe, daughter of —— Sharpe and Sarah A. Long. Mrs. Clara Worthington died May 26, 1886, and Dr. Worthington married, 2nd, Dec. 4, 1890, Lora Ellen Harvey (b. July 29, 1864, in Washington, Iowa), daughter of Archibald Harvey and Ellen Clapp.

CHILDREN BY 1ST MARRIAGE.

882. STELLA FLORENCE, born Sept. 18, 1884, in Fairfield.

541.

FRANK C. WORTHINGTON of Aurora, Ill., married Jan. 1, 1890, Effie Geese (b. Aug. 16, 1867, in Mt. Hamill, Ohio), daughter of William Geese (b. Dec. 18, 1832, in Pennsylvania,) and Clara Powell (b. Dec. 14, 1838, in Columbus, Ohio).

545.

FRANK WORTHINGTON of Oconomowac, Wis., married, 1st, June 15, 1876, Rosa Martin. Married, 2nd, Oct. 15, 1885, Emma F. Brown (b. June 28, 1862, in Lemonweir, Wis.), daughter of Thomas I. Brown and Lydia Ackerman.

CHILDREN BY 1ST WIFE.

883.	EDITH,	born June 6, 1877; died Feb., 1879.
884.	Ora B.,	born Jan. 20, 1880.
885.	BENIE,	born March 1, 1882.

CHILDREN BY 2ND WIFE.

886. THEODORE THOMAS, born Oct. 6, 1886.
887. GEORGE EDMOND, born March 28, 1888.
888. CORDELIA NELLIE, born Oct. 29, 1889.

546.

WILLIAM D. WORTHINGTON of Deep River, Connecticut died about 1888. Left one son and one daughter. The son, William A., is living at or near Deep River, Connecticut, but no record of the family can be obtained.

CHILDREN.

889. WILLIAM A.
890. A DAUGHTER.

561.

ELDEN WORTHINGTON of Elyria, Ohio, married, Sept. 16, 1857, Elizabeth Cornell (b. Feb. 14, 1836, in Eaton, Ohio), daughter of James Halleck Cornell and Betsey Dolbee.

CHILDREN.

891. EDITH BERTHENA, born Oct. 29, 1859.
892. CLARA AUGUSTA, born July 22, 1863.
893. FRANCES ASBURY, born Oct. 20, 1867.
894. NELSON ORR,   born Nov. 15, 1870.
895. LILA MAUD,   born Jan. 3, 1877; died Jan. 7, 1888.

564.

ELIJAH WORTHINGTON, a real estate dealer of Cleveland, Ohio, married, 1st, Aug. 13, 1864, Henrietta White (b. May 7, 1846), who died Nov. 22, 1876, and Mr. Worthington married, 2nd, Sept. 13, 1882, Emily I. Bradley.

CHILDREN BY 1ST WIFE.

896. GERTRUDE ISABELLA, born Aug 20, 1867.
897. EFFIE MAY,   born Oct. 29, 1869; died July 2, 1871.
898. MAUDE EVALYN, born Jan. 7, 1871.
899. NETTIE FLORENCE, born April 3, 1873.
900. HARRY ELIJAH,   born Nov. 22, 1876.

CHILDREN BY 2ND WIFE.

901. BENJAMIN FREDERICK, born March 27 1885.
902. CHARLES EDWARD, born Oct. 29, 1887.

565.

HENRY C. WORTHINGTON of New Boston, Mich., married Oct. 7, 1867, Euphema A. Wing (b. May 11, 1848, in Strongville, Cuyahoga Co., Ohio), daughter of Stephen P. Wing and Eliza Barnard.

CHILDREN.

903. JONATHAN BIRD, born March 29, 1885.

572.

BARTLETT MACK WORTHINGTON of Chicago, Illinois, married, Oct. 15, 1862, Frances E. Wood, daughter of Russell A. Wood and Fidelia B. Kinne.

CHILDREN.

904. ALICE WOOD,   born July 9, 1863; married, Nov. 21, 1888, George Beech Adams, son of Robert Galusha Adams and Mary Josephine Watson.

905. LENORE MACK, born Nov. 26, 1868; died Aug. 16, 1870.
906. ELSIE ELOISE, born Feb. 10, 1871.
907. JOSEPHINE DENISON, born Aug. 2, 1874.

574.

CHESTER BUTLER WORTHINGTON of DesMoines, Mo., married, Nov. 17, 1859, Mary Chapman (b. Aug. 15, 1845, in Rockport, Pa.), daughter of Joseph Chapman and Martha P Wooley.

CHILDREN.

908. EMERY CHAPMAN, born Nov. 23, 1870.
909. LEIGHTON COLEMAN, born Jan. 16, 1873.

578.

JAMES LACY WORTHINGTON of Albion Calhoun Co. Mich., married, Oct. 24, 1850, Elizabeth Curtis (b. June 7, 1829, in Stockbridge, Mass.), daughter of Henry Curtis and Phœbe Churchill.

CHILDREN.

†910. ALBERT CURTIS, born July 8, 1855, in Pittsford, N. Y.
†911. EDWARD LACY, born April 2, 1857, in Princeton Bureau, Ill.
912. JENNIE AMELIA, born Oct. 8, 1859, in Princeton Bureau, Ill.
913. FREDERICK HENRY, born Oct. 11, 1864, in Princeton Bureau, Ill.

582.

CHARLES CARTER WORTHINGTON of Homer, Calhoun Co., Michigan, married, June 2, 1874, at Cincinnati, Ohio, Clara Belle Evans (b. Jan. 7, 1855, in Cincinnati, O.), daughter of John Evans and Elizabeth Jones.

CHILDREN.

914. JUSTIN EVANS,   born Aug. 26, 1876.
915. ELIZABETH LAVINA, born March 21, 1878.
916. CLARA AMELIA,   born Jan. 21, 1880.
917. MARIA HELEN,   born May 15, 1882.

583.

JUSTIN WILLIAM WORTHINGTON of Hartland, Livingston Co., Michigan, married, Oct. 21, 1867, Elmira Snyder (b. April 21, 1838, in Parma, N. Y.), daughter of Jonathan Snyder and Yancy Mather.

CHILDREN.

918. ADA MAY   born June 6, 1869; died July 1 1887.
919. JOHN WATROUS, born Aug. 23, 1873.

584.

JAMES AMOS WORTHINGTON of Fowlersville, Mich., married, Dec. 6, 1860, Nancy I. Young (b. October 5, 1841, in Hartland, Mich.), daughter of David Young and Harriet Gleason.

CHILDREN.

920. HARRIET L.   born Sept. 30, 1861; married, Feb.
                      2, 1881, John W. Graham

921.	SARAH R.,	born Nov. 2, 1864; married, Nov. 30, 1882, Milo Z. Jeffrey, and died May 14, 1883.
922.	CORA E.,	born October 17, 1864.
923.	CHESTER C.,	born Dec. 24, 1870.
924.	EMMA J.,	born Jan. 25, 1875.
925.	JAMES R.,	born July 11, 1883.

586.

CHARLES NICHOLAS WORTHINGTON of Caro, Tuscola Co., Michigan, married, Nov. 28, 1880, Adelia Melissa Utter, (b. April 16, 1837, in Casanovia, N. Y.), daughter of Henry Utter and Polly Webb, and widow of Mr. Townsend.
No children.

588.

DELOS IOTE WORTHINGTON of Argentine, Wyandott Co., Michigan, married, March 5, 1889, Lucinda James (b. Nov. 30, 1862, in Muskingum Co., Ohio), daughter of Amon B. James and Martha Blunt.
No children.

590.

LESLIE WORTHINGTON of Spokane Falls Washington, married, Oct. 21, 1863, Sarah S. Lewis (b. April 16, 1843, in Batavia, N. Y.), daughter of Eli T. Lewis and Condace Kellogg.

CHILDREN.

| †926. | ALBERT, | born April 11, 1866, in Cannon City, Minn. |

927.	IRVING,	born June 19, 1868, in Grove Lake, Minn.
928.	WILLIAM,	born July 13, 1871, in Grove Lake, Minn.
929.	NELLIE,	born Aug. 13, 1874, in Tulore, Cal.
930.	RENE,	born Nov. 18, 1876, in Sank Centre Minn.
931.	LAURA,	born May 3, 1879, in Barrie, N. Dakota.
932.	LEWIS STARK,	born April 12, 1882, in Barrie, N. Dakota.
933.	MAY,	born Sept. 22, 1884, in Barrie, N. Dakota.
934.	ALBERTA,	born Feb. 1, 1887, in Barrie, N. Dakota.

599.

ALBERT SELDEN WORTHINGTON of Platte Michigan, married, April 20, 1887, Katie Goin (b. Dec. 9, 1860, in Seneca, Canada), daughter of Eber Goin and Abigail Drake.
No children.

609.

ENOCH BROWN WORTHINGTON of Colchester, Connecticut, married, March 24, 1868, at Salem, Conn., Lucy Adelia Bulkley (b. March 16, 1846, in Salem, Conn.), daughter of James Bulkley and Sarah A. Adel.
Mrs. Lucy Worthington died Oct. 10, 1890. No children.

611.

HON. JOHN WORTHINGTON of Cooperstown, N. Y., United States consul at Malta, married, 1st, Nov. 6, 1862, Jennie Cooper (b. March, 1844), daughter of Richard Cooper (son of Fennimore Cooper), and Mary Storrs of Cooperstown, N. Y.

Mrs. Jennie Worthington died Jan 12, 1863. Mr. Worthington married, 2nd, June 1, 1870, at Morris, N. Y., Cora Lull.

616.

DR. HENRY WORTHINGTON, a physician of Los Angeles, California, married, Dec. 7, 1875, Kate L. Heaver (b. Feb. 14, 1853, in Cincinnati, Ohio), daughter of William Heaver and Margaret Eyler.

CHILDREN.

935. JOHN RICHARD,   born Sept. 19, 1876.
936. MARY ALICE,   born Feb. 26, 1878; died March 6, 1879.
937. WILLIAM HEAVER, born Nov. 10, 1879.
938. HENRIETTA KATE, born June 14, 1883.
939. DORRANCE HENRY, born March 7, 1885.
940. FREDERICK TRUMBULL, born Sept. 17, 1889.

619.

ALBERT PAYSON WORTHINGTON of Durham, N. Y. married, Oct. 19, 1866, at Durham, N. Y., Addie E. Humphrey.

Mrs. Addie Worthington died Oct. 6, 1867, in Durham.

CHILDREN.

941. ALBERT HUMPHREY, born Oct., 1867, in Durham; died April 16, 1869.

622.

RALPH WORTHINGTON of Cleveland, Ohio, married, June 9, 1871, at Cleveland, Helen Harman Ely (born Sept. 26, ——, in Milan, Ohio), daughter of George Beckwith Ely and Gertrude S. Harman.

CHILDREN.

942. GEORGE ELY,   born May 7, 1872.
943. DAISY,   born Oct. 1, 1877.

628.

GEORGE WORTHINGTON, 2ND, of Cleveland, Ohio, married, Oct. 12, 1880, at Albany, N. Y., Lily Marie Smith (b. June 21, ——, in Auburn, N. Y.), daughter of John Wesley Smith, one of the proprietors of the *Albany Argus* (b. May 22, 1837, on the banks of the Hudson River, near the town of Milton, N. Y., son of William Clark Smith and Aner Lewis, and great-grandson of Captain Anning Smith. Died Oct. 31, 1885, in Albany, N. Y.) and Altia Downer.

CHILDREN.

944. GEORGE WORTHINGTON, 3RD, born July 10, 1890, in Cleveland, Ohio,

630.

GEORGE WORTHINGTON of Brooklyn, N. Y., a merchant doing business in New York, married, April 24, 1855, Charlotte Bloomer, daughter of Thomas Bloomer and Lea Maria Gillett.

CHILDREN.

945.	CHARLOTTE,	born Dec. 12, 1856.
946.	CATHERINE.	born June 18, 1860; married George M. Boardman. No. Children.
947.	GEORGE,	born Feb. 16, 1863.
948.	CHARLES,	born Oct. 20, 1868; died Aug. 13, 1891, in Hague, Lake George, N. Y. Unmarried.

631.

RICHARD PIERSON WORTHINGTON of Buffalo, N. Y., married, Feb. 13, 1872, at North East, Pa., Lottie Evangeline Dix, daughter of David Dix of North East, Pa.

Mrs. Lottie Worthington died Feb. 14, 1878.

Mr. Worthington died Sept. 19, 1878.

CHILDREN.

949.	DAN BELDEN,	born June 28, 1873, in Buffalo.
950.	GEORGE DIX,	born April 23, in Buffalo.

632.

· ROBERT CONE WORTHINGTON of Fowlersville, Michican, married, May 24, 1880, Lucy D. Raymer (b. March 6, 1833, in Allegheny, N. Y.), daughter of George Raymer and Susan Showers. No children.

633.

CHARLES GAD WORTHINGTON, fire and marine underwriter of Buffalo, N. Y., married, July 19, 1869, at Buffalo, Ella Maria Whitaker, daughter of Chauncey G. Whitaker and Delia Walworth Prescott.

CHILDREN.

951. LOUISE PRESCOTT, born Feb. 18, 1871; died August 12, 1871.
952. MABLE STAFFORD, born Jan. 5, 1873.
953. FANNY BURNETT, born Jan. 5, 1873.

640.

REV. EDWARD WILLIAM WORTINGTON, Episcopal clergyman, rector of Grace church, Cleveland, Ohio, married, June 17, 1880, Eleanor Lobdell (b. May 29, 1861, in Morris, Conn.), daughter of Rev. Francis Lobdell, D. D., and Julia Danforth.

CHILDREN.

954. ELEANOR,   born Sept. 1, 1881, in West Haven, Conn.
955. AGNES SEABURY born Nov. 14, 1884, in Mt. Morris N. Y.
956. EDWARD LOBDELL, born June 2, 1886, in Mt. Morris, N. Y.
957. DONALD,   born Jan. 13, 1893, in Cleveland, Ohio.

642.

ARTHUR WOODS WORTHINGTON married in 1882, Elizabeth P. Strong.

CHILDREN.

958. ROBERT STRONG, born
959. ARTHUR SINCLAIR, born
960. ELEANOR,   born
961. HOWARD,   born Dec. 22, 1889.

649.

FREDERICK WORTHINGTON of Portland, Oregon, married Feb. 20, 1882, Julia Pries (b. June 18, 1859, in New York city), daughter of R. F. Pries and Josephine Ziegler.

CHILDREN.

962. MARY EDITH,   born March 15, 1884, in Denver, Col.
963. RALPH,   born Jan. 20, 1886, in Denver, Col.

653.

AMOS FRANCIS WORTHINGTON, a merchant of Cincinnati, Ohio, married, Nov. 28, 1861, Ellen Steelman, daughter of Jeremiah Steelman and Jane Hunter.

CHILDREN.

964. FLORA ELLEN,
865. NELLIE DEZIER

655.

STEPHEN WOOD WORTHINGTON of Cincinnati, Ohio, married, in 1861, Camilla Edwardes (b. 1844, in Hamilton Co., Ohio) daughter of M. M. Edwardes.
Mr. Stephen Worthington died Jan. 12, 1890.

CHILDREN.

966. CHARLES,   born 1862 (?); died 1881.
967. OLIVE,   born 1866 (?).
968. JESSIE,   died in early life.

656.

James Gallup Worthington of Glenbrook, Nevada City, California. He went to California in 1858; married, Sept. 29, 1862, Luvia Damon (b. Oct. 3, 1846, in Coaticook, P. Q.), daughter of Aaron Upton Damon and Snsan Charlotte Sutton. Mrs. Luvia Worthington died Dec. 7, 1870.

CHILDREN.

969. James Frank, born Aug. 21, 1863. Lives in Nevada City, Cal.
970. Frances Elinor, born Sept. 9, 1865; married, in 1888, a Mr. Hartman of Nevada City, Cal.
971. William Albert, born May 5, 1867. Lives at Nevada City, Cal.

664.

Lewis Nicholas Worthington (in 1882 he changed his name from Lewis Sedam Worthington), of Canandaigua, N. Y.; was graduated from Y. C., 1860; studied law with Coffin & Mitchell in Cincinnati, Ohio. In 1861 he entered the Sixth Regiment Ohio Volunteers, and was honorably discharged on Aug. 1. Commanded a company of soldiers during the investment of Cincinnati by the troops of Kirbv Smith in 1863. Studied law at the Harvard Law School during the winter of 1862-3. Received the degree of M. A. from Y. C. in 1863. Visiting Europe in 1864 on account of failing health, he began the study of medicine in 1867 in the school of Medicine in Paris, France. Receiving his diploma as "Docteur en Médecine de la Faculté de Paris" in 1876, having previously, in 1871, received a diploma from the Miami

Medical College of Cincinnati, and been appointed house
surgeon of the Good Samaritan hospital in that city, which
position he was unable to accept. Dr. Worthington began
the practice of medicine in Paris in 1876, but was obliged to
return to Cincinnati in 1879, to assume charge of his father's
estate. In 1882 he removed to Canandaigua, N. Y. In 1888
he received the decoration of "Officier d'Académie" conferred
by the minister of public instruction in Paris. In 1891 he
published some "Notes concerning Nicholas Worthington and
certain of his descendants." On May 18, 1886, in Kensington,
London, England, Mr. Worthington married Emma Lucy
Jarvis Browne, daughter of David and Catherine W. Browne,
of St. John's, Antique, West Indies.

CHILDREN.

972. NICHOLAS WARNICK DENNIS, born Aug. 1, 1888, in
Paris, France.

666.

JOHN SHEPHERD WORTHINGTON of St. Paul, Minn., married,
1st, Sept. 16, 1888, Charlotte T. Lyon, daughter of George G.
and Frances M. Lyon; 2nd. May 21, 1885, Sarah M. Brown,
daughter of Lorenzo D. and Susannah Brown.

CHILDREN BY 1ST WIFE.

973. LIZZIE MAY,   born Nov. 12, 1869; died Feb. 12,
1871.
974. ROY LYON,   born Oct. 15, 1871.
975. FANNIE MAY,   born Feb. 6, 1874.
976. CLARENCE EDWARD, born April 18, 1880.
977. LOTTIE,   born Aug., 1882; died, Dec., 1882.

CHILDREN BY 2ND WIFE.

978. INFANT DAUGHTER, born Nov. 15, 1889.

675.

WILLIAM WATSON WORTHINGTON of Cincinnati, Ohio. When a young man he entered the military academy at West Point and completed the mathematical course, but was obliged to leave on account of poor health. He then lived a few years in Canandaigua, N. Y., assisting his father in the management of the Blossom Hotel. In 1851 he removed to Cincinnati and entered into partnership with his uncle, Lewis Worthington, who had purchased the "Globe Iron Works." Mr. Worthington married, Feb. 9, 1860, Marv Olmsted Howlett (b. Sept. 9, 1831), daughter of Alexander H. Howlett and Emily Jackson of Canandaigua, N. Y

Mr. William Worthington died Sept. 17, 1860, in Cincinnati, leaving no children.

676.

EDWARD FULLER WORTHINGTON of Toledo, Ohio, conduetor on the T., St. L. & K. C. R. R., marrried, November 6, 1872, Sarah Elizabeth Buckles (b. July 7, 1848), daughter of John Buckles and Harriet S. Voorheis of Mount Holly, O.

CHILDREN.

979. CHARLES LEACH, born Oct. 23, 1873, in Ft. Wayne, Indiana.
980. BESSIE NEAL, born Nov. 3, 1878, in Ft. Wayne, Indiana.
981. FANNY MILLINGTON, born Sept. 3, 1886, in West Bloomfield, N. Y.

681.

HENRY ROWLAND WORTHINGTON of Hartford, Conn., married, 1st. May 12, 1869, Rosetta O. Steele (b. Nov. 8,1849, in Ilion, N. Y.), daughter of Nicholas Steele and Sarah Paddock. Mrs. Rosetta Steele died Jan. 10, 1873, and Mr. Worthington married, 2nd, Jan. 15, 1874, Isabella Clark Gambell (b. Oct. 30, 1851), daughter of John Gambell and Elizabeth Clark of Providence, R. I.

CHILD BY 1ST WIFE.

982. LENA ROSE,   born April 6,1872 in Ilion, N. Y.; died Jan. 9, 1873.

CHILDREN BY 2ND WIFE.

983. IDA H.,   born Dec. 30, 1875.
984. JOSEPH E.   born Nov. 30, 1877; died April 23, 1882.
985. HENRY,   born May 16, 1880.
986. MINER A.,   born Jan. 1, 1886.
987. HORACE JOHN,   born Aug. 21, 1890.

683.

ALBERT EDWIN WORTHINGTON of Agawam, Mass., married, 1st, May 30, 1878, Mary A. Whitman (b. Aug. 24, 1860, in Agawam, Mass.), daughter of Louis L. Whitman and Martha Pepper. Mrs. Mary Worthington died May 24, 1883, and Mr. Worthington married, 2nd, March 17, 1887, Eva E. Bitgood (b. Dec. 13, 1860, in Bozrah, Conn.), daughter of Carl ton B. Bitgood and Charlotte L. Metcalf.

CHILD BY 1ST WIFE.

988. CARRIE ALBERTA, born June 11, 1882, in Agawam.

686.

CLARENCE M. WORTHINGTON married Fanny Hathaway of Suffield, Conn.

Mr. Worthington died Dec. 28, 1878.

692.

JAMES ROWLAND WORTHINGTON married, Sept. 9, 1881, Cora E. Ricker of Holyoke, Mass. (b. Aug. 22, 1856, in Branton, P Q.), daughter of Albro M. Ricker and Betsey Berwick.

CHILDREN.

989. BESSIE PRAY, born June 16, 1882.

694.

ALBERT EDWARD WORTHINGTON of Springfield, Mass., married, Sept. 13, 1883, Martha Lucy Pratt (b. Nov. 23, 1861, in Great Falls, N. H.), daughter of Edward Hartshorn Pratt, M. D., and Julena Hodsdon. No children.

695.

SOLON ROBERTS WORTHINGTON of Springfield, Mass., married Nov. 15, 1852, Esther Dearborn, (b. April 13, 1824, in Wentworth, N. H.), daughter of Peter Dearborn and Amanda Hayner.

Mr. Worthington died June 9, 1876.

Mrs. Esther Worthington died Sept. 2, 1880.

CHILDREN.

990. ABBIE JANE,   born March 9, 1855, in Agawam,
                      Mass.; married, Feb. 3, 1876,
                      Edwin Hall Langguth of Bos-
                      ton, Mass. (b. Aug. 3, 1844, in
                      Bridgeport, Conn.), son of
                      George E. Langguth and Eme-
                      line N. Parks.

CHILDREN.

1. Howard Worthington Lang-
    guth, b. Aug, 14, 1876.
2. May Worthington Lang-
    guth, b. May 10, 1878.

696.

RANSFORD WORTINGTON, 2ND, of Great Barrington, Mass.,
married, July 4, 1847, Elizabeth Fuller (b. Jan. 14, 1830, in
Suffield, Conn.), daughter of Rodrick Fuller and Elizabeth
Adams.

Mr. Ransford Worthington died July 30, 1892, at Canaan,
Conn.

CHILDREN.

991. JANE ELIZABETH, born July 15, 1848, in Agawam
                      Mass., married, March 28, 1877,
                      William Chiswick. No children.
992. ANISETTA,   born Oct. 15, 1851, in Feeding Hills,
                      Mass., married, Nov. 20, 1890,
                      Robert I. Miller (b. Dec. 25,
                      1857, in Chickopee, Mass.), son
                      of George Miller and Mary Ann
                      Burgess.

CHILDREN.

1. Robert S. Miller, July 22, 1872, in Westfield, Mass.
2. Benjamin T. Miller, born Jan. 1, 1874, in Westfield, Mass.
3. Jabina A. Miller, b. Sept. 10, 1875, in Westfield, Mass.
4. Archibald C. Miller, b. May 20, 1877, in Westfield, Mass.

993. GERALDINE, born May 20, 1856, in Agawam, Mass.; married Frank Fowler, son of Henry Fowler and Nancy Wing.

CHILDREN.

1. Hazel Fowler, b. Sept 8, 1886; died Feb. 8, 1890.

994. CORA, born June 24, 1861, in Feeding Hills, Mass.; died Nov. 8, 1862.

995. CORA LAURA born June 11, 1865, in Feeding Hills, Mass.; married June 20, 1884, Ruben Humphreville.

CHILDREN.

1. William A. Humphreville, b. April 11, 1885.
2. Bruce Humphreville, b. April 26, 1887.

996. ALGERON, born March 16, 1876, in Feeding Hills, Mass.

997. FRANK JUDSON born May 24, 1869, in Westfield, Mass.

699.

WILLIAM HENRY WORTHINGTON of Agawam, Mass., married, May 22, 1866, Ellen B. Pomeroy (b. May 4, 1839, in Agawam), daughter of Jonathan Remington Pomeroy and Jerusha Rease. Mrs. Ellen Worthington died Jan. 6, 1890.

CHILDREN.

998.	NELLIE M.,	born April 22, 1868; died Nov. 15, 1877.
999.	ALBERT J.,	born Aug. 31, 1871.
1000.	CHARLES,	born March 27, 1873.
1001.	LEROY	born Aug. 3, 1875.
1002.	JENNIE,	born Aug. 1, 1878.

704.

ALBERT WORTHINGTON of Saxton River, Vermont, married, May 19, 1847, Lestina Long (b. Dec. 2, 1819, in Marboro, Vt.), daughter of David and Melecinda Long, of Greenfield, Mass. No children.

710.

ALBERT WORTHINGTON of North Greenbush N. Y., married, May 3, 1882, Sarah Elizabeth Barringer (b. May 7, 1853, in North Greenbush, N. Y.), daughter of William Barringer and Maria Ostrander.

CHILDREN.

1003.   LENA BARRINGER, born Nov. 8, 1883, in North Greenbush, N. Y.

1004.   MARIA LOUISA, born Oct. 28, 1885, in North Greenbush, N. Y.; d. April 23, 1886.

713.

JOHN WORTHINGTON, merchant of Troy, N. Y., married, 1st Oct. 16, 1867, Jennie Elizabeth Loomis, (b. Oct. 9, 1843, in Schodack, N. Y.), daughter of Moses Forbes Loomis and Hannah Mahale Poyneer. Mrs. Jennie Worthington died May 20, 1878, and Mr. Worthington married, 2nd, Dec. 12, 1880, Sophia Adelaide Whidden (b. April 7, 1851, in Antigonish, Nova Scotia), daughter of George William Whidden and Sarah Adelaide Witter.

CHILDREN BY 1ST WIFE.

1005. JESSIE ELIZABETH, born Oct. 4, 1868.
1006. MAHALA LOOMIS, born Nov. 27, 1870; died July 15, 1871.
1007. DAVID LOOMIS, born Sept. 12, 1874; died March 1, 1875.

CHILDREN BY 2ND WIFE.

1008. EFFIE RICHARDSON, born Dec. 22, 1881.
1009. JENNIE ADELAIDE, born Nov. 18, 1883; died March 15, 1888.
1010. DOROTHY, born Aug. 28, 1887.

721.

AARON AMBROSE WORTHINGTON of North Adams, Mass., and Petersburgh, N. Y., married, 1st, Feb. 29, 1872, Ida F. Green (b. Feb. 16, 1856, in Petersburgh), daughter of Martin and Sarah Green. Married, 2nd, Abbie C. Williams of Clarksburg, Mass.

CHILDREN BY 1ST WIFE.

1011. AMBROSE A.,   born April 30, 1873.
1012. KATE   born Nov. 8, 1875
1013. MINNIE MIRANDA, born Oct. 28, 1880; died July 30,
                      1881.

CHILDREN BY 2ND WIFE.

1014. NELLIE,   born Aug. 18, 1884.
1015. JENNIE,   born Nov. 9, 1886; died July 26, 1887.
1016. ALFRED,   born Aug. 1, 1888.

725.

WINFIELD SCOTT WORTHINGTON, 2ND of New York, married, July 3, 1883, Minnie A. Gooler, daughter of Henry Gooler.

CHILDREN.

1017. PEARL MAY,   born May 7, 1884.

729.

ELLIOTT HOAGE WORTHINGTON of North Bennington, Vermont, married, June 3, 1866, Adelaide Scrivens (b. March 23, 1847, in Hoosic, Vt.), daughter of Samuel and Louisa Scrivens.

CHILDREN.

1018. ALICE L.,   born July 30, 1867, in Petersburgh,
                     N. Y.
1019. HELEN MAY,   born Dec. 29, 1870, in Petersburgh,
                     N. Y.

1020.	SANFORD E.,	born Dec. 1, 1873, in Petersburgh, N. Y.
1021.	MARTHA J.,	born Aug. 29, 1878, in Petersburgh, N. Y.
1022.	EDMUND J.,	born Nov. 7, 1883, in No. Bennington Vt.

730.

JOHN LINUS WORTHINGTON of Grafton, N. Y., married, July 8, 1847, Elsie Jennette Durkee (b. May 22, 1848, in Grafton, N. Y.), daughter of Aliel Durkee and Harriet Wagar.

CHILDREN.

1023. EFFIE LUELLA, born May 11, 1870.
1024. ALBERT SETH, born Nov. 1, 1876.

731.

THOMAS SETH WORTHINGTON of Rural Hill N. Y., married, Januarv 1, 1884, Rose Electa Hagadone (b. April 10, 1863), daughter of Martin C. Hagadone and Anna B. Curtis.

CHILDREN.

1025. HATTIE, born April 18, 1885.

743.

FREDERICK ALFRED WORTHINGTON of Greenfield, Mass., married, Mav 19, 1887, Sophia Smead Powers, daughter of William Brown Powers and Sarah Adell Newton.

CHILDREN.

1026. HAROLD POWERS, born Feb. 24, 1888.
1027. ELSIE MAY,   born Aug. 24, 1889.

748.

CLARLES EDWARD WORTHINGTON of Norton, Kansas, married, Oct. 13, 1886, Edith Shaw, (b. Nov. 14, 1855, in Bridgewater, Vermont), daughter of Elihu M. Shaw and Maria Davis.

CHILDREN.

1028. A DAUGHTER,   born Jan. 10, 1888; died Jan. 13, 1888.
1029. LESTER SHAW, born Jan. 12, 1889.
1030. DOROTHY,   born Oct. 7, 1890.

756.

HARRY A. WORTHINGTON married, Oct. 18, 1888, Lora L. Birchard. No children.

760.

WILLIAM HENRY WORTHINGTON of Rockford, Illinois, merchant, married, May 29, 1879, Cynthia Adelle Shaw (b. Aug. 17, 1852), daughter of Calvin Shaw and Clarissa M. Stowell.

CHILD.

1031. GRACE ADELLE, born April 23, 1883.

765.

WILLIAM HENRY WORTHINGTON of Indianapolis, Indiana, married, Dec. 25, 1868, Blanche Wall (b. June 8, 1848, in Columbus, Ohio), daughter of Thomas Wall and Lottie Boyne.

CHILDREN.

1032.	ERNEST,	born Dec. 26, 1867.
1033.	LILLIE	born June 3, 1878.

766

MELVIN WORTHINGTON of Cherryvale, Kansas, married, June 16, 1882, at Dowangiac, Michigan, Amy Hunter (b. Aug. 9, 1861, in Buchanan, Mich.), daughter of Thomas Jefferson Hunter and Elizabeth Glover.

CHILDREN.

1034.	ROY HENRY,	born Aug. 9, 1883.
1035.	ROBERT ARTHUR,	born Feb. 8, 1885.
1036.	HUGH MELVIN,	born May 20, 1889.
1037.	LULU HAZEL,	born July 29, 1890.

767.

ALBERT ARTHUR WORTHINGTON of Buchanan, Michigan, married, April 12, 1882, Luella E. Van Riper (b. Jan. 13, 1862, in La Grange, Mich.), daughter of Jacob J. Van Riper and Emma E. Brunner. No children.

783.

MYRON WORTHINGTON of Henry, Illinois, married, August 27, 1857, Jane A. Greeley (b. March 23, 1839, in Rochester Ill.), daughter of M. T. Greeley and C. A. Barnes.
Mrs. Jane Worthington died July 20, 1891.

CHILDREN.

1038. JAMES TRUE,   born Sept. 23, 1859.
1039. MAY ADELL,   born May 4, 1862; died March 29, 1868.
1040. AMY MORIAH,   born March 13, 1866.
1041. CHLOE ANN,   born Nov. 17, 1868.
1042. CHARLES MYRON, born Feb. 10, 1876.

784.

JOHN WORTHINGTON of Sandusky, N. Y. married July 12, 1864, Mary A. Howe (b. Sept. 8, 1835, in Yorkshire, N. Y.), daughter of John Howe and Elizabeth Fish.

CHILDREN.

1043. EDITH,   born Aug. 7, 1867.
1044. MERTIE,   born Aug. 14, 1871.
1045. ADDIE,   born Aug. 31, 1873.

787.

CHARLES WORTHINGTON, a merchant at Lawrence, Kansas, married, April 9, 1863, Malinda J. Cool (b. Jan. 9, 1840, in Herkimer Co., N. Y.), daughter of James Cool and Betsey J. Sweet.

794.

JACOB WORTHINGTON of Fairmont, Nebraska, married, June 24, 1861, Leydia Jane Ames (b. May 15, 1840, in Rushford, N. Y.), daughter of Abel Ames and Mary Waterbury.

CHILDREN.

1046. FREDERICK AMES, born Aug. 5, 1862, in Farmersville, N. Y.; died Jan. 1, 1863, in Port-ville, N. Y.

1047. ALLAN SAMUEL, born June 1, 1867, in Portville, N. Y.

1048. CLARK ABEL, born Nov. 6, 1869, in Farmersville, N. Y.

1049. INFANT DAUGHTER, born Aug. 28, 1877, in Farmers-ville, N. Y.; died same day.

1050. BYRON GROVE, born Oct. 4, 1878, in Farmersville, N.Y.

795.

RUSSELL WORTHINGTON of Farmersville, N. Y., married, April 1, 1861, Amanda Worthington (b. March 20, 1838, in Freedom, N. Y.), daughter of Thaddeus Worthington and Sally Ann Wilkes of Yorkshire Center, N. Y.

797.

MILES WORTHINGTON of Freedom, N. Y., farmer, married, Aug. 31, 1879, Rosetta Lau (b. Oct. 21, 1858, in Farmerville, N. Y.), daughter of Eliphalet Lau and Mary Strong.

CHILDREN.

1051. LENA MAY, born Jan. 30, 1881, in Farmersville, N. Y.

1052. MILES ELMER, born Aug. 27, 1887, in Freedom, N. Y.

798.

REV. DE BIAS WORTHINGTON of Olean, N. Y., clergyman in the Methodist Episcopal Church, married, August 20, 1860, Ruth A. Mattice (b. July 10, 1834, in Schoharie Co., N. Y.), daughter of Frederich M. Mattich and Clara M. Driggs.
Rev. Mr. Worthington died Sept. 25, 1865.

CHILDREN.

1053. LELLA LEWIS, born April 9, 1863, in Olean; died June 12, 1866, in Buffalo, N. Y.

799.

REV. GEORGE WASHINGTON WORTHINGTON of West Randall N. Y.; a local preacher in the Free Methodist Church; married, 1st, 1854, Beattie Latitia Cooper (b. Nov. 26, 1833, in Holland, N. Y.), daughter of Leonard Cooper and Eliza Humphery. Mrs. Beattie Worthington died, 1862, and Rev. Mr. Worthington married, 2nd, 1862, Narcissa Lodorscia Cooper (b. Nov. 26, 1833, in Holland, N. Y.), daughter of Leonard Cooper and Eliza Humphery.

CHILDREN BY 1ST WIFE.

1054. JOHN LEONARD, born July 5, 1855.
1055. FLORA BELLE, born July 29, 1859.

CHILDREN BY 2ND WIFE.

1056. MARIA ANTOINETTE, born May 5, 1872.

WILLIAM FRANK WORTHINGTON.

800.

Rev. Randolph Worthington of Jamestown, N. Y., a preacher in the Free Methodist Church, married, 1st, April 21, 1859, Julia Thompson (b. Sept. 9, 1840, in Holland, N. Y.), daughter of John Thompson and Elizabeth Harmon. Mrs. Julia Worthington died Dec. 21, 1871, and Rev. Mr. Worthington married, 2nd, Ruvina Elizabeth Freeland (b. Feb. 13, 1837), daughter of James and Lucinda Norwood.

CHILDREN BY 1ST WIFE.

1057. Carl De Bias, born Jan. 27, 1867.

CHILDREN BY 2ND WIFE.

1058. Arlie Mabel, born Feb. 4, 1875.
1059. Benjamin James, born August 7, 1877; died April 4, 1891.

801.

William Frank Worthington of Buffalo, N. Y., was born in Farmersville, Cattaraugus Co., N. Y., on December 18, 1836. "His boy life was identified with the drudgery of the farm, but, like most American boys, he had opportunities to acquire a common school education. Having removed to Rushford when quite young, he attended the academy there, and was graduated with credit. He then devoted himself to teaching, first in Rushford, then in Franklinville, and finally in Sardinia. Afterwards he studied law in the office of Charles Woodford at Rushford, and continued his legal studies with Henry W. Box of Buffalo, from whose office he was admitted to practice in the courts of the state of New York in 1864, and in the United States courts in 1868. He enlisted in a company of Sharpshooters in 1862, rose to the rank of lieutenant, and was subsequently mustered out of service on account of an affection of the eyes, and during all his after life was obliged to wear glasses, returning to Buffalo in 1863. During 1866 and 1867 he served the city of Buffalo as assistant city attorney, under the Hon. George S. Wardwell. He was contemporary with Grover Cleveland, being admitted to the bar about the same time. They tried their first case together, as council for the opposing sides to the suit. Late in 1867 he removed to Richmond, Va., where he had been offered an appointment in the U. S. internal revenue service. He was soon made commonwealth attorney of Albemarle, Goochland and Fluvanna counties, and after the state was readmitted to the Union he became chief magistrate of Chesterfield county, residing at Manchester, Virginia. Subsequently he served two years as assistant United States district attorney. In 1875 Mr. Worthington returned to Buffalo and resumed practice there. In 1885 he was elected city attorney, which office he held until his death. During his first term the law department was reorganized, the title of its chief being changed to corporation counsel. Personally Mr. Worthington was a well beloved and most popular man. He had a gentle and kindly disposition that no ordinary mind could rufle, a brightly, buoyant spirit and a tongue that spoke ill of no man. He was the sunniest-hearted man one would meet in many a long day's journey, and the sunlight in his heart made life bright for all who knew him."

Mr. Worthington married, Dec. 23, 1863, in Buffalo, Margaretta Douglas Taggert (b. June 16, 1835, in Weybridge, Vt.), daughter of William Taggert and Anne Runier.

Mr. Worthington died Nov. 15, 1890, in Buffalo N. Y.

CHILDREN.

1060. WILLIAM FRANK, born Oct. 4, 1864, in Buffalo.

801.

IRA CATLIN WORTHINGTON, a builder of Griswold, Kansas married, June 13, 1873, Alpha Howard (b April 13, 1852, in Franklinville, N. Y.), daughter of Benjamin Howard and Tryphena Gifford.

Mrs. Alpha Worthington died May 22, 1888.

CHILDREN.

1061. CARRIE E.,   born May 17, 1874; died May 14, 1880.

1062. GEORGIE M.,   born April 29, 1877.

802.

LEONARD MASON WORTHINGTON, a farmer of Yorkshire, N. Y., married, Aug 15, 1866, Sarah I. Van Dozen (b. Feb. 27, 1847, in Freedom, N. Y.), daughter of John B. Van Dozen and Sally E. Stevens.

CHILDREN.

1063. NINA E.,   born June 14, 1867, in Rushford N. Y.

803.

SYLVESTER B. WORTHINGTON, a farmer of Farmersville, N. Y., married, Feb. 14, 1861, Louisa M. Holmes (b. in Farmersville), daughter of Peter Holmes.

Mr. Sylvester Worthington died Sept. 12, 1865.

Mrs. Louisa Worthington died Dec. 17, 1866.

CHILDREN.

1064. GERTRUDE E.,   born August 8, 1862, in Farmersville,
N. Y.

805.

HENRY WORTHINGTON, a farmer, of Farmersville, N. Y., married, Jan. 1, 1867, Anna E. West, daughter of Samuel West.

CHILDREN.

1065. LELLA A.,   born Feb. 13, 1871, in Farmersville,
N. Y.

EIGHTH GENERATION.

811.

CHARLES ALFRED WORTHINGTON of Detroit Mich., married, Jan. 16, 1877, Mary Viola Alexander (b. June 15, 1850, in Utica, Mich.), daughter of James Alexander and Eunice Davis of Utica, Michigan.   No children.

813.

HENRY FRAZIER WORTHINGTON of New York married Frances Fenton.

CHILDREN.

1066. ELIZABETH.
1067. VALERIA.

814.

CHARLES CAMPBELL WORTHINGTON of New York city married, April 16, 1879, Julia A. Hedden, daughter of Edward L. Hedden and Elizabeth C. Apgar of New York.

CHILDREN.

1068. JULIA H.
1069. HENRY ROSSITER.
1070. CHARLES CAMPBELL, 2ND.
1071. EDWARD H.
1072. WILLOUGHBY
1073. REGIBALD STUART.

831.

CHARLES ELLIS WORTHINGTON of Chicago, Ill., married, Sept. 12, 1882, at Newton, Lower Falls, Mass., Eliza E. Jenkins (b. April 23, 1852, in Wellesley Hills, Mass.), daughter of Ebenezer C. Jenkins and Mary L. Coller.

CHILDREN.

1074. ELLIS JENKINS, born July 11, 1883, in Newton, Lower Falls, Mass.; died Oct. 5, 1883.
1075. ISABEL, born May 6, 1885, in Newton, Lower Falls, Mass.

833.

GEORGE WORTHINGTON of Fitchburg, Mass., married, Oct. 15, 1877, Cora Jane Snow (b. Feb. 27, 1854), daughter of Jerome B. Snow and Naomi L. Reckard.

CHILDREN.

1076.   BERTHA OLIVE,   born Sept. 2, 1878; died Aug. 13, 1879.
1077.   LUCIUS JEROME, born Sept. 5, 1882.

836.

LUCIUS WORTHINGTON of Chelsea, Mass., married, Nov. 1, 1883, Martha Adaline Clinger (b. April 18, 1860), daughter of Robert Clinger and Henrietta Elizabeth Stoner.

CHILDREN.

1078.   ETHEL HENRIETTA, born Oct. 10, 1884.
1079.   CAROLINE MAY, born Sept. 8, 1888.

850.

CHARLES EDWARD WORTHINGTON a carpenter, of Alpena, Mich., married, Oct. 26, 1881, at Alpena, Millie Stearnes (b. June 23, 1860, in Detroit, Mich.), daughter of Joseph Alonzo Stearnes and Margaret Wright.

· CHILDREN.

1080.   EDITH MAY,   born May 19, 1883, in Alpena.
1081.   CHARLES LORENZO, born Jan. 19, 1885, in Alpena.
1082.   MILLIE MAUD,   born Aug. 22, 1887, in Alpena.
1083.   MYRA FARWELL, born July 26, 1889, in Alpena.

851.

DAVID LORENZO WORTHINGTON of Alaska, Mich., married, March 9, 1886, Amelia Buell (b. March 2, 1858, in Amanda Mich.), daughter of Marcus Buell and Mary Glvcerria Bennett.

CHILDREN.

1084. LEONA,   born June 6, 1888.

910.

ALBERT CURTIS WORTHINGTON of Albion, Mich., married, April 3, 1884, Elizabeth Campbell (b. Dec. 9, 1862, in Aberdeenshire, Scotland), daughter of William Campbell and Isabella Webster Spence.

CHILDREN.

1085. NELLIE ELIZABETH, born Aug. 10, 1886, in Minneapolis, Minn.
1086. FREDERICK CAMPBELL, born July 5, 1888, in Minneapolis, Minn.

911.

EDWARD LACY WORTHINGTON of Albion, Mich. married, March 18, 1885, Effie May Nethercott (b. July 11, 1863, in Albion, Mich.), daughter of Richard Nethercott and Mary Ann Conway.

CHILDREN.

1087. HOWARD RICHARD, born May 5, 1889, in Albion, Mich.

926.

ALBERT WORTHINGTON of the State of Washington, married, June 1, 1887, Rachael E. Zacharesen (b. Nov. 10, 1865, in Norway), daughter of Nicholie Zacharesen and Jabobea Nelson.

CHILDREN.

1088. GERTRUDE,   born Aug 14, 1888.
1089. LULA ELIZABETH, born Jan. 19, 1890.

ADDENDUM.

Page 23, number 25, Rev. John Hooker succeeded President Edwards as Pastor of the Northampton Ch. Was b. 1729 in Kensington, Conn. Was grad. from Y. C. 1751. Ordained in 1753. Was a
descendant in the fourth generation of the renowned Rev. Thomas
Hooker of Hartford. Died in Northampton, Mass.

Page 24, number 6, From "Recollections of a Life Time," S. G.
Goodrich. Rev. William Worthington "preached for a time in
Stonington, Conn., and was settled in Saybrook, West parish, then
called Pachoug, in 1726. He was the first minister of the parish,
and was ordained in the dwelling-house built for himself, but then
unfinished, the people sitting on the beams and timbers to witness
the ceremony." . . . "He was a popular preacher and a most
faithful pastor. His influence was eminently persuasive to love and
good works, and was long visible after his death, in the religious
character of his people, and in the tone of feeling prevalent in the
business and courtesies of life. He preached the election sermon in
the year 1744, the following being the title page, "The Duty of
Rulers and Teachers in unitedly leading God's people, urged and ex-
plained in a sermon preached before the General Assembly of the
Colony of Connecticut, at Hartford, on their Anniversary Election,
May 10th, 1744." The sermon is a logical and well written dis-
course. In his social and ministerial intercourse, he was a gentleman
of great blandness, gracefulness and urbanity of manner—attributes
which he transmitted to many of his descendants. Some of his
people said that they had but one thing against him, and that was,
"he walked as if he were a proud man," but Mr. Lay, one of his
parishioners, seeing him walking in the woods, and supposing himself alone, with the same dignity and gracefulness of bearing as when
in the presence of others, came to the conclusion that his "manner
in public was natural to him." His four daughters were celebrated
in their day for their accomplishments. The traditions of their
superiority of air, manner and appearance still linger among the old

people of Westport. Their father's mode of educating them was to keep one of them, in succession, at domestic employments with their mother, while the others were at their studies with himself.

The following is told among the legends of the family: "Mr. Worthington had a slave named Jenny. After his death she lived with his children, one after another. When she died, it was ninety years from the time that the first bill of sale given. She had two children in Guinea before she came to this country, and must therefore have been considerably over a hundred years old. When she was on her deathbed, at Mr. Elnathan Chauncey's, in Durham, Dr. Goodrich conversed with her. 'Jenny has strange notions,' said he, when he came out of the room. She said to me, 'I shall go to Heaven. I shall knock at the door, and ask for Massa Worthington; and he will go and tell God that I had always been an honest, faithful servant, and then he will let me in, and I will go and sit in the kitchen.'"

Page 29, number 4, Dr. William Mason Eliot settled at Goshen, N. Y.

Page 55, number 31, Sarah Worthington (Ely) is thus described by her grandson, Samuel Griswold Goodrich, about the year 1803: "My grandmother Ely was of the old regime—a lady of the old school, and sustaining the character in her upright carriage, her long tapering waist and her high heeled shoes. The costumes of Louis XV.'s time had prevailed in New York and Boston, and even at this period they still lingered there, in isolated cases, though the Revolution had generally exercised a transforming influence upon the toilet of both men and women. It is curious enough that at this moment 1855—the female attire of a century ago is revived; and in every black-eyed, stately old lady, dressed in black silk, and showing her steel-gray hair beneath her cap, I can now see semblance of this, my maternal grandmother." "She sang me plaintive songs; told me stories of the Revolution—her husband, Col. Ely, having had a large and painful share in its vicissitudes; she described Gen. Washington, whom she had seen; and the French officers, Lafayette, Rochambeau and others, who had been inmates of her house. She told me tales of even more ancient date, and recited poetry, generally consisting of ballads, which were suited to my taste. And all this lore was commended to me by a voice of inimitable tenderness, and a manner at once lofty and condescending."

Page 57, numьer 1, Worthington Ely was graduated from Yale College in 1780.

Page 59, numьer 2, Samuel Goodrich was, on the 22nd of Jan., 1811, "dismissed from his charge at Ridgefield, at his own request, and on the 29th of May following he was installed at Worthington, a parish of Berlin," (Connecticut).

Page 61, numьer 6, Lucretia Elv m. Dr. Gregory of Sand Lake, near Alьany, N. Y.

Page 62, numьer 8, Edward Ely, a lawyer, settled at Goshen, N. Y.

Page 62, numьer 1, Also called Stephen Augustus, removed to Richmond, Va.

Page 62, numьer 2, George Hopkins, was a "well known printer and puьlisher."

Page 62, numьer 3, Silvia Hopkins, "was a celeьrated ьeauty."

Page 85, numьer 10, Capt. Elijah Worthington was a representa tive from Colchester, Ct., to the General Assemblv of Connecticut in 1757-58-59, 1760-61-62.

Page 113, numьer 21, The parish of Worthington in the eastern part of Berlin township, Conn., was so called as a memorial of the judicious efforts of Col. John Worthington of Springfield, in settling the long standing difficulties, which finally ended in the parish of Kensington ьeing divided, the western portion retaining the name of Kensington, and the eastern taking the name of Worthington.

Page 123, numьer 33, Colonel William Worthington was appointed ьy the General Assemьly held at Hartford, Ct., in May, 1767, Lieutenant of the 10th company or train ьand in the 7th regiment of the colony. Was appointed Captain of the same company in May, 1771. Was appointed Major of the 7th regiment of militia in the colonv, Oct. 1774, and in March, 1775, Lieutenant-Colonel of the same. On June 6, 1776, at a meeting of the Governor and Council of Safety at Hartford, he was appointed Lieutenant-Colonel of the first ьattalion. He was a Justice of the Peace during the years of 1772-3-4-5-6, and representative from Sayьrook to the General Assemblv in 1771-2-3-4-5-6-7-8-9-81-ϙ-3-5-6-90-1. In May, 1773, he was appointed, with others, bv the General Assemьly at Hartford, a committee to receive the sums to ьe raised by lotterv granted for erecting ьuoys and other monuments on Sayьrook Bar, for the more easy and safe navigation over said ьar, and having received said sums, the same to lay out for the purpose aforesaid

according to their ɔest discretion, and if they see cause, to use and
improve for the said purpose, the stone remaining of the old fort at
Sayɔrook. On Oct., 1774, he was appointed, with others, to hear,
enquire and examine into all the matter upon the memorial of
Benoni Hilliard of Sayɔrook against James Wright, dec., and report
same to the next General Assemɔly.

Page 124, numɔer 35, Elias Worthington of Colchester, Ct., was
appointed on Feb. 14, 1765, ɔy the selectmen, to take charge of the
affairs of Moses Dodge, who ɔy his "imprudence and mismanagement
ɔeing likely to waste his estate and ɔecome chargeaɔle to said town."
In 1767 he was deputy to the sheriff of Hardford County; was
representative from Colchester to the General Assemɔly in 1770-1-7-
9-81-3-4-8-90-1. By the General Assemɔlɔ', Oct. 1770, he was ap
pointed and impowered to sell so much of the real estate of Jonathan
Harrison of Colchester, dec., as shall procure the sum of £133 3s 6d,
and £6 10s 0d, together with incident charges theron arising, taking
the direction of the Court of Proɔate for the district of East Hadam
therein, and he is directed to pay said sums to said creditors, and
settle his account thereof with said Court of Proɔate. In May,
1771, he was appointed, with Henrv Champion, trustee, with full
power and authority, to receive from one Amasai Jones, petitioner, a
conveyance of all the estate of said Jones to and for the use and
ɔenefit of his creditors. In May, 1772, he was appointed, with
Joseph Isham, trustee of the estate and effects of John Clark of
Colchester, for the ɔenefit of his creditors. He was appointed, May,
1773, to sell the lands of Zipporah Chapman of Colchester, dec., to
pay the deɔts.

Page 145, numɔer 53, Capt. Elijah Worthington of Colchester
was appointed ɔy the General Assemɔly, at Hartford, May, 1771,
Ensign of the seventh company or trainɔand in the 12th regiment of
the colony. In Oct., 1773, he was appointed Lieutenant of the
same company. In May, 1775, he was appointed Captain of the
same companv.

Page 174, numɔer 97, Mr. Joel Worthington represented Colchester, Ct., in the General Assemɔly, Oct., 1804; Mav and Oct.,
1806; May, 1807; Oct., 1808; May, 1810.

Page 221, numɔer 143, Doctor Charles Worthington of Lenox,
Mass., "was an active memɔer of the Berkshire Medical Society, and
held various responsiɔle positions in it, and he appears to have had

the respect and esteem of his medical brethren."—*History of Berkshire Co.*

Page 221, number 300, Hon. John Zacchrus Goodrich of Stockbridge, Mass., who married Sarah, dau. of Dr. Charles Worthington of Lenox, was educated at the Lenox Academy, and studied law with Judge H. W. Bishop of that town. On being admitted to the bar, he united his profession with that of editor, purchasing a journal called *The Argus,* published at Pittsfield, and uniting it with the *Berkshire Star* of Lenox, giving the consolidated paper the title of *The Berkshire Journal,* and afterwards *The Eagle.* In 1847, he engaged in the "Glendale Woolen Company," in which he was concerned during the largest portion of his remaining active life. In 1848 he represented Southern Berkshire in the State Senate. He served in Congress during two terms, being elected from the Eleventh District. He was one of the originators of the Republican party in 1856. In 1860 he was elected Lieutenant-Governor of Massachusetts, and was appointed by Governor Andrew one of the peace commissioners of the state who met at Richmond, Va., in the futile effort to forefend the threatening War of the Rebellion. In the same year, he was one of the Presidential electors. In 1861 he received the appointment of Collector of the Port of Boston, and held it for four years. Thenceforward his energies were devoted mostly to personal, town and county affairs. Was President of the County Bible Society and the Housatonic Railroad; a trustee of Williams College, to which college he gave, in 1870, Goodrich Hall, a stone building, the upper story of which furnished a most ample and well-provided gymnasium. He also gave the library building to Stockbridge."—*From History of Berkshire County.*

Page 227, number 149, Doctor Robert Worthington of Lenox, Mass., " was well known as a physician, having long resided in the county. He was for years Secretary of the Berkshire Medical Society, and was highly honored and esteemed. Not only was he well known in the walks of professional life, but in those of Christian benevolence. He was a member of the Congregational Church in Lenox, and one on whom much was imposed, and sustained with ability and constancy. He was for many years Treasurer of the Berkshire Bible Society, and was made a life director of the American Bible Society. He was Secretary of the County Seaman's Friends Society, and an earnest friend of every measure of popular reform.

His Christian faith was vital, energetic, active, and the true
that works bv love. His memory will always ɔe cherished
honor. He was ɔorn in Colchester, Conn., and removed to Len
the earlv part of the centurv."—*Historv of Berkshire Countv.*

ERRATA.

On page 13, line 7, 1870 should be 1670.
On page 21, Top of page should ɔe figure 4, instead of IV.
On page 22, line 21, 1825, should ɔe 1725.
On page 22, line 26, V. should ɔe 5.
On page 24, line 2, VI. should ɔe 6.
On page 25, line 19, haring should ɔe having.
On page 101, line 15, Maɔle should ɔe Marɔle.
On page 132, line 22, Clark should ɔe Wright.
On page 173, line 6, Francis should ɔe Frances.
On page 196, line 26, Beginning at children, which should bɛ
and all that follows should ɔe in smaller tvpe, to "Children bv
Husɔand" on page 197.
On page 216, 12, line Xenɾietta should ɔe Henrietta.

INDEX.

CHRISTIAN NAMES OF WORTHINGTONS.

A.

Aaron, 159, 249; Aaron Ambrose, 344, 395; Aaron Ferre, 247, 257, 341, 342; Aaron Seth, 258.

Abaline A.....................254

Abbie, 159; Abbie Jane, 392.

Abigail, 82, 149, 217, 219, 312; Abigail Maria, 319, Abigail Ross, 344.

Ada May.....................379

Addie.....................296, 400

Adelaide.....................302

Adelbert.....................273

Adoniram Judson.....................335

Affa.....................188

Agnes Seabury.....................385

Albert, 215, 236, 286, 310, 315, 337, 339, 340, 353, 369, 369, 380, 394, 394, 410; Albert Arthur, 354, 399; Albert Brownell, 212, 311; Albert Curtis, 378, 409; Albert D, 259; Albert Edward, 332, 334; Albert Edwin, 332, 390; Albert Henry, 307; Albert Humphrey, 382; Albert J, 394; Albert Payson, 316, 382; Albert Selden, 178, 311, 381; Albert Sigourney, 306; Albert Seth, 397.

Alberta.....................381

Alcott.....................174, 362

Aldula.....................374

Alfred.....................161, 205, 263, 298, 396

Algeron.....................393

Alice, 321; Alice Augusta, 340; Alice Elizabeth, 365; Alice Jane, 371; Alice Josephine, 272; Alice Julia, 366; Alice L., 396; Alice Roae, 348; Alice Trumbull, 314; Alice Wood, 377.

Allen Samuel.....................401

B.

D.

E.

F.

I.

J.

K.

L.

MALE CONNECTIONS BY MARRIAGE. '

A.

B.

E.

F.

G.

H.

I.

J.

W.

FEMALE CONNECTIONS BY MARRIAGE.

A.

B.

K.

L.

M.

N.

O.

P.

Y.

Z.

ALL OTHER NAMES.

A.

D.

F.

G.

I.

J.

K.

L.

243; Mary Blanch, 243; Martin Clum, 243; Robert E., 242; Robert Henry, 243; Winifred Ada, 243.

N.

O.

Q.

R.

U.

Index.

V.

W.

Y.

Z.

CPSIA information can be obtained
at www.ICGtesting.com
Printed in the USA
LVOW10s2245080518
576526LV00026B/93/P

9 781333 626198